CALLOWAY COUNTY PUBLIC LIBRARY
710 Main Street
MURRAY, KY 42071

D1509381

90993

331.7
Time   Time-Life Books

Odd jobs
                      090993

DISCARD

Calloway County Public Library

710 Main Street

Murray, KY 42071

1.   Books may be kept two weeks and may be renewed once
for the same period, except 7 day books and magazines.

2.   A fine is charged for each day a book is not returned according to the above rule. No book will be issued to any person in-
curring such a fine until it has been paid.

3.   All injuries to books beyond reasonable wear and all
losses shall be made good to the satisfaction of the Librarian.

4.   Each borrower is held responsible for all books charged
on his card and for all fines accruing on the same.

ODD JOBS

Cover: Against the silhouettes of bustling New York City commuters, a precariously perched Mohawk high-steel worker aligns bolt holes 48 stories above Manhattan.

Donated 9-9-93

ODD JOBS

By the Editors of Time-Life Books

TIME-LIFE BOOKS, ALEXANDRIA, VIRGINIA

CONTENTS

RISKY BUSINESS

Perhaps nothing is as certain as death and taxes, but for most people the dire necessity to earn a living runs a close third. Around the world, the simple equation of work for pay has yielded any number of occupations, some fulfilling and others soul-destroying, jobs that inspire, jobs that dull. Most are familiar variations on the office, the factory, the shop, or the field. But that same spectrum of employment comprises a species of workers who seem drawn less by opportunity than by what Scottish author Robert Louis Stevenson called "the bright eyes of danger." Toward the end of World War I, for example, the life expectancy of a young aviator on the Western Front was reckoned in weeks; neither side, however, feared a shortage of volunteers: While patriotism and the exhilaration of flight no doubt played a part, the airmen found the hazard irresistible.

Danger lures as seductively in peacetime as it does in time of war for those who choose to peer into its bright eyes. Their specialties, which seem stunningly reckless to the safely sedentary worker, form a blazing scarlet corner on an occupational map that is mostly gray. For some, the motive may be humanitarian or economic need; others simply deny that there is risk. No doubt there are jobs whose apparent riskiness lies in the dazzled eyes of the outsider, but many are as dangerous as they seem, recurring rites of passage—the spice, and stuff, of life.

1

Shellseekers

Little has changed for the ama divers of Japan in two millennia of harvesting shellfish and edible seaweed from the seabed near their island country. Mostly women, they still work some 10 fathoms below the waves, unencumbered by breathing apparatus and tethered to their boats by single ropes that can trap and drown an unwary diver. Each morning in the spring and summer they venture out to their watery hunting grounds, where they may dive 200 times—and spend a total of several hours submerged—before the day ends.

For all the time they spend at the bottom of the sea, and despite the inherent risks of diving, the amas have had relatively few casualties. Since they work without tanks of pressurized air, and rarely dive deeper than 60 feet, they are virtually free of the bends, a potentially deadly complication in which nitrogen bubbles form in the blood. Many suffer ear damage early in their careers from the rapid pressure increases during their weighted descents. And, although some have adopted neoprene wet suits, prolonged exposure to the cold water can result in hypothermia, a potentially deadly lowering of body temperature. On-board hot drinks and stoves help combat this threat, however, and women are less susceptible to cold because of a thin layer of fat under their skin absent in men, which explains the predominance of women among the amas—and of wet suits among male divers.

In fact, most amas continue diving well into their fifties. In the past, not even pregnancy kept divers away from their work; veterans tell of women who continued diving right up to the day of delivery. More than one baby was born on the deck of a diving boat.

The amas' impressive safety record comes partly from a lifetime of informal training. Although fewer young divers are joining the profession now, those who do generally began playfully diving from shore for rocks tossed by their mothers when the future amas were three or four years old. By the time they enter the profession in their late teens, they are as comfortable in the water as on land.

Although specific customs vary from island to island, amas generally begin their professional diving in relatively shallow water, perhaps 20 feet deep, staying underwater about 40 seconds. As their skills and confidence grow, the divers work up to deeper, longer dives, achieving top professional competence at about the age of 30.

Many work with their own boatmen, usually a husband or a brother. As she leaves the boat, a diver speeds her descent by holding on to a weighted rope paid out by the boatman. After being submerged as long as 60 seconds, she tugs on a second line, tethered to her waist, and the boatman hauls her up. While she rests on the boat, the boatman pulls up the weighted line to prepare for the next dive.

Throughout their careers, amas occasionally sight large sharks, but the predators evidently pose little real risk. Japan's cold seas support less life than tropical waters, so the shark population tends to be small. Also, the large predators prefer to attack from below, so surface swimmers are at greater risk than divers. Still, even the amas were unnerved in the spring of 1992, when a fisherman using a helmeted diving suit in the Inland Sea was killed by a great white shark. Although no amas have ever been attacked, this news was alarming enough to keep them out of the water for months. □

Trailing thin lifelines and brandishing prying tools called *tegane* on one of many minute-long descents, three traditionally clad ama divers search the seabed off Japan for awabi, or abalone.

A team of rescue miners in Draeger breathing gear—called draegermen in Nova Scotia—prepare to search for survivors trapped by a 1956 coal-mine explosion in Springhill, Nova Scotia. Their efforts brought 88 miners out alive.

The Draegerman Will Get You

Since large-scale coal mining began in the 17th century, mines have ranked among the riskiest of work sites, a prey to cave-ins, seeping poisonous gases, and airborne particles that degrade the lungs. Terribly hazardous for all who enter them, coal mines offer profound danger to an elite of specialists—the miners who go into the pits not to dig coal, but to find their lost comrades. They are the first to revisit underground disaster areas from which all but the trapped have fled. Along the treacherous coal seams of Nova Scotia, they are called draegermen.

The rescuers take their name from Bernhard Draeger, the German engineer who, early in the 20th century, invented the bulky oxygen breathing apparatus that first allowed rescuers to enter the subterranean nightmare of a collapsed, gas-choked mine shaft. Draegermen work in teams around the clock, struggling to clear debris and reach their trapped fellows. The battle is fought against great odds. A shattered mine can be a maze of fallen rock and twisted steel, filled with smoldering coal, rising water, carbon monoxide, and hair-trigger concentrations of explosive methane gas. Claustrophobia nibbles at one's nerve. "There's just enough room for men to go through," one draegerman said after probing a 1992 explosion. "Just a little hole—that's all. You don't look behind you, you don't look up, you just go in. If you start looking around, you're going to get scared—real scared." Moving through that dark minescape with a 35-pound breathing pack, according to one expert, is like "climbing a steep hill in the dark wearing scuba gear." Because a single spark can cause a methane explosion, the draegermen use no electrified equipment. All of their probing must be done with pick and shovel, in the full knowledge that time works against the desperate men who may be waiting on the other side. As they find their way through the unstable clutter of a ruined mine, they blaze a trail and restore ventilation for teams of "bare-faced" rescuers following them.

Sometimes the painstaking effort discovers life, after all. When a coal-dust explosion ripped ◊

through Nova Scotia's Springhill Number 4 Colliery in 1956, draegermen rescued 88 men. Of the survivors, 54 had been trapped more than a mile below the surface for five days, breathing from compressed air pipelines in chambers sealed against deadly coal gases. Two draegermen were killed early in the rescue. The rest, exhausted and with blistered shoulders from their breathing packs, had no trouble explaining why they had risked their lives. "You won't find a more clannish bunch than miners," one told a reporter. "If you were trapped down there, you'd want the others to help you."

Often, however, nothing can be done. At Plymouth's Westray Mine in May 1992, a methane-triggered explosion along the rich Foord Seam buried 26 miners in the shaft. The detonation was felt for miles around the mine and shattered the interior. Enormous steel doors were crumpled by the blast, and the probing draegermen crept through tunnels where rocks tumbled continually around them. Some of the miners caught in the explosion had been seared where they stood or sat, suspended in place like the residents of ancient Pompeii. Others had been hurled hundreds of feet by the explosion, to break upon the tunnel wall.

Draegermen retrieved 11 bodies a day after the disaster and continued the search for 15 other men. In the end, only 15 bodies were recovered, and the search for others was abandoned. The exhausted draegermen said little to outsiders of the horrors they had seen in Westray, but they spoke with their brothers in coal. "My God, the stories," one young miner said afterward. "My God, the stories." □

Steeple Chasing

Centuries ago, steeples were the highest structures in most European and American communities, soaring from churches built on hills in the town. But their heavenward reach exposed the spires to damage from wind, hail, ice, sun, and lightning—damage that was difficult to repair, given the preference of most carpenters, masons, and metalsmiths for work on solid ground. Accordingly, the job of healing injured steeples passed into the hands of iron-nerved generalists of repair: steeplejacks.

Like many other risky jobs, steeplejacking is often shared by a single family. Skyline Engineers of Massachusetts, for example, employs sons, cousins, and brothers of its founder, John Douglas Quinn, now semiretired, who trained all his boys to become steeplejacks. Chief among the skills Quinn has passed along is his own style of rigging, which he learned from his wife's uncle. The rigger is the first steeplejack to go up on a job, setting blocks and tackles into place. Doug Quinn's rigging techniques, like those of other steeplejacks, are closely guarded by his family. "We tell people that we use trained mice," quips Quinn's son Stephen, a Skyline vice president, "and they run up a little tiny string." More than that he is reluctant to divulge.

Working on steeples, the jacks go as high as they can inside before moving, through an access door or specially bored hole, to the exterior; on such jobs as tall chimneys, they must often scale the whole structure outside. Rig-

ging lines laced to the structure support boatswain's chairs, wooden seats dating to the days of tall-masted ships; many steeplejacks today customize their chairs with cushions and stereos. Ropes, pulleys, and chairs are checked daily, and any questionable cordage or other material is replaced immediately. Steeplejacks are urged to pay equally close attention to their own condition: One who feels unwell or just does not want to climb is summarily grounded. "There's never any questions asked," one Skyline veteran says. "You have to feel good about being up here."

Indeed, attitude is everything in the steeplejack trade, where complacency or carelessness can lead to a fatal fall. Steeplejacks can even be startled to death by the unexpected charges of angry birds, bats, or insects. Doug Quinn has been attacked inside a steeple by an owl defending its nest. "Once I had to get rid of a 13-foot honey bee nest," Steve recalls, adding, "When bees are swarming you, yes, there is the possibility of your losing your balance."

Many jobs require steeplejacks to repair the very structures that are holding them hundreds of feet in the air, such as the crumbling concrete cap at the top of a chimney. Some steeples are so fragile, says Steve Quinn, that it is best to take them off their churches and repair them on the ground.

The same forces of nature that cause such damage may also threaten anyone unlucky enough to be on the steeple at the wrong time. One of Doug Quinn's admonitions is succinct but often repeated: "Get the hell down when you see a storm." Steve says that he failed to heed these words only

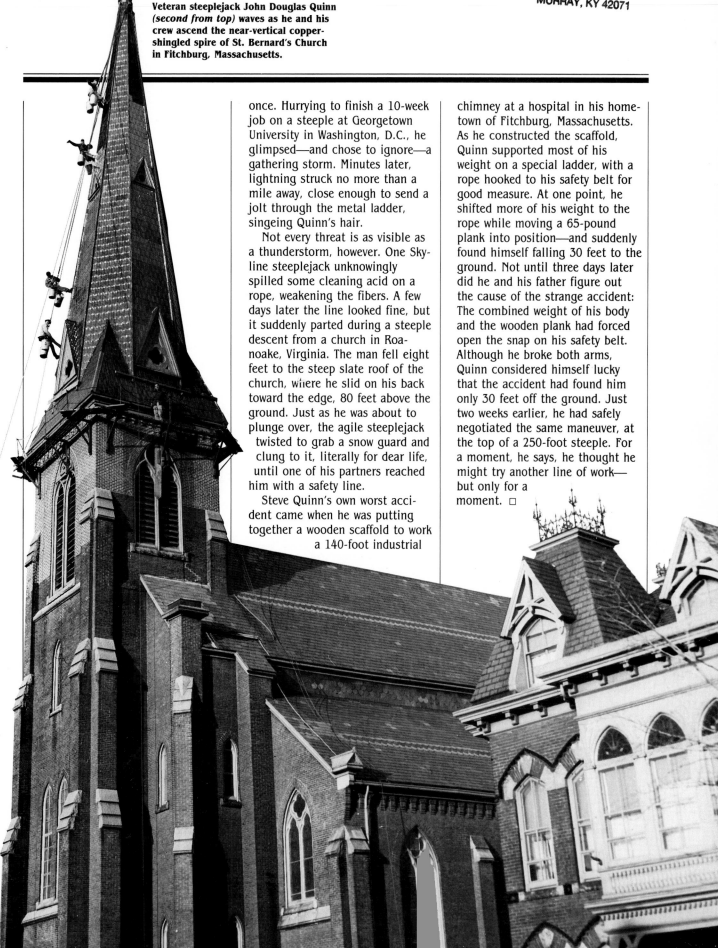

CALLOWAY COUNTY PUBLIC LIBRARY
710 Main Street
MURRAY, KY 42071

Veteran steeplejack John Douglas Quinn *(second from top)* waves as he and his crew ascend the near-vertical copper-shingled spire of St. Bernard's Church in Fitchburg, Massachusetts.

once. Hurrying to finish a 10-week job on a steeple at Georgetown University in Washington, D.C., he glimpsed—and chose to ignore—a gathering storm. Minutes later, lightning struck no more than a mile away, close enough to send a jolt through the metal ladder, singeing Quinn's hair.

Not every threat is as visible as a thunderstorm, however. One Skyline steeplejack unknowingly spilled some cleaning acid on a rope, weakening the fibers. A few days later the line looked fine, but it suddenly parted during a steeple descent from a church in Roanoake, Virginia. The man fell eight feet to the steep slate roof of the church, where he slid on his back toward the edge, 80 feet above the ground. Just as he was about to plunge over, the agile steeplejack twisted to grab a snow guard and clung to it, literally for dear life, until one of his partners reached him with a safety line.

Steve Quinn's own worst accident came when he was putting together a wooden scaffold to work a 140-foot industrial chimney at a hospital in his hometown of Fitchburg, Massachusetts. As he constructed the scaffold, Quinn supported most of his weight on a special ladder, with a rope hooked to his safety belt for good measure. At one point, he shifted more of his weight to the rope while moving a 65-pound plank into position—and suddenly found himself falling 30 feet to the ground. Not until three days later did he and his father figure out the cause of the strange accident: The combined weight of his body and the wooden plank had forced open the snap on his safety belt. Although he broke both arms, Quinn considered himself lucky that the accident had found him only 30 feet off the ground. Just two weeks earlier, he had safely negotiated the same maneuver, at the top of a 250-foot steeple. For a moment, he says, he thought he might try another line of work— but only for a moment. □

Burrowed Time

Guests in fancy dress promenaded through the Thames Tunnel at its formal opening in 1843. Queen Victoria and Prince Albert graced the masterwork with a visit. The *Illustrated London News* declared that the London structure, the first modern tunnel under a navigable waterway, "probably will have no parallel for many ages."

The celebrated achievement had not come cheap. More than 18 years of dirty, dangerous work had gone into constructing the 1,200-foot tunnel beneath the Thames River. To get through the clay and silt under the river, workers had chopped away with picks and shovels through slots in a cast-iron shield, 38 feet wide and 22 feet high, that filled the head of the tunnel to prevent cave-ins. As they hacked out the earth in front of the shield, the metal plate was pushed forward by screw jacks braced against brick tunnel walls continually extended by a crew working behind the diggers.

On May 18, 1827, the tunnelers hit a loose patch of earth. Suddenly, water and mud from the river, 14 feet overhead, spurted through the wall in front of the shield. The powerful discharge knocked some of the men down; the rest ran for the stairs at the tunnel mouth, the torrent close behind. The flood snuffed out gas lamps, and some men found themselves swimming in darkness to reach the stairs. Miraculously, all escaped alive.

The people who dig underwater tunnels—workers called sandhogs in the United States—have rarely been so lucky. When geologic fore-casts turn out wrong, a barrier fails, or new tunneling techniques prove faulty, sandhogs reap the often disastrous consequences. A memorable case in point came when a seemingly innovative approach was applied to building a web of underwater tunnels to the island of Manhattan.

The first tunnel began in the 1870s under the supervision of Dewitt Clinton Haskin, a Californian who proposed to burrow under the Hudson, connecting Manhattan with Jersey City by rail. But instead of using the customary slotted shield, Haskin planned to fill the tunnel with compressed air, which would keep water out of the shaft until workers stabilized the emerging tunnel with timbers and finished it with iron and brick.

To keep the tunnel's pressure up, Haskin added a sealed chamber called an air lock, where men and materials could wait until the chamber's pressure was adjusted to match the pressurized work site on one side or the open atmosphere on the other. At first, his scheme seemed to work. Then, one day in July 1880, the compressed air began to bubble up through a flaw in the mud heading. As pressure dropped, water and mud poured back through the breached barrier of air. Of the 28 workers in the shaft, only 8 made it to the air lock before the door jammed. The rest waited stoically for death in the slowly rising water.

Although Haskin abandoned the

The Anglo-French counterparts of American sandhogs position segments of a concrete liner *(left)* inside the underwater tunnel linking Britain and France, as workers *(below)* renew the propeller-like "teeth" of a tunnel-boring machine.

project, and those tunnel workers went back to using shields, his method gradually won acceptance as the best way to prevent leaks in underwater tunnels through soft rock and mud. Compressed air posed a new danger, however. The deeper the tunnel, the greater the air pressure needed to sustain a barrier. Working in such high pressures, sandhogs soon faced another hazard: the bends, formerly known only to deep-sea divers. Caused when pressurized nitrogen dissolved in the blood forms bubbles at normal pressures, the excruciating disorder can be fatal.

Some relief came with decompression chambers, which restored normal atmospheric pressure slowly enough that nitrogen remained dissolved in the blood. But the bends still killed about a fourth of New York's river-tunnel workers and remained a threat to sandhogs for years afterward.

By 1987, when work began on the world's longest underwater tunnel—the so-called Chunnel linking England and France beneath the Channel—the risks had changed. The bends were not a hazard, because the shaft was vented directly to the atmosphere—the tracked tunneling machines themselves *(left, below)*, not a bubble of high-pressure air, sealed the shaft

head, a technique that also reduced chances of a catastrophic leak. Still, Chunnel sandhogs—nicknamed Tunnel Tigers by the British press—remain the infantry of modern underwater tunneling and continue to pay the price of being underground, underwater.

Since the giant burrow began, seven workers have died in the Chunnel, and hundreds have been injured. But none was harmed by the kind of accident that once plagued sandhogs; most casualties fell afoul of the equipment itself, struck down by the powerful machines maneuvering in the cramped confines, which left the workers no space to dodge even if they had warning. To make matters worse, locomotives used in the construction process regularly derailed, visibility was dangerously low, and carbon dioxide levels proved hard to control. "Construction and mining are two of the most dangerous jobs," summed up one reporter. "The Chunnel combines both."

Nevertheless, modern methods have banished some of the grand accidents befalling sandhogs. It is unlikely, for example, that today's sandhog will share the experience of Richard Creedon, who worked in a pressurized shaft under New York's East River in 1905. When a weak spot in the roof gave way, a blast of compressed air blew Creedon out of the shaft and propelled him through 17 feet of silt and 10 feet of water like a human missile. Later fished from the river unharmed, Creedon shrugged off his strange flight. "It didn't amount to such a lot," he said with the modest composure of the sandhog. "Before I came down I had a fine view of the city." □

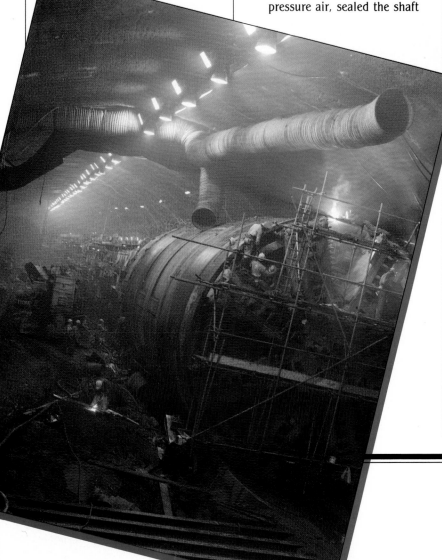

This Caughnawaga cross is one of three memorializing the Mohawks who earn their living on the high iron. The crosses are made of structural steel of the type used on the unfinished Quebec bridge, which killed 33 Mohawk workers when it collapsed in 1907.

Men of Steel

In the summer, scores of pious tourists once made their way across the St. Lawrence River to Caughnawaga, the settlement of the Mohawk Indian reservation. Their destination was the small, centuries-old Jesuit mission church that still houses a shrine to Caughnawaga's most famous resident, Kateri Tekakwitha, the 17th-century Mohawk holy woman whose reputation for sacrifice and self-denial has set her on course for canonization. Her spirit is credited with healings and other miracles.

Kateri's is one of several local Mohawk shrines; the second consists of a small forest of 41 iron and steel crosses. There, and at two other Caughnawaga sites, stands a large cross made of metal beams. This is the kind of steel used on bridges and skyscrapers; the crosses commemorate those who died on the steel—the legendary high-iron workers of the Caughnawaga Mohawks.

The men of this band are descendants of one branch of the wide-ranging Iroquois Nation that once ruled much of present-day New York and the province of Quebec. Though converted to Christianity, the Mohawks of Caughnawaga were never "tamed." Instead, they adapted their traditional regard for strength and daring to new pursuits. Although the Jesuits encouraged them to become farmers, the Mohawks became scouts, guides, and navigators for European explorers. As the St. Lawrence valley became more settled, the Mohawks established themselves as river pilots and log raftsmen, guiding huge flotillas of timber downstream through dangerous rapids to the sawmills in Montreal.

Their entry into the exotic and dangerous world of high iron was due more to happenstance than design, but it was hardly surprising, given the Mohawk's appetite for hard work and hazard. In 1886 the Dominion Bridge Company was building a railroad bridge across the St. Lawrence River near Caughnawaga. Naturally, the builders hired several local Mohawks. The Indians were not intended to work on the high girders, but, in their curiosity about bridge building, they wandered all over the project—often strolling casually across narrow beams high above the river to question an ironworker about a tool or process.

Many high-iron workers of the time were former sailors who had learned to work aloft on the swaying masts and yardarms of square-rigged ships. But the age of sail was almost over, and the supply of trained seamen was drying up. When the Mohawks began to pester their foremen for a chance at the high-paying high-iron work, the Dominion Bridge Company decided to train a few. The Indians—proud, prodigious workers—proved to be natural-born bridgemen. By the turn of the century, scores of Mohawks had taken up bridge building, and a new tradition was added to those of earlier days. Mohawk boys listened raptly to tales of heroism on the high iron—of jobs too dangerous for any but an Indian.

The danger was by no means mythical, and in time it took its toll. Joe Diabo was the first casualty, falling to his death from a bridge at Sault Ste. Marie, Ontario, in 1888. Then in 1907 the Caughnawaga Mohawk reservation was stunned by an event so terrible that, for years, it was referred to simply as "the disaster."

The calamity occurred on a bridge being built over the St. Lawrence River near Quebec City. After eight trouble-plagued years, the bridge was near completion. Two spans were cantilevered from either shore, 300 feet above the St. Lawrence, to be joined by a central section that would be floated into the river on a barge, then raised into position. The project never quite reached that stage; one day in August, as a train carrying steel made its way out on the incomplete south span, rivets began popping like gunfire. Within sec-

High above Manhattan streets, a Mohawk connector (*inset*) aligns bolt holes on a 48th-floor corner of the Equitable Insurance Building's metal skeleton, while two fellow Indians (*right*) ride a hanging steel beam into position.

onds, iron girders twisted and plunged into the river. Thirty-three of the 96 men killed were from Caughnawaga. Nearly every family lost a father, son, or uncle—a devastation that staggered the community. To prevent a recurrence, the women of the reservation decreed that the men would never again work in such large numbers on a single job. The rule was honored for decades.

Despite its effects, the disaster only height- ened the young men's desire to work on high steel, and within two decades Caughnawaga Mohawks were erecting skyscrapers all over North America, from the George Washington Bridge to the Golden Gate. They put up the steel for the Empire State Building, New York's World Trade Center, and hundreds of smaller buildings. Although they constitute less than 1 percent of the U.S. population, Indians now form about 10 percent of its high-iron work force.

In the early days, ironwork was connected by rivets, heated cherry red, then pounded home with heavy hammers. Today, high-strength bolts have largely replaced rivets, but little else has changed. Most members of a seven-man raising gang work on the floor nearest the top, where steel for the next level is stacked and lifted by crane, piece by piece, to a pair of connectors at the top of the nascent building. These men balance in the wind on a foot-wide beam as they grab the next swinging one-ton girder, muscle it into place so its bolt holes line up with those on the column, then secure it with two bolts at each end. The connectors often work outside the skeleton of the building. Work rules insist that they wear lifelines; another safety consideration—the need for complete freedom of movement to handle the swinging girders—dictates that they do not. The Mohawks take the latter road, even though a connector's fall is nearly always fatal.

Work on the floor, while safer, requires constant attention to swinging beams and proximity to the edge, where nothing but a stainless-steel cable lies between complete safety and utter disaster. But danger is an afterthought. Among the Mohawks, the capacity for hard work is a virtue. Although there is no shame in choosing other careers, great honor resides in the high skeletons of buildings. As retired iron man Norton Lickers put it, "If you're scared, no use in going up; you might as well stay on the ground. But if you're going up on the iron, you might as well go all the way up. That's where the work is. On top." □

Friendly Fire

Fireworks have fascinated multitudes since the Chinese began fashioning skyrockets with gunpowder in the ninth century AD. Since then, pyrotechnicians have added brilliant colors, dramatic visual choreography, and remote control. Pyrotechnics are still explosives, carefully packed and rolled by hand, fired into the sky in celebration. In their way, those who make and display them are as conservative as munitions makers, and for the same reason—a slight misstep can blow their factories, and employees, sky high.

These specialists are careful to protect such arcana as chemistry and fuse length, keeping the secrets of their success within families devoted to the craft. In the United States, most of the great fireworks families are from Italy, where fireworks have enlivened festivals for centuries. One of the best known is the Zambelli family of New Castle, Pennsylvania, which operates what may be the nation's preeminent fireworks company, founded after the first Zambelli

arrived in the United States in 1919. Three generations later, the secret recipes, still written in Italian, remain locked in the company safe.

If safeguarding secrets is a concern in the industry, safeguarding lives is an obsession. The Zambellis train their workers carefully, with safety as an ever-present concern. In addition to knowing the chemistry of colored fire, every worker must master all the steps of safely making each kind of shell by hand. George Zambelli, the second-generation president of the company, quotes his father on the subject: "It takes longer to be a fireworker than to be a medical doctor." So far, the Zambellis' method has paid off. The family makes hundreds of thousands of British Hummers, Big Willows with Strobing Stars, Stromboli Volcanoes, Shimmering Shamrocks, and other colorful perennials for more than 3,000 displays each year but experiences few accidents. Their last fatal manufacturing mishap occurred in 1950, when a brother-in-law died in a factory that spontaneously exploded. "What he was doing," George Zambelli said, "to this day we don't know."

Fireworks accidents have been much worse. In 1930 one of the greatest industry disasters occurred when an explosion at a Pennsylvania factory killed 10 workers, injured dozens more, tossed cars off a nearby road, and shattered windows for miles. In 1983 the Bellport, New York, factory of the Gruccis, a strong competitor of the Zambellis', blew up. The spring and summer of 1985 were particularly deadly; two separate

fireworks-manufacturing accidents killed a total of 32 people, 11 of them in an illegal Ohio plant. The destructive appetite of black powder, still the key explosive ingredient in fireworks, is a steady hazard, despite elaborate precautions.

Like all American pyrotechnicians, the Zambellis' work year revolves around the weeks before and after the Fourth of July, when they fire more than half of their displays. To prepare for that week, a fluctuating work force of 11 family members spends the rest of the year working singly or in pairs in small buildings, widely dispersed to limit the effects of any explosion. Two to three inches of sawdust cover the work floors, to stabilize stray powder that might float to the floor and to prevent sparks created by friction or static electricity; for the same reason, all tools are made of wood or brass.

The shells manufactured under these circumstances hold a variety of components. Each includes an ignition fuse, a propellant charge, a time-delay fuse, and such special effects as colored stars, which are gunpowder-coated pellets the size of sugar cubes, meant to ignite and scatter brilliantly when a shell explodes. Workers put the parts together with papier maché, then stuff the bundles into prepared cardboard tubes. They then wrap the shells in twine and kraft paper and dry the finished pyrotechnics in the sun. Produced in batches of 1,000 or more, shells may be several weeks in the making. One reporter likened a visit to a Zambelli plant to a "step back into pre-industrial Europe." But such employees are a vanishing race. "It's tedious, hazardous work," says George Zambelli. "There aren't more than a dozen experienced hand-rollers left in the country."

Launching the fireworks is less subject to catastrophe than making them, but it remains a hard and dangerous activity. Preparations begin several days before the display, when pyrotechnicians start digging holes for the metal launching tubes, or mortars. Where holes are inappropriate, sturdy wooden frames are used instead. The mortars and frames are positioned and aimed to keep the fireworks well away from the spectator area and to shield the operators.

The operators spend the night moving among the mortars, wearing protective goggles, hard hats, and fire-resistant suits. One, known as the loader, shuttles to and from the box where the fireworks are stored, carrying shells to reload mortars. The loader tips a shell into its tube,

then moves back toward the box. A second operator then lights the shell's long fuse and immediately retreats a few feet, dropping to one knee to get under any unexpected explosive spray. Eight seconds later, if all goes well, the black powder propellant charge goes off with a hiss, sending the shell hundreds of feet high.

Like the aerial displays, movements on the ground must be precisely choreographed to prevent collisions between the loader, carrying explosives, and the lighting operator, carrying a flare. Furthermore, the loader must be wary of sparks. Flammable debris in the mortar can detonate a shell prematurely, and embers drifting into the shell box can ignite a huge explosion. Premature ignition poses the greatest risk for the loader and is the reason for the cardinal rule of loading: Never put any part of the body over the barrel of the mortar. A slow-burning fuse during a 1980 Zambelli display in Butte, Montana, drummed that lesson home. An employee, anxious when the shell failed to go off, forgot the rule for a fatal moment. He leaned over the mortar to check it just when the fuse burned its way to the propellant—and was killed.

Modern technology has begun to make this aspect of pyrotechnics safer by allowing operators to fire shells from a distance. Triggering electronic relays that fire already-loaded pyrotechnics in the desired sequence, the operator plays an electronic console, like an organist whose instrument produces a music of light. □

Walking on Air

Wing walker Johnny Kazian called it "Breaking the Ground Barrier." Hanging by his feet from a rack on the upper wing of an upside-down Waco biplane, Kazian grabbed a ribbon stretched from one side to the other of a 30-foot-deep drainage ditch. The ribbon was tied 16 feet from the bottom of the ditch, and the plane was going about 185 miles an hour. Declining to press his luck, Kazian performed the unprecedented feat only once. "If my pilot was not excellent," he later reflected, "this act could have made a mess of me."

Although Kazian was strapped securely in place for that stunt, he is more often seen walking untethered on the wings of biplanes, keeping alive an American art born in aviation's barnstorming era. During the 1920s, bands of freelance pilots ranged across the United States, swooping into towns for a few days at a time to give residents the thrill of their first flight for five dollars or more. Within a few years, most adventuresome citizens had been up for a spin, and the fliers, desperate for customers, began performing stunts to bring them back. Flying with someone out on the unprotected wings was guaranteed to do the trick—especially when the imperiled person was a woman.

Few walked wings better than Jessie Woods, who took to the air in 1929 with the Flying Aces aerial circus, which she had founded with her husband, Jimmie. Her maiden trip was almost her last, but not from nearly falling. Her spouse had tethered her to the ship with a ◊

Joseph Zambelli, a master pyrotechnician at his family's New Castle, Pennsylvania, fireworks firm until his death in 1988, loads whistles into the cardboard casings of skyrockets that scream.

Wing walker Johnny
Kazian (right) struts his
stuff on Dave Dacy's Stearman, preserving the act
pioneered in the 1930s by Jessie
Woods (inset), about to perform on a
Travel Air flown by husband Jimmie.

heavy safety rope, one end tied
in the plane's front cockpit, the
other around her waist in a knot
"as big as a coconut." As Woods
moved around, the rope caught in
the struts between the biplane's
top and bottom wing. She worked
herself loose, returned to the cockpit, and gave her husband a piece
of her mind.

This first marital spat ended
with Jessie's declaration of independence: She would walk on
wings her way, or not at all. Thereafter she used a rope only during
aerobatic maneuvers. A bulky parachute was even more dangerous
because of the risk that one of the
wires on the wings would accidentally catch and pull the rip cord,
opening the chute into the wing
structure—an almost certain reci-
pe for a crash. Woods wore a parachute only when an aviation official might see her or when jumping was part of the day's show.
More often, she ostentatiously wore
the chute while climbing into the
plane, but left it in the cockpit
when she began her act.

The regulations came to her
rescue, however, during the filming
of a newsreel near Oklahoma City.
Woods had resigned herself to
wearing a parachute that day because its absence would have been
all too clear on the screen. As she
later recalled, wing walking for the
cameras proved unexpectedly tir-
ing, since each stunt had to be
flown again and again. But Woods
did not know just how fatigued she
was, until she suddenly realized
she was falling. She pulled her rip
cord and floated to a soft landing
at a farm—ankle-deep in manure
in a pen filled with rambunctious
calves. Woods climbed on the
fence and waited for her crew.

Like his colorful predecessor,
Johnny Kazian shuns a parachute
or a safety cable, one of very few
wing walkers—his son Tony is another—to do so. Kazian, who
trained as a trapeze artist in his
youth, uses only toeholds and a
steel rack similar to a ladder that
is mounted on the top wing. He
also has a belt to hold him to the
rack during four-point rolls and
other maneuvers that would otherwise snap him off the plane.

One stunt that Kazian always
buckles up for is the rarely performed Lomcevak—Czech for "ber-
serk headache"—during which the
plane tumbles horizontally nose
over tail through the air. Kazian
remains the only person ever to
ride the top wing through this violent maneuver, experiencing forces
equal to five times his weight.

In the course of a more ordinary
show, Kazian may climb up the
rack, then extend his arms and
legs, letting the force of the 110-
mile-per-hour slipstream hold him
in place. Other stunts include

standing on his
head, braced against the rack, and
climbing out on a lower wing to
hang on to the end struts while
the plane loops and rolls.

For all the apparent risk of falling, Kazian maintains that the
greatest danger he faces is a mechanical failure on the biplane he
rides. Once, at a 1990 airshow, the
engine did fail. "It's the most
deafening quiet you have ever
heard," Kazian remembers. Following a prearranged emergency plan,
he climbed down from the top

wing and straddled the fuselage while the pilot lined up the runway for a dead-stick landing. Kazian then tucked his head under the top wing in case the plane flipped onto its back once on the ground. Fortunately, that part of the plan went untested; the touchdown was so perfect that the audience thought it was part of the act. Kazian and his pilot took a bow and then worked until 3 a.m. getting the plane fit for the next day's show.

Nearing 60 in 1992, Kazian was still working dozens of airshows a year. "I have never used a cable," he said. "The day that I have to, or feel that I have to, is the day that I'll stop doing wingwalking and become an announcer." □

White Death

The clear ocean off Australia is a paradise for divers—and sharks. For some, the submarine prowling of the big predators might be a reason to stay out of the water. To Australian cinematographers Valerie and Ron Taylor, however, the presence of sharks—the voracious great white sharks especially—is a magnet and a living.

The Taylors have specialized in filming great white sharks, whom they see not as mindless marauders, but as the perfect fish—beautiful, sleek, superbly equipped by evolution about 150 million years ago for mastery of the seas. Patrolling for their elusive subjects, the cinematographers draw sharks to their boat with offal and a slurry of chopped bait called chum. Propelled by their enormous appetites, sharks swim up this river of

blood to begin their feeding; the Taylors and their cameras slip into submerged steel cages to begin filming. The result is a kind of cruel poetry in motion, the grace of the ultimate predator contrasted with its awful power to destroy.

Much of the world first saw the Taylors' astonishing photography in their 1971 movie, *Blue Water, White Death,* on which they served as divers, camera crew, and actors, often filming from outside the protective cages. In a published diary extract written during the filming, Valerie Taylor recalled one day when she guarded a cameraman. A few feet away, huge sharks ripped chunks of meat and entrails from the bait—a whale carcass tethered to the cage for the shoot. The fish darted in to tear at the body, retreated with blood streaming from their gills, then hurtled back to strip off more. Dozens of other sharks clung to the whale, gulping their way into its flesh in a gluttonous frenzy. Valerie kept them at bay with a power head, a spearlike prod tipped with a .303-caliber or shotgun cartridge at one end; the creatures often respond to poking by the sticks, and in an emergency the armed end of the power head, properly applied, can kill even a large shark. "I whacked, hit, and thumped as hard and as fast as I could," she wrote, but still the big fish pressed in. "Another shark about seven feet in length bumped me

gently in the side. The first I knew of it was when it hit me. He actually mouthed my waist and a terrible tingle went over my body, but he apparently decided I was not what he wanted and moved on into the whale. At one stage, I rubbed against a feeding shark. Its vibrating body next to mine felt terrible, like some primitive shuddering monster in a nightmare."

The Taylors also filmed the real shark sequences for *Jaws, Jaws II,* and a killer-whale thriller called *Orca,* among others. Although such assignments often require them to work among feeding sharks, the couple have few scars. Valerie gives credit to constant alertness: Look a shark in its lidless eye, she asserts, and it will never attack. Her own run of luck ended in 1980, when a six-foot blue shark approached from behind during filming off the California coast. It clamped its jaw on Valerie's lower left leg, letting go only after she struck him four times on the ⟡

Submerged in the Coral Sea in 1988,
shark follower Valerie Taylor puts
her "chain mail" protective suit to the
acid test—a gnawing by a whitetip shark
attracted by the chunk of fish Taylor
holds in her free arm.

nose. Although the six-inch gash required three layers of stitches, Valerie was back in the water—with sharks—three weeks later.

Eager to avoid bites, the Taylors helped develop a shark-proof suit of heavy metal mesh, similar to medieval chain mail. Testing the suit, Valerie turned herself into living bait, swimming among hungry sharks with a handful of dead fish. For the most part, the tests were successful; Ron shot plenty of footage of sharks chewing ineffectually on Valerie's arms. She said she felt only the initial impact and a sense of pressure. Occasionally, larger sharks tried to shake or wrench off a piece of this new delicacy, but Valerie repelled them with blows to the eyes and gills.

During one shallow-water trial in the Coral Sea, however, Valerie and the suit got more of a workout. Swimming into a horde of sharks with a tuna in her arms, she suddenly felt a tremendous impact against her head, followed by a grinding noise. A shark had struck her, getting his mouth around her face. The mesh hood protected the top of her head against the grating upper teeth, which gave off a sound that made her think the shark was tearing off her face. Fortunately for her, it was not, but beneath her chin the shark's lower teeth had inflicted bloody cuts.

Dismayed by its prey's unexpectedly hard shell, the shark quickly disengaged. Temporarily shaken, Valerie sank several feet to the bottom, feeling as though she had been punched in the jaw. But she resurfaced wearing a broad smile of success: Not only had the shark suit kept her face intact, but Ron had captured the whole spectacular episode on film. □

The Face of War

"It's not easy to take a shot of a man crying," photographer Larry Burrows once said, "as though you have no thoughts, no feelings as to his sufferings." Burrows (*opposite*) saw, photographed, and felt more than his share of suffering. In 15 years as a combat photographer he moved his cameras, and his admiring audience, ever closer to the shocking life-and-death realities of battle. Driven by memories of his youth in Blitz-torn London, Burrows sought out conflicts around the world, hoping that his pictures might shock viewers into "realizing and facing the horrors of war."

From a technical standpoint, that ambition was easier for Burrows to pursue in the 1950s and 1960s than it had been for earlier generations of war photographers, who used cameras so slow and bulky that they could capture only still scenes. Civil War photographer Matthew Brady's most famous images, for example, are portraits of carefully posed soldiers and the static horror of a battle's aftermath. As cameras became lighter and more versatile, however, photographers moved closer to the action, always homing in on those fateful human moments that are the true essence of war. "If your pictures are no good," said Robert Capa, a *Life* photographer who first won fame with his front-line images of combat in Spain and China during the 1930s, "you aren't close enough." Getting close enough made photographers virtual partners in the action—and brought them into harm's way. Then and now, bombs and bullets do not differentiate between photographers and their subjects. Nor are battles the only dangers; in the tense military standoffs that pass for peace in much of the world, a momentary misunderstanding can trigger sudden, deadly violence. Some combatants today, ignoring the presumed immunity of journalists, torture and kill them.

Among the host of talented men and women driven to illuminate the terrible face of war—to die doing it—Larry Burrows remains a towering figure. Working in the midst of such mayhem in the Congo, Cyprus, India, Iraq, Iran, and Lebanon, Burrows never willingly passed up a chance to document, in his words, "the suffering, the sadness, that war brings." When an angry mob beat him and smashed his four cameras during unrest in the Congo, Burrows retreated to the American embassy—only to sneak back out to take pictures with a camera pieced together from the wreckage of the original four. When he was not photographing war, the sensitive Briton composed images—buildings, cities, landscapes—of enduring beauty.

Burrows was already a seasoned professional in 1962, when he first went to Vietnam. But it was there that he won his reputation as a premier war photographer. Tall, gaunt, and bespectacled, he went where he wished, regardless of the dictates of his military handlers. When an army officer insisted he wait until mines had been cleared from a road to the scene of an important story, Burrows refused. The risk of missing the breaking story, he believed, outweighed the danger of the mines. At the end of such days, colleagues said, he invariably dressed for dinner.

During his nine years in Vietnam, Burrows won his first two Robert Capa awards, given for top-notch photography taken under dangerous war conditions. One prize honored a 1965 photo essay about the crew of a Marine helicopter, *Yankee Papa 13*. After a week of rising before dawn to shoot frames on hazardous missions, Burrows completed the assignment with a climactic ride into a maelstrom of enemy fire. Four Marine helicopters had been shot down ferrying South Vietnamese troops into a battle zone. When his own chopper landed to rescue the crew of a downed craft, Burrows leaped out to record the effort. While a machine gun sprayed the area from a building 70 yards away, Burrows shot pictures of his crew chief trying to pull the trapped pilot from the wreck, then giving up when he realized the man was dead. Burrows and the crew chief sprinted back to their helicopter, which fluttered skyward as soon as they were aboard.

Back in his usual position by the door, Burrows discovered three large holes in the fuselage—holes that would have gone through him had he remained aboard rather than running to the crashed chopper. "I could easily have been killed," he recalled later. "It is all a matter of fate."

As it turned out, fate waited for Burrows somewhere else. In 1971, balked at the border of Laos for several days while South Vietnamese troops invaded that country, Burrows finally wangled a ride aboard a Vietnamese helicopter to the scene of the fighting. The chopper, which was carrying four other photographers, strayed over a powerfully defended valley in the rugged Annamite Mountains. Hit by fierce antiaircraft fire, the craft crashed and burst into flames. No one survived.

"There is always this urge to go have a look and see what

is happening," Burrows had written of his work in Vietnam. "I can't resist it." The urge that had carried him to his death also brought him a final honor: His story about an American bombing run that accidentally hit a friendly position won him a third Capa award. He had shot the prize-winning images just a few days before his death. □

Rivers of Stone

"There are two kinds of vulcanologists," Maurice Krafft once told a French interviewer. "The first sort sounds out the entrails of a volcano like a doctor with a stethoscope, working from a vulcanological observatory using sophisticated technical apparatus which investigates the heart of the mountain. If the volcano has been dormant for a long time, then it is a bit like standing on the platform of a railway station waiting for a train but not knowing if it will arrive in one minute or in a hundred years. The second kind of vulcanologist acts; he does not foresee an eruption but arrives when the volcano explodes. A 'grey' volcano," he went on, referring to the ashy color of an eruption, "is like a very fast train—you can feel the wind, and if you are in front of it, it is as if you were standing on the railway track as the train hurtles past."

Maurice Krafft, and his colleague and wife, Katia, were vulcanologists of the second kind. From Vulcain, the volcano-alert center they founded in 1968 in Cernay, France, they waited for news of major eruptions. When it came, they dropped everything to race to the scene. The pair worked to good effect: In a quarter-century, the Kraffts witnessed nearly 150 eruptions, more than any of their less mobile colleagues around the world. They were not, however, merely volcano-obsessed. The Kraffts were trained scientists—Maurice a geologist and Katia a geochemist—whose longtime fascination with volcanoes had led them to specialize in photographing and filming eruptions and flows at very close range. Their images greatly advanced scientific understanding of volcanoes, and the incomparable pictures—along with lectures and several books—also helped the Kraffts earn a living studying what they loved. Both had fallen for volcanoes as children, Maurice at 7 during a picnic at the edge of Stromboli, an Italian volcano active for the last 2,000 years, and Katia at 14.

Of all the pyrotechnic offerings of erupting volcanoes, pyroclastic flows, the deadliest products of vulcanism, most drew the Kraffts. A devil's stew of ash and boulders mixed with hot gases, pyroclastic flows boil down slopes at speeds of 60 to 80 miles an hour, knocking down and incinerating whatever they hit. It was a pyroclastic flow that killed 28,000 people in Mount Pelée's 1902 eruption on the Caribbean island of Martinique.

Wearing suits resembling those worn by airport firefighters, the Kraffts took cameras and sampling

gear closer to these rivers of stone than anyone had done before. The resulting data—and the daring closeup photography—put them at the top of their profession and made them the high-wire artists of vulcanology. "Life is an adventure that you don't get out of alive," Maurice said. "When we know everything about the subject in question, we will throw ourselves into the first crater we find."

In their close pursuit of a kind of volcanic intimacy, the Kraffts inevitably found themselves in one dangerous fix after another. They spent a hellish five days in 1979, for example, trapped alone on a tiny island not far from an erupting volcano on the Indonesian island of Krakatoa, the site of a catastrophic eruption in 1883. "Volcanic bombs, incandescent rocks which are thrown several dozen kilometers high, were falling everywhere," Maurice recalled. "We were stuck there for five days with explosions occurring every two or three minutes. The bombs as they fell described perfect parabolas, so we knew where they would fall," he explained. "We had to take turns in watching day and night."

When Alaska's Augustine volcano erupted in 1986, the Kraffts helicoptered to the fiery mountain, guided by University of Alaska vulcanologist Juergen Kienle. "They came home with spectacular footage of things no one else has because they got closer than anyone else," Kienle recalled, adding with mingled relief and regret: "I probably will never be that close again."

The Kraffts took risks with their eyes wide open. They had seen a great deal, and the prospect of death on a volcano was perfectly acceptable. Maurice thought of the mountains as living creatures, understood only by careful attention to all their actions and moods. The best observation point, he felt, was in "the belly of the beast," but he did not judge others who declined to join him there. "To study volcanoes as closely as I do," he once said, "you have to be mad, and tough and qualified as well. One is either born mad, or one is not."

In May 1991 the Kraffts followed their obsession to restive Mount Unzen in southwest Japan. Dormant since a disastrous eruption in 1792 that claimed 15,000 lives, the volcano was again oozing lava and disgorging as many as 35 pyroclastic flows each day.

Harry Glicken, an American vulcanologist at Tokyo Metropolitan University, joined the Kraffts as guide and translator. Glicken knew the danger better than most; in 1980 he had helped monitor Washington's newly active Mount St. Helens. His shift on a ridge eight miles north of the mountain had ended the day before the volcano exploded, engulfing the observation post and killing his successor.

At Unzen, the vulcanologists stationed themselves on the mountain's east flank, near the Mizunashi River. As white smoke billowed hundreds of feet above the mountain, huge chunks of sticky lava near the summit broke off and tumbled down the steep canyon walls, exploding into smaller pieces and releasing pent-up gases in a flow that surged down the riverbed.

Once again, the Kraffts moved in for the closest possible look, accompanied by Glicken. At first, Unzen obliged by sending down a succession of moderate flows. But on the afternoon of June 3, another mass of lava boulders broke away, and a searing tempest raged through the valley. Nothing in its path escaped. Buildings and cars burned to cinders, and 43 people died. Among them were Harry Glicken and the Kraffts—finally in the true belly of the beast. □

Protected by aluminized asbestos material, vulcanologist Maurice Krafft *(left)* strolls near a lava flow at Iceland's Krafla volcano in 1984. Above, he and wife Katia monitor vapor temperatures in a volcanic fumarole in Japan.

Bonds with Stock

Millionaire zoo founder John Aspinall *(left)* sits with Djoum, one of 39 gorillas in Aspinall's Howletts Zoo, where keeper Nicolas Marx *(below)* cavorts with three Indian tigers.

Zookeeper Nicolas Marx was stroking the friendly female Indian tiger one summer day in the mid-1970s when her jealous mate appeared, spoiling for a fight. The big cat circled aggressively, and Marx turned to keep facing him. When the tiger moved in to take a bite, Marx was ready: He slapped his adversary's head. Abandoning the man, the chastened cat went off to quarrel with the tigress instead.

Knowing how to act around animals, friendly and otherwise, not only keeps Marx alive—it is the essence of his job at the unusual Howletts Zoo Park near Canterbury, England. One of two such facilities founded by John Aspinall, a multi-millionaire casino owner with a passion for preserving endangered species, Howletts follows a contro-versial philosophy of close contact: Keepers are encouraged to enter the animals' enclosures and be-friend them. The goal is to estab-lish a bond between humans and their charges, based on affection and mutual understanding. Accord-ingly, keepers do more than tend their animals' physical needs—they routinely work inside the enclo-sures of elephants, gorillas, and even Siberian tigers, the zoo's largest carnivores, with the resi-dents close beside them.

Some zoo specialists have ex-pressed doubts that such animals can be trusted to develop and hon-or bargains with humans. Their skepticism is fueled by three fatal accidents. A plaque near the entrance at Howletts commemo-rates Brian Stocks and Bob Wilson, carnivore keepers killed by a Siberian tiger named Zeya in separate inci-dents in 1980. Brought to Howletts from Canada at the age of 14 months, Zeya rebuffed all friendly advances; keepers were wary of her and never entered her enclosure alone. Given that caution, the de-tails of Brian Stocks's fatal maul-ing in the tiger pit remain a mys-tery. The second incident was witnessed by two other keepers. Zeya scaled a "tiger-proof" fence some 10 feet high, then ran down Wilson as he tried to flee, catching him with a leap just three feet from the gate and safety. She still had his body in her mouth when Aspinall, despairing of her rehabili-tation, shot her dead.

Such clearly intentional acts are not the only danger. In 1984 at Aspinall's other zoo, in Port Lympne, near Dover, a good-natured 13-year-old Indian bull elephant named Bindu, who had recently been seen roughhousing

with the other elephants, playfully grabbed keeper Mark Aitken by the waist. Lifting Aitken off the ground, Bindu inadvertently smashed him into an iron girder. The keeper died instantly.

Despite these tragedies, the staffs at the two zoos agree with Aspinall's reading of what hap-pened. The keepers who died, he wrote to a newspaper in 1990, per-ished in the course of their regular work, "the protection and propaga-tion of endangered mammals," which they considered worth the risk. But Aspinall left no doubt about his feelings for his employ-ees, either: "A healthy, skillful and affectionate keeper is just as im-portant in my view as the animal he keeps, and often about as rare."

But, as proponents of the Aspi-nall method are quick to point out, accidents occur in all zoos. Some pursuits—breeding bull ele-phants, for example—are inherently dangerous. The real result of his zookeeping technique seems to be that the animals are treated and respected as individuals, not as herds of livestock, and their social ties with one another and their keepers are respected. "At Howletts and Port Lympne," wrote wildlife biologist Ian Redmond, "it is possible to see more natural behaviour than in almost any other zoo I have visited (which includes almost a hundred around the world)."

Proof that the Aspinall zoos are doing something right lies in their success in breeding certain species. Howletts was the first zoo in the United Kingdom to breed an African elephant and raise the calf, and experts consider its gorilla colony, with more than 39 animals, to be one of the best in the world. The gorillas have enjoyed a breeding success rate two and a half times that of ordinary zoos.

The most important factor in these and other achievements, according to Aspinall, is that the animals are not only healthy and happy, but also stimulated. "Boredom is the zoo animal's worst enemy," Aspinall says. "They must associate their keepers with entertainment and pleasure, not fear."

The animals' human friends try hard not to impose their presence where it is not wanted, however. Although Nicolas Marx spends most of his workday inside their enclosures, he never approaches tigers, instead allowing them to come to him. His friends among them, always glad to see him, come by to rumble a hello; when they do not, he respects their decision. The more aggressive tigers have learned to leave him alone—provided he does not show them his back for too long. □

Aided by Australian visitor Mike Thompson, alligator biologist Kent Vliet draws a blood sample from a 600-pound reptile at Florida's St. Augustine Alligator Farm. The samples are used to correlate stress and reproductive hormone levels.

Alligator Tag

Kent Vliet no longer swims with alligators, but it is not because of something they did. One of the world's few alligator biologists, Vliet spent the early 1980s observing the huge reptiles in their watery habitat, studying their subtle body language, including the tactile cues of courtship. Early in the study, however, Vliet realized that, to understand his subjects, he would have to get into the water with them. He subsequently spent an estimated 44 hours floating more or less inconspicuously a few feet from alligators as they met, bellowed, bumped, and mated.

The biologist's fascination with crocodilians grew out of a boyhood interest in the snakes and lizards of his native Oklahoma. Arriving in Florida as a graduate student in 1979, he planned to study gecko lizards but found alligators so intriguing—and so abundant—that they became the focus of his doctoral research. Although he knew nothing about handling the reptiles, he plunged right in.

For his first foray at the St. ◊

Augustine Alligator Farm, Vliet donned a diving mask one morning and slipped into the water. Immediately a very large alligator sped toward him. Trying to outswim an alligator is futile, so the stocky, powerfully built Vliet stood up, hoping to intimidate the beast. It stopped 10 feet away. After a brief exchange of stares, Vliet drove off his adversary with a splash—and quickly made for land.

Later that morning, Vliet went back into the water, and the same scenario took place. He was on his way to his first alligator insight: The reptiles are most "troublesome," as Vliet puts it, early in the day. He began observing them in the late afternoon, carrying a big stick to poke the snouts of those who displayed any dangerous curiosity about the man in their pond.

Cataloging and correlating what he saw on a computer, Vliet discovered 49 alligator behaviors related to mating, including remarkably tender courtship rituals. Alligators examine prospective mates in several ways, he says, such as bumping noses, ramming heads and necks, and submerging one another. There is also a good deal of communication using infrasound—sounds at frequencies too low for humans to hear.

One informal statistic belied the gators' reputation for ferocity: Since sliding into alligator-infested waters in 1981, Vliet has suffered just five bites, four of them while working on land with the farm's exhibitors to teach them how to handle the reptiles. Only one of those bites, on his wrist, merited a trip to the emergency room.

The single injury received in the water occurred when an alligator tagging session suddenly went sour. Vliet was seated on a 10-foot-long alligator, trying to rope it in order to tag it, when the animal suddenly headed out of the three-foot shallows and into the deeper waters where the farm's alligators like to gather. With Vliet still aboard, the alligator then chose to dive under the surface and ram another alligator from below. The second animal bit back—and got Vliet's arm, puncturing the skin with its teeth. Luckily, the animal did not clamp down with its powerful jaws and drag Vliet to the bottom.

Finding himself released, the wounded Vliet abandoned his amphibious mount and hurried back toward shallow water, diving over floating alligators who blocked his way and forcing himself between the creatures. Although alligators continually nip and push at one another with no ill effects, the middle of a floating crocodilian mob is no place for a human. Vliet finally managed to reach dry land.

When his studies of alligator courtship and mating were completed, Vliet got out of the water. He stopped going in, he later told a journalist, "because I didn't need to do it anymore. Anyway, it was starting to become a circus. People went crazy when they saw me out in the water, up to my neck with the gators." But alligators are still his specialty and his life. His more recent studies require capturing the big crocodilians to tag them, determine gender, and take blood samples. He is analyzing alligator hormones to see if crowding in captivity disrupts their reproductive cycle. He still rides and wrestles the occasional alligator in the name of science, but Vliet is no longer in the swim. □

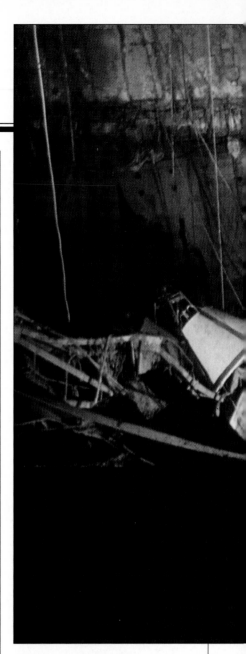

The Heart of Chernobyl

Early on the morning of April 26, 1986, unit number four of the Soviet Union's Chernobyl nuclear complex failed catastrophically, destroying the reactor hall and spewing tons of radioactive material into the atmosphere. At great sacrifice, technicians, firefighters, and soldiers contained the resulting fire and restored much of the

Blurred by his motion, a member of
Chernobyl's Complex Expedition works
inside the Sarcophagus, a 28-story
tomb for the ruined number four reactor. His garment keeps out some hazards but is transparent to deadly gam-
ma radiation near the reactor.

ejected uranium fuel and shattered
graphite to the reactor's core.
Then the radioactive wreck was
encased in a mixture of lead, sand,
neutron-absorbing boron carbide,
and thousands of tons of cement.
The result was an eternal monu-
ment to an accident whose nuclear
fires will smolder for a thousand
centuries: the Sarcophagus. But,
lethal as it is, this hastily constructed, leaky, 28-story tomb remains a workplace for a handful of
scientists and technicians—dedi-

cated people who are very likely
doomed by their current jobs.

In the aftermath of the explosion, scientists discovered that all
204 tons of the uranium fuel could
not be accounted for. Some, melted by the 5,000-degree fire, had
disappeared into the rubble. Physi-
cists feared that under certain conditions the escaped fuel might
become the critical mass required
to ignite a new—and perhaps explosive—chain reaction. Someone
would have to go into the Sarcoph-

agus and find the missing fuel.

The Complex Expedition, as it
was originally called, began probing the inside of the reactor in
1987. Clad in cotton suits, respira-
tors, and gloves—in especially
high-radiation areas, an additional
plastic suit was worn—members of
the expedition had little real protection against the surrounding
nuclear emissions. "We were going
into fields of 100 and 200 and 250
roentgens per hour," recalled Kiev
physicist Victor Popov, "and such
situations might spring up quite
unexpectedly. You walk down a
corridor and there's one to five
roentgens, and then you turn the
corner and there is 500 roentgens.
So of course you turn back right
away. You have to run. It was really
dangerous." Named for the discov-
erer of x-rays, the roentgen is a
unit of exposure to radiation; nuclear workers in the United States
are limited to five roentgens per
year, and a lethal dose is between
500 and 900 roentgens.

Proceeding at a deliberate pace,
never rounding a corner or entering a room before measuring the
radiation field, the team gingerly
picked its way through the jum-
bled, dust-covered wreckage,
searching for the vanished fuel.
Finally, in the once-flooded base-
ment below the wreckage of the
reactor, they came upon a glassy
mass more than six feet across and
weighing many tons; it was called
the elephant's foot because of the
odd shape it assumed in cooling.
Unable to approach the fuel because of its lethal radioactivity,
scientists used a rifle to shatter
samples from its surface. The
shards, scooped up by a specialized type of robot, proved to be a
new crystalline formation of ◊

fused sand and uranium, never seen in nature. The scientists took time from their task to give the material a name: chernobylite.

The rest of the missing fuel was found in similar glassy formations, reducing fears of a spontaneous chain reaction. But the expedition also discovered a new, equally serious, threat. The Sarcophagus, intended to endure for centuries, was already beginning to fall apart. When the explosion occurred in 1986, the 2,000-ton steel lid on the reactor was blown upward, then settled back, balanced precariously on broken piping and structure. Named Yelena by the Complex Expedition, the great steel lid will almost certainly fall inward as its supports deteriorate with time. This will trigger another latent hazard stored in the Sarcophagus: some 30 tons of highly radioactive plutonium dust. Every time something falls inside the tomb, a cloud of the lethal particles rises on the still air; if Yelena falls, the resulting cloud will squirt into the atmosphere. The collapse of the entire Sarcophagus would create a veritable storm of ''hot'' dust.

Faced with such adversities, the team remaining at Chernobyl's unit four faces others that are almost as formidable. ''We have difficulties with literally everything,'' Victor Popov told a journalist in 1991, ''the shortage of working clothes and even socks, and of course an invincible bureaucracy.'' The expedition has been reorganized since the breakup of the Soviet Union and now reports to the Academy of Sciences of the newly independent nation of Ukraine, where the nuclear complex is located. The expedition's name has been changed to Ukrytie, which means ''Cover''—an

effort to entomb further the ruins of Chernobyl number four.

Team members are less forthcoming about their greatest enemy. Asked whether they received extra doses of radiation as a result of poor equipment, Popov replied, ''That's our secret.'' Later, he expressed the expedition's amiable fatalism. ''The fact that a team of scientists working here is able to persevere under these conditions is a type of natural selection,'' he explained. ''We don't throw ourselves headlong into areas of high radiation. We don't pick up anything we see, we don't go wherever we want, by no means. We know very well where work has to be done quickly, and where we should not go at all. It takes time, but we are not robots, we're living people, and our endurance is not unlimited. We're fully aware that at some point our strength will fail, and then we shall have to leave.''

Since that 1991 interview, one expedition member was diagnosed with leukemia before dying of a heart attack; two others have suffered heart attacks, and a third is in a coma, all apparently as a result of their high-stress work. The expedition members undergo regular medical exams that include analyses of their blood, urine, feces, and sweat. Popov himself has since retired on disability as a result of radiation-induced cataracts. Yet the work continues. ''We know that it's not doing our health any good,'' said Popov before his retirement, ''but somehow the problem must be solved. There is no way around it. In time of war, things are also bad. Bullets are flying around, it's better to stay home. But someone has to go to war. This is a similar situation.'' □

Extremist

The French have a word for it: *ski extrême.* For most people—including those who ski moderately well—the scenario has the frightening texture of a recurring dream. Skiing down a convex dome of powdered snow, the skier sees that, just ahead, the slope has shattered into a sheer precipice that drops to a not-quite-naked lip of granite 80 feet below. Instead of waking up, the skier sets up for the calamity, flies over the rim, and, half-skiing, half-falling, soars through the air until the angled skis touch the earth again, and the downhill run continues. No dream at all, this outer envelope of skiing is the regime that Montanan Scot Schmidt explores for a living.

Although he is not the only person to do what he calls steep technical skiing, Schmidt ranks among the best in a highly specialized business. Once a promising downhill ski racer, he moved from Montana to a training camp at Squaw Valley, California, in 1979. There, the 18-year-old learned he could not afford to travel the ski-racing circuit without substantial backing. He also experienced the exhilaration of pitting his skills against the rocky, clifflike slopes beyond the reach of the chairlifts.

By 1983 word had reached ski film producer Warren Miller that a young man was carving out new lines at Squaw Valley. One particularly impossible run had been dubbed Shmidiots after its fearless conqueror. Miller sent a camera crew to record the action, and Schmidt's career took off. Since then, film assignments have taken him to menacing slopes in Switzerland, Canada, France, and New

Wearing a backpack full of mountaineering gear, Scot Schmidt *(right)* begins his run down a 50-foot snow-speckled cliff for the cameras, as he pioneers a near-vertical slope in the little-skied Chugach Mountains of Alaska.

Zealand, among other places. Sometimes he plays himself; now and then, he doubles for actors chasing, or being chased, on skis.

Getting to the site is often the first challenge; trams or helicopters take him most of the way, but Schmidt says he must then climb farther up, sometimes for as long as half a day, to reach the point from which his descent is to begin. Within the planned location, Schmidt picks each filmed run himself, studying the slope from all angles for days and taking snow conditions and rocks into account. A large part of his approach is aesthetic—he is not interested in the short traverses with which many extrême skiers pick their way down an unskied cliff. "I'm not a real mountaineer," Schmidt told one interviewer. "I'm not out to break records. I'm out there to have fun and to be real explosive and dynamic—to use a lot of style in my skiing." The camera crews position their equipment to catch the best angles. Schmidt has found some sites with great potential for filming but minimal snow; he says in some cases he has had to wait for years for snow to cover just the right rocks so that he can make a particular descent.

Schmidt has also, on occasion, suffered from too much of the white stuff. Avalanches are always a threat when one skis on an undisturbed, precariously balanced crust. In 1986 a large block of snow crumbled around him while he was on location in Verbier, Switzerland. "Somehow I stayed with it," he later told a reporter. "I was riding down on giant snow blocks, watching them crumble as we went. It finally swallowed me." Curiously at peace with the experi-

ence, Schmidt "felt my skis running with the snow. I kept them running, kept my weight back, and then, at the bottom where the chute opened into a bowl, the avalanche just dissipated. I put an edge on my skis and skied out."

Despite that close call, which he recalls with more awe than terror, he considers the bulk of his exploits relatively safe. Speed is both a tonic and a threat. "On some of my hundred-foot jumps," he said in 1986, "the speed is just unbelievable. The landing comes up so

fast. It really freaked me out on my last big jump. I must have been going 100 when I hit the ground." Still, he knows his is a hazardous business. "Adventure skiing is dangerous. I'd be really scared if I didn't know what I was doing. People who want to try the sport should constantly check their fearmeters. Be ready to back out if you push too far into the red." His own final check before going off a jump reveals no anxiety. "Just before I go, if it's a rowdy maneuver, I usually give a yip and yell." □

Cave Man

The bugs and salamanders that Andy Grubbs collects in the course of his work are perfectly harmless. Not even the occasional blind scorpion poses much of a threat. Getting to them, however, is another story, for Grubbs is a biospeleologist—a specialized student of nature who examines life as it is lived far underground, in total darkness. To follow his biological specialty—and his powerful interest in caving—he has lowered himself thousands of feet into vast, rocky rooms that have never seen daylight, rappelled down sheer faces, scrambled over and through wastelands of shattered rock, squeezed through openings that would destroy a claustrophobe, and waded through chill subterranean pools and streams with only an inch or two between the water and the rock ceiling. Along the way, he probes for blind scorpions, springtails, ant spiders, and, his favorite, a large arachnid resembling a mashed tarantula. For many it would be a nightmare. For Grubbs it has become a grueling, but very satisfying, occupation.

Clearly not for the insect squeamish or the faint of heart, biospeleology is in fact a way of studying evolution—in reverse. While most creatures become less alike with each evolutionary step—a process called divergence—the pale, eyeless creatures retrieved by Grubbs demonstrate the opposite effect of convergence. As the rigors of cave living force similar adaptations from all inhabitants, different species of cave dwellers begin to look more and more alike.

Although Grubbs himself may study what he collects, he sends most samples to colleagues with less enthusiasm for subterranean adventure; their expertise identifies new species and tracks the distribution of known types. This is not to say he plies his underground trade in isolation. In the deep caves, teamwork drives the expedition. Hauling and rigging ropes and other gear needed for a long descent requires a well-coordinated group effort; the deepest explora-

On the lookout for cave-adapted insect species, biospeleologist Andy Grubbs traverses along the rocky flank of a 2,000-foot-deep chasm during a 1985 expedition in Mexico's Cueva St. Augustine, one of the world's deepest caverns.

tions require two or three teams of three to six people each. Dropping down through the perpetual night of the caverns, the explorers follow the flow of air that tells them whether apertures are blind alleys or openings to discovery.

Teams provide some security in the event of a sprain or more serious injury, but nothing can completely eliminate the risks. In March 1991 a spelunker friend of Grubbs's named Chris Yaeger died in Mexico's Cueva Cheve, one of the world's 10 deepest caverns and a site Grubbs had explored several times in the past. As Yaeger was changing ropes above a 70-foot drop, a piece of rappelling equipment let go and he fell to his death; Grubbs helped recover the body in an expedition a year later.

A caver for 20 years, Grubbs's closest call came in 1989; it involved falling rock, another common hazard. Standing in the so-called bomb zone below a descent route—the impact zone for falling rocks dislodged by previous climbers—Grubbs took a direct hit from a football-size rock that fell 70 feet from a ledge when another climber accidentally freed it. The rock broke to pieces on Grubbs's helmet, saving him from serious injury or death.

The rewards for all this effort and risk range from hard-won scientific knowledge to the sheer exhilaration of exploring new caverns never before seen by humankind. But for Grubbs the work has also brought a slice of immortality. Among the nearly 60 new species he has brought back are 10 that carry his name, including a six-millimeter-long California pseudoscorpion known to science as *Apochthonius grubbsi.* □

Fly-by-Night

In California's Imperial Valley, humans have added the water of irrigation to the fertile soils of an ancient seabed, producing, with the help of intense, year-round sunlight, one of the world's agricultural marvels—a cornucopia of lettuce, broccoli, sweet corn, asparagus, and other vegetables that spill onto the tables of the nation throughout the year. This fountain of food requires constant tending. Not only water must be added to the valley's soil, but tons of pesticides. In the Imperial Valley, as across the Midwest, the Mississippi Delta, and California's great Central Valley, only chemicals can protect the fields of corn, cotton, rice, and produce from destruction by peckish aphids, grubs, and beetles. The predations of these insects are fought by two winged creatures: insectivorous birds and crop dusters.

Flying more than 120 miles per hour at head height across the fields, the duster holds one of farming's dirty, physically exhausting, mentally demanding, and dangerous jobs. Modern dusters—or aerial applicators, as they are known by officialdom—feel that their world is far removed from that of their predecessors. These were often itinerant pilots, hard-drinking, hard-talking men who flew rickety aircraft—often carelessly and fatally. Today's crop dusters are closely regulated and have acquired better equipment and better skills using it. Nevertheless, some concede that theirs is still a dangerous occupation.

In fact, danger envelops them. Crop dusters fly at an altitude of about six feet above the crops, at speeds between 120 and 140 miles per hour. There is usually a road at the end of the field, however, and roads provide a convenient route for telephone and electric wires. Low-flying crop dusters sometimes snag the wires; with luck, the plane stumbles on, trailing yards of wire whistling in the slipstream. But Carl Payne, who runs a crop-dusting operation in Katy, Texas, in the heart of rice-growing country, has watched a fellow duster crash in flames after hitting power lines with his aircraft's windshield. Payne himself once plowed into the top of an elm tree after snagging a telephone wire.

Engines can quit suddenly and airplanes fall apart. Texan Terry Porter cannot remember the crash that followed when his Stearman's 450-horsepower engine tore itself from its mountings; he only recalls standing next to the smoldering wreckage. Flying at an altitude of six feet, the pilot has little time to think or space to maneuver before his plane hits the ground. Birds zig when they should zag, smashing windshields and pilots' faces.

But perhaps the greatest enemy of the crop duster is his or her—there are a very few women in the business—fatigue. During the busiest months of the season, an ag pilot flies from dawn to dusk, seven days a week—long days spent bathed in the fumes of poisonous chemicals, hot engines, and the sweat of hard labor. The cockpit of a crop-dusting airplane is one of the busiest workplaces in the world, where inattention and carelessness are punished swiftly and brutally. It is not unlike the cockpit of a fighter plane in a dogfight, which may explain why many former fighter pilots have ◊

been attracted to the business.

From the time he first spots his target until he leaves for the next, a crop duster will spend about an hour treating a square 150-acre field measuring one-half mile on each side. In that time, the pilot will fly 55 to 65 passes over the crops, each consuming less than 20 seconds. On each pass the pilot must turn the chemical flow on and off, adjust the throttle, maintain a precise track, determine the effect of wind on the drifting spray, watch for obstacles ranging from birds to shovel handles sticking up from the ground, and execute a steep climb to clear the inevitable power lines. As the climb slows the heavily loaded aircraft to near stalling speed—the speed at which the wings no longer provide lift—the pilot carves a sharp, precise turn that leaves him exactly on course for the next run. Hands and feet are in constant

Crop duster Jim Newman *(inset)* prefers to work California's Imperial Valley in the cool, calm air between dusk and dawn *(above),* flying his Piper Brave along rows marked by a ground crew.

motion manipulating rudder pedals, stick, throttle, and chemical valves. The pilot's eyes scan ground and sky for obstacles and the instrument panel for any sign of mechanical difficulties.

Although experienced crop dusters express love for their work and respect for its dangers, they are not eloquent about their reasons, leaving it to outsiders to express the subtle gravitation of their trade. A hint of what attracts them may be detected as Jim Newman flies a 300-horsepower Piper Brave in the ovenlike atmosphere of the Imperial Valley. Because of the valley's triple-digit daytime tem-

peratures, Newman prefers to fly at night. The air is calmer then, he says, as well as cooler. It is also more dangerous; power lines and other obstacles are less visible. But the darkness also provides a perfect stage. Witnessed from a nearby field, Newman's work becomes a show of sound and light that, in its way, is as moving as the play of colors on the fountains of Versailles.

Newman's arrival over his darkened target field is abrupt. The curtain of silence opens quickly to reveal the rumbling baritone of an airplane engine. Amid the stars, three lights appear: one red and flashing, bracketed by two steady lights glowing like the unblinking eyes of a giant beetle—red on one wing, green on the other. The plane is invisible as the show begins. A torrent of white light gushes forward, blinding all in its path, illuminating a field of produce and tracing strands of electric wires that delineate the field. Still cloaked by darkness, Newman's plane sweeps head-high across the crops behind a wave of light, the trailing plume of chemicals barely visible in the reflected glow.

At the end of the field the brilliant white light abruptly winks out. A dimmer bulb flicks on and off, briefly picking out a line of wires as the plane rushes toward them. The engine's sound falls in intensity, and the small red and green lights spring back into focus against the blue-black sky, leaping upward, tilting and twisting above the wires, then turning sharply back for a second run.

The aircraft itself remains invisible throughout. Another white light flashes on momentarily, pointing downward; it is attached to the wing tip, and Newman switches it on in mid-turn to provide a fleeting view of the ground. When the wing tip light winks out, red and green are again visible, descending rapidly. No sooner are they level than another breaker of light floods the field, illuminating a thin cloud of insecticide that hovers over the crops. The show continues until the field is fully covered. The entire performance consumes less time than a single movement of a symphony. But, in the rise and fall of the engine's sound, and the twist, arc, blink, and plunge of the aircraft's lights, there is a dangerous kind of art. □

Micromurderers

Given the nature of contagious disease, doctors are always at some risk of becoming patients, especially those who study rare viruses that cause illnesses for which there is neither vaccine nor cure. Sometimes the risk can be controlled. For example, at the Maximum Containment Center of the federal Centers for Disease Control (CDC) in Atlanta, Georgia, researchers examining such tiny killers don pressurized, full-body spacesuits before entering the center's laboratories through a series of air locks; when they leave, they take a chemical shower with the suits still in place. High-efficiency air filters screen out even the tiniest particles, and to guard against accidents, no glassware or flames are allowed in the lab. Most of the hypodermic needles are dull, to prevent accidental jabs.

But, rarely, a CDC researcher must leave this containment for the real world, where there is no protection. All the risks the CDC labs are designed to mitigate are everywhere in the field for virologists trying to comprehend little-known diseases. For CDC virologist Joseph McCormick, the hazards of fieldwork have special resonance—during most of his 20-year career, he has specialized in the deadly hemorrhagic fever viruses of Africa. Victims of such viruses invariably run high fevers and in the worst cases suffer extensive internal bleeding. Most deaths come when, in shock from being starved of blood, vital organs fail.

During the 1970s and 1980s, McCormick was often one of the first outside doctors to reach the remote sites of new fever epidem-

ics. While he treated victims and tried to limit the spread of the disease, he also studied its properties and patterns of infection. Where ordinary physicians would diagnose an individual, McCormick would diagnose a community and map the viral wildfire as it leaped from person to person. For the virologist, epidemics are a kind of uncontrolled experiment.

One of McCormick's deadlier adversaries was the Ebola virus he encountered during its first known outbreak, in Zaire in 1976. Named after a Zairian river, the Ebola strain is the deadliest of all known African fever viruses, killing many of its victims in a matter of days. "It's frightening because the disease is so dramatic," McCormick has said. "People get sick and die fast, and they bleed and it scares the daylights out of you."

The virologist had been working in Sierra Leone on a CDC study of another of Africa's viral illnesses, Lassa fever, when rumor told of a strange epidemic in Zaire. Since he had worked there as a teacher before going to medical school and knew local languages, customs, and governments, McCormick decided he was the right person to go to the stricken area. Once in Zaire, he searched out fever victims in far-flung villages and found that terror was as pervasive as the virus. Families rebelled against bringing their sick to hospitals, preferring that the almost inevitable death happen at home. Because the virus evidently needed close personal contact to spread, McCormick believed lives could be saved by separating patients from their families. But nothing ◊

worked well against the disease.

Of the 318 people diagnosed with Ebola fever in Zaire during the 1976 outbreak, 290—91 percent—died. This fatality rate, astonishing even for the Ebola virus, had the medical world holding its breath. The virus appeared to be spreading easily, leading to fears that it might break out of rural Africa into the cities—and into the world at large. Noted one observer, "Hiroshima would have looked like a picnic in comparison."

In the end, however, the Ebola epidemic sputtered and died out. Its original virulence, physicians later discovered, had been amplified by the extremely unhygienic procedures used to treat the sick. In one remote, poorly funded hospital almost all medication had been administered with the same five needles and syringes, without any sterilization. Once a needle was used on an Ebola fever sufferer, many subsequent patients were infected. While some who contracted the disease from friends or relatives survived, all who got it from needles died—the body evidently could not win against Ebola inject-

ed directly into the bloodstream.

McCormick had reason to remember that epidemiological detail three years later, during another Ebola epidemic in southern Sudan. Again, the local population was reluctant to cooperate, and few guides would take him to the stricken areas. In one village, he landed at dusk in a police aircraft, its pilot eager to escape but forced by darkness to delay takeoff until morning. McCormick rushed to examine all the patients that night, taking blood samples to ship back to CDC for analysis; he knew that weeks might pass before another plane arrived—the government had quarantined the region.

Working by a kerosene lantern in the thatched, mud-walled hut that served the village as a clinic, McCormick knelt to examine the patients lying on reed mats on the dirt floor. One delirious patient, an elderly woman, began to thrash about as he took a blood sample. As McCormick withdrew the needle, the woman knocked his hand, causing him to stab his own thumb. Days from real medical care, possibly infected with a dis-

ease that would take only a week to incubate, and scarcely longer to kill, he spent a long night considering his situation, helped, he recalled later, by "a substantial portion of a bottle of scotch."

McCormick stayed. "I decided that I wasn't going to do anything about the epidemic somewhere else," he said afterward, "and there wasn't anybody else who could do it, so I decided to stick around and if I got sick I would somehow get word out." In the days that followed, he kept a close watch over the elderly woman. Soon, to his great relief, her fever broke and her condition improved; unlike most of the patients in the hut, she had been infected by a less deadly virus than Ebola.

That close call did not prevent McCormick from rushing back to Africa whenever an isolated case of Ebola fever appeared. During the early 1980s, however, he learned that some of Zaire's rich were flying to Belgium for treatment of another deadly illness: AIDS. Conscious that the appearance of AIDS among the wealthy few in that impoverished country signaled a larger epidemic among the many poor, McCormick helped found Projet SIDA—SIDA is the French acronym for the lethal disease—the first African AIDS research project, in 1983. Then, early in the 1990s, McCormick turned away from the viral diseases of Africa to confront one of humankind's ancient tropical enemies: malaria, the infectious parasitic disorder Western medicine has been fighting since the 1700s. □

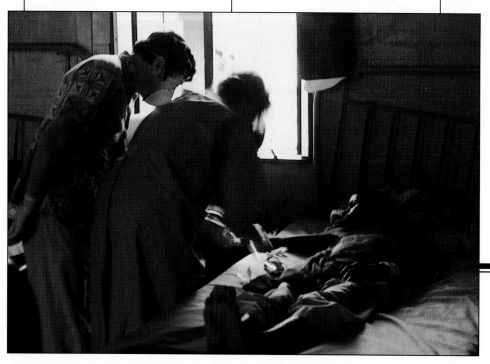

At a Sierra Leone hospital in 1979, virologist Joseph McCormick *(far left)* assists colleague Patricia Webb with a victim of Lassa fever, one of the hemorrhagic diseases in which McCormick specialized.

Protected only by a burlap shawl, Nepalese honey hunter Mani Lal braves swarms of angry bees to lever honey and comb into a bamboo basket, which will be lowered to helpers who are waiting on the rocks below.

Sweet Danger

Deep in the Himalayan foothills of central Nepal, villagers often depend on small-scale farming and trading to earn their living. In 1984 a husband-and-wife team of photojournalists began documenting one such tiny business, the collection of honey and wax from bees' nests located on high cliffs.

Australian Eric Valli and his French wife, Diane Summers, have chosen to document the work of Mani Lal, an aging honey gatherer from the village of Danra Gaon who was born to his centuries-old role. According to Valli and Summers, Mani Lal always prays before going to work, scattering rice to invoke the protection of Pholo, god of the forest. Then he climbs down a cliff to the nests of angry bees. Only his tight grip on a fragile, swaying ladder of bamboo fibers keeps him from tumbling more than 300 feet to his death.

In Danra Gaon, a select few are sanctioned to collect the wax and honey of the Asian honeybee, the world's largest. Each has his own inherited role. Some manage smoky fires used to disorient the bees, others filter the honey, still others relay equipment down the ladder from the cliff top. But only Mani Lal descends to the nest.

From his tenuous perch, Mani Lal drives the bees away from ◊

their nests with smoke from a bundle of burning leaves. Those that stay to defend their nest find a relatively easy target: The honey hunter wears nothing more than a pair of secondhand army pants and a cape draped loosely over his head. Mani Lal's faith in Pholo has protected him so far, but the danger of a destructive attack is palpable. He believes his father's faith must have faltered on the day he was attacked by thousands of bees, whose stings destroyed the vision in one eye. But thus far, Mani Lal's faith has not been shaken.

Surrounded by the fearsome buzzing of the dispossessed bees, Mani Lal cuts up the honeycomb at arm's length using bamboo poles. He quickly fills a dangling goatskin-lined basket with thick slabs, and his helpers above lower the prize to the helpers below. Melted down and filtered, the wax and honey from this and scores of other nests provide Mani Lal and his comrades with a modest income. Beeswax can be sold for use in the Katmandu bronze-casting industry, while honey is traded locally for milk, grain, or labor.

Honey hunting was a worldwide practice long before humans learned to husband bees. About 10,000 years ago, a cave painter in what is now Spain depicted a hunter climbing a ladder to a bees' nest, bucket in hand; similar images have been found in Africa and India. But, ancient as it is, the hunt is nearing its end. As he gets older, Mani Lal finds himself hunting for honey a little less each year, according to Valli and Summers, and his sons have no interest in succeeding him on the frail, swaying ladder far above the rocks, fighting angry bees. □

Cool Miners

In modern warfare, an armistice stops the shooting, but the killing goes on for years. All wars have littered their battlefields with munitions that did not explode as intended, remaining dormant until triggered accidentally. World War I artillery shells have lasted long enough to kill the grandchildren of the original combatants. But the problem of this lethal litter has never been worse than it is today. It is now routine for combatants to sow tens of thousands of small mines intended to maim or kill anything that passes. Even duds are more deadly—an unexploded high-technology weapon may suddenly detonate for unfathomable reasons. Peace brings an expensive harvest, one few war-torn nations can afford. Still, where there is money to do it, the slow and dangerous cleanup attracts a rare species of employee, who reckons success in terms of survival.

In the tiny, oil-rich Persian Gulf state of Kuwait, the locus of the 1990-1991 Gulf War in which Kuwait was first invaded by Iraqi forces, then recaptured by the forces of a United Nations coalition, that harvest has only begun. Quickly resolved by overwhelming force, the conflict strewed death across Kuwait. The retreating Iraqis left hundreds of square miles of dense minefields and vast quantities of munitions deteriorating in the sun. The massive air strikes by the U.N. allies added about 30,000 tons of unexploded bombs—a third of the total dropped. Some were experimental weapons that evidently did not function as designed; others, designed for hard targets, were not detonated by their softer landing in damp desert sand. In the first year of peace, unexploded weapons left behind by both sides killed

A two-man team (left) works one of Kuwait's Iraqi-laid minefields in 1992. As the lead man discovers mines with his gunlike metal detector, his partner marks their locations with red and white flags, indicating a safe path through the field.

and wounded 1,420 civilians, by Kuwaiti estimates; other experts believe that figure is far too low.

Within several weeks of the end of fighting, a new multinational force began arriving in Kuwait: specialists from Pakistani, Egyptian, French, English, and American organizations hired by the Kuwaiti government to clear various sections of the country. Most who answered the call were former military men such as 44-year-old George Kramer, a retired United States Air Force explosive-ordnance disposal—EOD—technician who left his job as a safety supervisor at Cape Canaveral to come to Kuwait. Drawn by fairly high pay—a good EOD specialist earns from $50,000 to $90,000 a year, paid monthly—and a well-developed sense of adventure, Kramer joined a British company that had landed a contract to clear mines around oil wells, roads, and power lines. "Our training involves basically anything from a .22-caliber bullet on up to and including nuclear weapons," explains Kramer. "We're trained to handle both ours and foreign countries'." In Kuwait, he is working mainly on duds and land mines from both sides.

"The hard part," Kramer says, "is when you first go into a mine field. The mines are all laid in specific patterns—once we get a breach through the side of a mine field, when we can go from one side to the other, we will find out what the pattern of the mines is, and then we'll know really within about a foot of where each mine is supposed to be." For example, a preferred pattern used by NATO and Iraq implants an antitank mine—triggered only by some 400 pounds of pressure—guarded on at least three sides by antipersonnel mines, which are detonated by just 5 to 15 pounds of force. In a properly laid minefield—often an area several miles long and a few hundred yards wide—a step or two in any direction risks setting off an explosion. "There is very little surface area," says Kramer, "that is not covered by mines."

Many of the land mines deployed by the Iraqis in Kuwait were placed on the ground and gradually covered by windblown sand. In these minefields, Kramer and his colleagues usually work in two-person teams, each wearing a 40-pound bomb suit designed to allow the wearer to survive the detonation of a charge smaller than seven pounds—though probably not without serious injury. Most antipersonnel mines contain less than one pound of explosive. But the antitank mines in Kuwait usually contain about 15 pounds. The suit, Kramer admits, is as much for "peace of mind" as for protection.

Given the stakes involved, mine-clearing teams work slowly and deliberately, one technician sweeping a swath a yard or so wide with a metal detector, the other sticking small flags into the sand to designate the safe path. The leader usually "safes" mines when they are found, by removing their detonators. The number-two person watches from a few steps away; in the event of an accident, the observer might be able to report what went wrong and prevent recurrences.

Antipersonnel mines are relatively simple to disarm and set aside for later collection and destruction, but antitank mines must be checked for booby traps by digging carefully under them with a trowel. Mines too dangerous to move are destroyed in place, sometimes by means of additional explosives; the team can set a plastic explosive beside or on top of a piece of ordnance, then detonate the two explosives at once from a safe distance, using a long wire and an electric blasting cap.

Because a single misstep can be fatal, the work requires constant concentration, a state of mind difficult to maintain in 120-degree desert heat while wearing a stifling bomb suit. Usually a mine-detecting team works just a half-hour at a time before stopping for a rest of an hour or more, while another team takes over.

High-technology duds are in some ways worse than mines, especially those containing hundreds of smaller bomblets—sub-munitions—that remain unexploded in the sand. "There are any number of reasons why a sub-munition did not go off," explains Kramer. "If you walk up to it ◊

In the Kuwait desert, explosive-ordnance demolition technician John Lowe prepares to disarm a concealed Italian-made antipersonnel mine guarding larger antitank devices like the one in the foreground.

and cast a shadow over it, the shadow may set it off." Anything can trigger such devices, he says, especially after the explosive has been rendered unstable by a year or two in desert temperatures.

Although many, like Kramer, were drawn by the adventure of explosives demolition, the task itself is tedious, nerve-jangling work, performed seemingly with no end in sight. And despite all the precautions, it is indeed extremely dangerous. In the eleven months after demolition began, 84 EOD technicians died in Kuwait.

Environmental Chemical Corporation, the British EOD company that Kramer originally worked for, enjoyed good luck until one day in August 1991, when the firm was clearing a path through a minefield more than a third of a mile across. Kramer's partner, Bruce Tincknell, was disarming a Soviet antipersonnel mine when it inexplicably detonated. Tincknell fell forward screaming, his hands in shreds; Kramer was spun about by the blast and dropped to the sand.

Raced to a hospital, Tincknell was eventually evacuated to the United States; he ended up losing one hand and several fingers from the other. Kramer miraculously emerged with minor shrapnel wounds in his arms, body, and legs and missed just one day of work. The incident took a further toll as well. In the next three weeks, five of the company's EOD technicians decided to take their pay and go home. Kramer left the company less than a month later but not the profession. After a short vacation, he found employment with another firm, where he resumed his dicey harvesting of latent death from Kuwait's battlefields. □

Fire Breather

When Lauren Muney ignites the gasoline-soaked ball of cotton gauze stretched on a small wire frame and sticks the resulting lollipop of flame into her mouth, she is not really eating fire, although that is what the trick is called. The flames go out the moment she closes her mouth, depriving them of oxygen; only the sour taste of white gasoline lingers.

Fire-eating is not as simple as it seems, however. Muney cautions amateurs never to try the seemingly easy tricks she performs. Many fire-eaters—even professionals—suffer severe burns of the esophagus and face and often lose beards and eyebrows when the stunt goes wrong. Muney herself was apprehensive at first. "I had to stare at the fire to get over the fear of it," she recalls. "But understanding the science behind fire-eating made me more comfortable with it. When you close your mouth over the fire and the fire's in there, the fire will go out." Urgently she adds, "This may sound corny, but . . . don't try it at home."

Even Muney often singes her long hair and regularly suffers mouth burns similar to those produced by too-hot melted cheese or coffee. She also admits to an upset stomach after some performances, a result of swallowing small amounts of white gasoline—about a teaspoon after each meal of fire. Many of her colleagues prefer alcohol as the flaming agent.

Fascinated as a child by tales of medieval troubadors and jesters, Muney began her professional life as a graduate of the Ringling

Brothers and Barnum & Bailey Clown College. Clown College regards fire-eating as too dangerous to teach, so Muney picked up that skill from a juggling colleague later on. A working fire-eater since 1989, when she was 25, Muney fulfills her childhood dream by performing at renaissance fairs, festivals, parties, banquets, and casinos around the United States and the world.

Like other fire-eaters, she does more than swallow flames by quenching them in her closed mouth. In one crowd-pleasing trick called the Dragon's Breath, she lowers a burning torch into her mouth, withdraws it, and suddenly belches a flame as much as a foot long, made of vapors she has drawn into her mouth and blown out again. Her most hazardous act is called the Volcano, which involves sipping gasoline and then blowing it across a lit torch to create a massive blast of fire. Unless she spits the gasoline just right, the flame can shoot back along the stream to burn her.

Although that kind of backfire has never happened to Muney while performing the Volcano, she did once suffer a "small burn" on her chin during a less demanding torch trick. The act had been going well, she recalls, until someone unthinkingly turned on the air conditioning, which blew burning liquid into her face.

Muney usually limits her fire-eating performances to two days a week, with five performances each day, to minimize long-term dangers: Gasoline is carcinogenic, so ingesting it regularly is a bad idea. Frequent exposure to flames also diminishes Muney's voice, essential to her one-woman show, which includes stilt walking, juggling, pantomime, stage combat, and spectacular feats with a bullwhip. On flameless days, Muney also toys with a new trick based on one described by the legendary magician Harry Houdini. She puts a few razor blades in her mouth, together with a ball of string. When she pulls out the string, if all goes well, the razor blades are threaded onto it. And, should her audience's attention seem to wane, there is always the awe-inspiring fiery puff of the Dragon's Breath. □

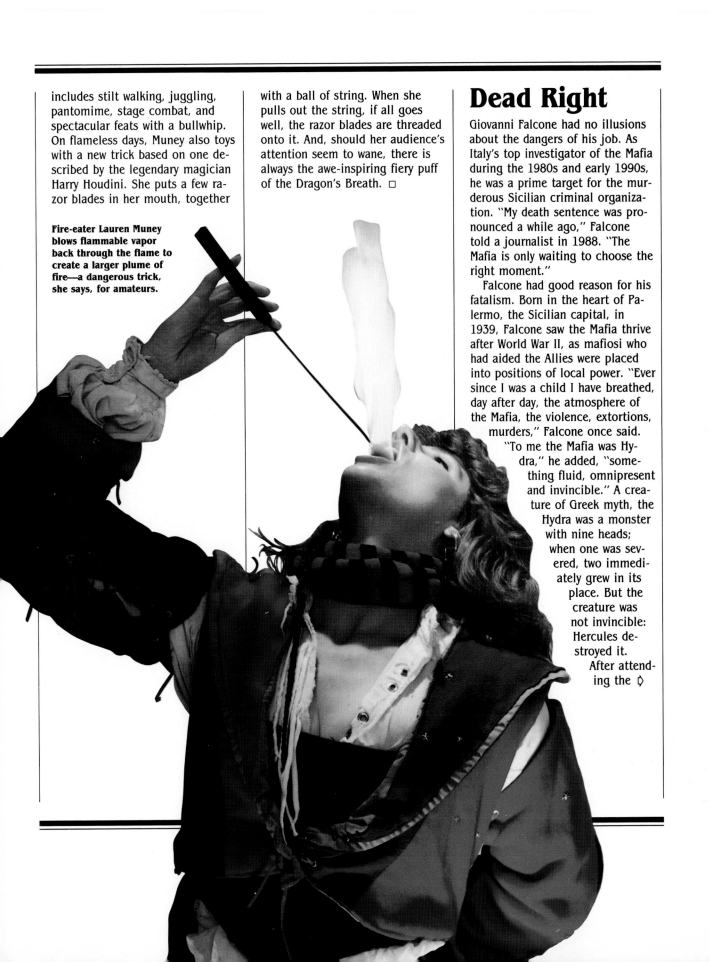

Fire-eater Lauren Muney blows flammable vapor back through the flame to create a larger plume of fire—a dangerous trick, she says, for amateurs.

Dead Right

Giovanni Falcone had no illusions about the dangers of his job. As Italy's top investigator of the Mafia during the 1980s and early 1990s, he was a prime target for the murderous Sicilian criminal organization. "My death sentence was pronounced a while ago," Falcone told a journalist in 1988. "The Mafia is only waiting to choose the right moment."

Falcone had good reason for his fatalism. Born in the heart of Palermo, the Sicilian capital, in 1939, Falcone saw the Mafia thrive after World War II, as mafiosi who had aided the Allies were placed into positions of local power. "Ever since I was a child I have breathed, day after day, the atmosphere of the Mafia, the violence, extortions, murders," Falcone once said.

"To me the Mafia was Hydra," he added, "something fluid, omnipresent and invincible." A creature of Greek myth, the Hydra was a monster with nine heads; when one was severed, two immediately grew in its place. But the creature was not invincible: Hercules destroyed it.

After attending the ◊

Mafia prosecutor Giovanni Falcone *(below)* takes laptop notes at a 1991 conference on criminality, a year before a remotely detonated ton of dynamite killed him and several others on a Palermo motorway *(right)* in May 1992.

Italian Naval Academy, Falcone followed the wishes of his father and attended law school—entering a profession that would prove far more hazardous than a military career. He began his anti-Mafia mission in 1966 as assistant public prosecutor in the gang-infested Sicilian city of Trapani, where he received the first of many death threats in the form of postcards covered with caskets and crosses.

In Trapani he witnessed the long arm of the Mafia, with its far-reaching interests in drug dealing, construction scams, extortion, smuggling, and illegal gambling. To defend its vast illicit earnings, the organization had no qualms about murder, even at the highest levels. In the 1970s alone, five top law-enforcement officials in Sicily died at the Mafia's hands.

Despite the danger, Falcone went cheerfully and effectively about his work. In 1979 his zeal brought him to the attention of Rocco Chinnici, a chief investigating magistrate who brought Falcone back to Palermo to work in the front lines of anti-Mafia prosecution. Two years later, Falcone became one of a special anti-Mafia group of eager young Sicilian magistrates organized by Chinnici. The team's efforts were soon spurred by the 1982 murder of General Carlo Alberto Dalla Chiesa, who was gunned down in his car with his wife four months after arriving in Palermo as the newly appointed anti-Mafia high commissioner. The murders marked a new level of violence: The mob had previously spared the female relatives of the officials they assassinated.

In the wake of the Dalla Chiesa killing, Chinnici trained his protégés to pool their findings, both to provide mutual support and to reduce their own vulnerability. With shared information, an investigation could no longer be snuffed out by a single murder. Chinnici fell victim to a car bomb in 1983, but the investigation he had launched continued.

Falcone stepped in to handle the arrest and indictment of more than 300 alleged mafiosi on warrants Chinnici had signed before his death. The young prosecutor traveled to Brazil, where he persuaded Mafia boss Tommaso Buscetta to break *omertà*, the traditional code of silence, to become the first ranking Sicilian mafioso to testify against his associates.

In February 1986 a highly publicized "maxi-trial" of hundreds of accused mobsters began in Palermo in a massive, specially built concrete courthouse guarded by tanks. By that time, Falcone was

leading a sequestered life in an apartment building monitored by cameras and patrolled by five guards. Police blocked off the neighborhood when he came and went. His girlfriend Francesca Morvillo, a magistrate who later became his wife, bought Falcone's clothes to keep him off the streets.

By the trial's end, 338 mafiosi had been sentenced to nearly 2,700 years in prison, and Falcone was a hero. But the fruits of victory were bittersweet. Appeals courts overturned many of the convictions and reduced other sentences. And because he had led the prosecution team, Falcone knew more secrets about the Mafia than any other outsider, a fact that marked him for almost certain death.

In response to that threat, Falcone lived in bombproof quarters inside a police station whenever he was in Rome. A detail of 58 police officers guarded him and his wife, who had remained childless because of the danger. The Falcones also had armored cars in Rome and Palermo, and they traveled in aircraft flown by a secret government agency.

Though Falcone viewed his possible murder as one of the job's risks, he was shaken in 1989, when police found 58 sticks of gelignite, a powerful explosive, in a gym bag left on a rocky pier behind his rented summer villa. The bomb ◊

A ton of dynamite transformed the interior of Giovanni Falcone's armored sedan into a mass of twisted leather and metal, killing the crusader and his wife. Riding in the backseat, the chauffeur somehow survived.

was fitted with a radio-controlled detonator investigators assumed was to have been activated from a passing boat. Friends reported that for the first time Falcone seemed nervous and pale, pacing the house with drink in hand.

Four years later, the Mafia chose its moment. Arriving at the Palermo airport in an unmarked government jet early one May evening in 1992, Falcone hopped behind the wheel of his armored car and sped from the airport along the A29 autostrada. His wife sat beside him in the passenger seat, and his chauffeur was in the back. Guards were in cars ahead and behind.

At 5:50 p.m. a huge explosion engulfed the convoy. The lead car was hurled into an olive grove 200 yards away, instantly killing the three policemen inside. Falcone's car, its front end ripped off, perched on the brink of a 30-foot-deep crater. Falcone died in an ambulance, Francesca in the hospital five hours later. Astoundingly, the chauffeur survived, although seriously injured—Falcone's desire to drive that afternoon had saved the driver's life.

Police later determined that a ton of dynamite hidden in a storm drain beneath the road had been detonated by remote control. The explosion was especially powerful, investigators found, because both ends of the storm drain had been crammed with bedframes and mattresses to increase the upward force of the blast.

Although some witnesses reported seeing motorway workers in suspiciously clean clothes hard at work near the blast site for weeks before the explosion, the culprits were never identified. A possible clue came from an anonymous call. The assassination, according to the caller, had been a wedding present for Salvatore Madonia, a son of boss Don Ciccio ("Fat") Madonia; Salvatore had married on the day of the explosion—in prison. Father and son were serving lengthy sentences for murder as a result of Falcone's efforts.

The death of Giovanni Falcone prompted an outpouring of grief and rage in Sicily, where many people had placed their hopes for a peaceful future squarely on the magistrate's shoulders. Newspaper editorials thundered, an unprecedented crowd of 40,000 gathered in Palermo to protest Mafia violence, and the national government pushed through the arrests of more than 700 suspected southern Italian mobsters.

Yet the bloody cycle of Mafia vengeance continued. Just two months after Falcone's death, his friend and potential successor Paolo Borsellino died in yet another car-bomb attack that killed five bodyguards as well. The blast, which was heard for miles, tore apart Borsellino's car, two police vehicles, and a nearby building, pelting pedestrians with shards of glass and metal. The Hydra that Giovanni Falcone died fighting had still not met its Hercules. □

HIDDEN HANDS

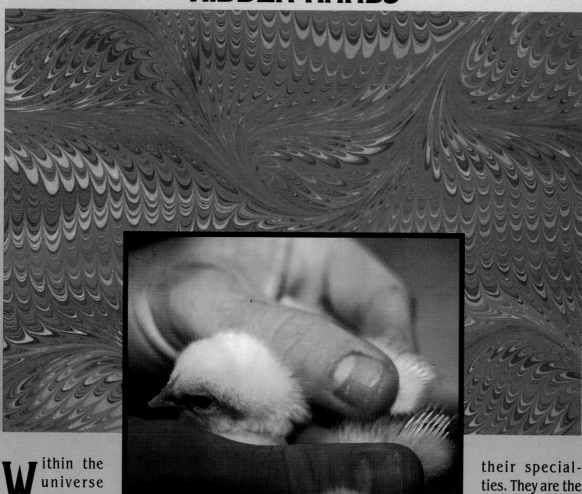

Within the universe of occupations lies a narrow, largely undiscovered realm of workers rarely seen or recognized outside the boundaries of their trade, although the fruits of their labor are in plain sight, for anyone to see. Working literally behind the scenes, these incumbents hold positions so obscure that few besides themselves even know their jobs exist.

If they embody the phrase "out of sight, out of mind," however, these little-noted workers keep whole corners of the world turning with their specialties. They are the artists who work in ice or diamonds, who calibrate colors and tastes, who advise and escort, all more or less unseen. They are the doll tailors and fish butchers, the sound of baseball, the modeled body parts, the scribes. They seem scarcely to exist, so far has their specialization removed them from the mainstreams of employment. And yet, were they to cease their labors, the world would subtly dim, for part of its luster comes from the deft touch of such hidden hands as these.

Impeccable Taste

Every year approximately 180 million pounds of tea enter the United States, and about 180 thousand pounds are rejected as unfit for consumption. As it has standards for everything else, the American government has a standard for tea. But unlike most standards, this one is embodied less in a canon of regulation than in a single person: Robert H. Dick, who has been the arbiter of tea since 1947.

Unknown to most residents of the United States, Dick is the nation's chief tea examiner. From his New York City office he evaluates all the tea that arrives on the Atlantic seaboard or through Oregon and Washington State; an associate in New Orleans tackles tea that comes through California or the Gulf of Mexico. Both of their positions were created nearly a century ago by the Import Tea Act of 1897.

That unusual law, which began as an attempt to regulate the flourishing China tea trade, makes tea the only product to enter the United States that is judged by the process of tasting.

Sipping tea, as many as 400 cups a day, is therefore one of Robert Dick's chief responsibilities. Every business day, in his Brooklyn waterfront office, he sits at a round antique table covered with plain white bowls and various tea samples. As the tasting ritual proceeds, he puts about a twelfth of an ounce of each tea to be tasted into its assigned bowl, then covers it with exactly five ounces of boiling water.

Dick first looks at the wet tea leaves to check color and consistency, then considers the color of the brew itself. Because exact hue is crucial, the teataster's office, at his insistence, has good north light. Then he dips in a silver-plated spoon—stainless steel has too metallic a taste—and sucks in a spoonful with enough vigor to send spray back onto the palate and scented steam up the nose.

After sloshing the sample around his mouth, Dick spits it into a large cuspidor known as a garboon and decides whether the tea will pass or fail. Then it is on to the next; each tasting takes only a few seconds. What is not obvious in the process is the examiner's refined palate and capacious memory for flavors. Robert Dick's taste buds and expertise are unmatched and only rarely challenged.

Although the variety of tea blends is almost too numerous to count, there are only three basic teas: green, black, and oolong. The division is based on their degree of fermentation. In practice, 98 percent of the tea arriving in the United States is black. Most is shipped as loose leaves in wooden crates, leaving it susceptible to

Federal tea examiner Robert Dick (above) pours out one of the hundreds of cups he tastes every day but rarely swallows—the samples are ejected into an hourglass-shaped garboon that stands beside the brewing table (left).

moisture—the single most common cause for rejection. But taste also plays a role: Dick can simply decide that a tea tastes too awful for American consumers. Without a teataster's signature of approval, no shipment can legally pass through customs. Rejection means either destruction or a costly trip back to the point of origin.

Under the same 1897 law, Dick and six industry specialists form the National Board of Tea Experts, which is charged with setting minimum standards for tea imports for the coming year. Their meeting, which takes place each spring as the new tea crop becomes available, is much the same as Dick's daily tea ceremony, except that the board's job is to pick the very worst-tasting brew that will be allowed into the country. Once they have made this decision for each of the basic tea categories, they do the same for flavored, scented, and instant teas. Samples of the minimum-quality baseline teas are kept in pastel canisters in Dick's office. Whenever he tastes a new batch of imports, he brews a cup of the appropriate standard as a comparison.

For all his superb qualifications as teataster, Dick's entry into the trade was largely accidental. After graduating in chemistry in 1937, he became a seasonal seafood inspector for the U.S. Food and Drug Administration. When the season ended, he worked as an FDA laboratory analyst and went on to serve in the army as a laboratory officer during the war. After his return to the FDA, Dick was transferred to tea inspection, where he discovered a talent for tea tasting that, experts agree, is very likely unequaled in the world. □

Giving a Hand

Although top fashion models are celebrated like movie stars, other equally photogenic posers labor in relative obscurity. These faceless figures earn comfortable and even handsome livings on the basis of their hands, feet, and legs, without anyone in the outside world knowing who the body parts belong to. Most of those who model their feet are to be seen in shoe advertisements, while leg models are often found showing off stockings. But those who model hands are by necessity generalists, whose flawless palms and fingers adorn advertisements for everything from rings to power planers to detergents.

John Carthay, a Long Island native who is unknown from the wrists up, has profited greatly from this little-known field. He earns upwards of $100,000 per year as, by general agreement, one of the best hand models in the world. His hands have clasped everything from American Express cards to Dunkin' Donuts to martini glasses filled with Bombay Gin, while his equally elegant wrists have served as the backdrop for Piaget watches. While Carthay insists "no talent" is involved in his job, directors comment on the ability of his hands to signal different personalities when they are in contact with different products.

He is also "steady,"

says commercial director Andrew Unangst. "A hand model who is not coordinated can cost $20,000 in overtime." Carthay himself puts the demands of his trade simply: "You have to be very professional, stand very still and you can't be a comedian."

A sociology graduate, Carthay entered the modeling business through the back door in the 1970s. He was working as a gofer in a film studio when the director suddenly needed a shot of a hand holding a suede brush for a Hush Puppies shoe commercial. Since he had sent all the models home, the director did an impromptu canvass of the staff and decided Carthay's thumb was the best looking.

Carthay's hands are insured for $500,000, and like all hand models he goes to great lengths to keep them in perfect shape, since even a bad cuticle can cost him a job. Among other things, he constantly manicures his nails and moisturizes his hands, using mortician's wax to hide any blemishes. Carthay wears lined gloves outside the house and gardening gloves inside and assiduously avoids the sun, to avert the twin evils of liver spots and too much tan. ◊

Photographed for a Christmas 1985 jewelry catalog, hand model John Carthay's prized extremity rests under the pale, pampered palm of Pat Tilley.

Seldom photographed from the wrist up, top model Pat Tilley presents a fan of cosmetics in one perfect, nearly translucent hand—the only part of her that will appear in the finished ad.

Hues In, Hues Out

Carthay's female peer is Pat Tilley, a New Jersey native whose hands have substituted for those of such top models as Christie Brinkley, Cheryl Tiegs, and Lauren Hutton. Tilley is generally credited with raising hand-model salaries to more than $300 an hour, up from about $40. The cost of excellence is also high for the model: Tilley finds a number of ordinary tasks too risky to perform, refusing to shake hands, cook, or use a knife. In restaurants, she avoids breaking her own bread; her husband does it for her. She shuns zippers and buttons on her clothes—they might leave a nick or break a nail—and, she says, "I'll suffocate before I open a window."

Although Tilley has reached her 40s—old age for most models—the results of her regimen continue to be stunning, according to those in the know. Part of her visual appeal is that her hands appear virtually boneless and thus ageless. In the flesh, the effect may be almost eerie. "Some people," Tilley admits jokingly, "have asked me if I'm alive." On camera, the same look is utterly right. "If the Venus de Milo had hands," says one admirer, "they'd be Pat Tilley's." □

Like clothes, cars, and other consumer goods, house paints follow the muse of fashion. Making sure his company's paints keep up with the times is the task of Kenneth Charbonneau. As color and merchandising manager for Benjamin Moore Paints, Charbonneau, now in his 50s, has been selecting voguish paint colors and giving them suitable names since the days of Lilac Pizzazz, Far-Out Blue, Crazy Coral, Go-Go Green, Live-It-Up Yellow, and Wild Lime in the 1960s.

The New Jersey-based nomenclator of color must know, from trend to trend, which of his employer's 2,000 or so hues are in. "When you go to the mass merchant and everything is rose, mauve, and gray with a touch of teal," he told one reporter, "you know that's the end of that trend." To another he said, "There is a certain cleaning up of the palette. Teal has evolved into turquoise, slightly brighter, slightly greener, very rich. And the mauving of America, it's finished, it's over, we can kiss it goodbye. Mauve is maudlin. Take the gray out of it and it becomes pink, magenta. Now isn't that a happier palette?" Reflecting the more conservative mood of a 1990s recession, Charbonneau helped redecorate America in such muted hues as English Hyacinth, Venetian Rose, and Gray Flannel.

A paint's name is almost as important as its color, in Charbonneau's view. The name Ivory, for example, once breathed associations of romance and wealth; by the 1980s it had come to evoke slaughtered elephants. After Charbonneau rechristened the same color Oriental Silk, the paint rose from 20th to 6th on the firm's sales charts. He has applied the same touch to several other old standbys with encouraging results. Chalk White, for example, has become the more distinguished China White, and Lead Gray—with its implicit link to lead poisoning—was long ago quietly transformed into the inoffensive Slate Gray. A similar fate may await Tobacco Brown. And, in today's environmentally preoccupied society, colors with such names as Mesquite, Rainforest, and Coral Reef are in.

Charbonneau, who works with a staff of six in an office painted Abingdon Putty—a pale lime that might be called Margarita—avidly absorbs newspapers, magazines, books, movies, television, and advertising in his quest for trends that may require new paint names and colors. The hue master himself has come to favor Linen White, a soft, glare-free shade with a name that implies coolness, formality, and possibly even virtue. "When you get to Heaven," he once told an interviewer, "you'll discover it's Linen White." □

Moving Pictures

Ollie Johnston wanted to be an illustrator, but he lacked the cash to finish art school. In January 1935 the 23-year-old tried out for Walt Disney Studios, where his friend Frank Thomas had found work. As a test, he was asked to draw sample "in-betweens" for a previously released animated film, *Three Little Pigs*. In-betweens are the frames that smooth an animated character's change of position. With sound film moving through the camera at 24 frames per second, a sudden change may require only a single in-between; a sustained motion may require hundreds. By the end of a week, Johnston could produce a usable frame in half an hour, and Disney offered him a job. He accepted, assuming he would stay a year, then return to school. But within two weeks, he recalls, "I was hooked. I thought, 'Gee, what Leonardo and Michelangelo and Daumier and all those guys missed. Somebody should have invented this for them.' "

Johnston had been inducted into one of the least visible professions—that of animation artist, the deft hand behind the expressions, motion, and look of richly imaginary characters. The job held him for 43 years. He moved from little pigs to Pinocchio—Johnston's first major character—and on to a host of other Disney cartoon figures. His youthful enthusiasm for the task never waned, partly because his career coincided with the golden age of Disney animation. In addition to creating ◊

Moving with the times, Kenneth Charbonneau (*above*) helped christen 1975's "deep and daring" palette of such "Now Colors" as Tie Dye, the lavender hue at 9 o'clock on the color wheel at left.

Ollie Johnston

figures for *Pinocchio,* he drew the coquettish centaurettes of *Fantasia,* released in 1940, the mischievous rabbit Thumper in 1942's *Bambi,* the title character of the 1951 *Alice in Wonderland,* and the bumbling Mister Smee in the 1953 *Peter Pan.* Smee bore a slight resemblance to Johnston, who had followed the Disney adage to draw what he saw. He often modeled characters' expressions in a mirror. "It's a fascinating business, because you're breathing life into something," says Johnston.

It was also, as it still is, an extraordinarily labor-intensive business. An hour of animated film translates into 86,400 frames and may require as many individual illustrations. The animators work partly in a studio, and partly in a graphics factory, where a kind of creative assembly line turns the illustrated product into pictures that seem to move. After four months spent proving his speed and technical ability as an inbetweener, Johnston became an assistant animator on *Snow White,* cleaning up and clarifying the quick strokes of more senior animators, who were encouraged to draw roughly, for spontaneity. As assistant animator, he also made sure there was consistency in the appearance of each of the seven dwarfs since each dwarf emerged from several animators' pens.

In those days, the animator's drawings went next to the ink-and-paint department, where the figures were outlined in bold strokes of ink, then filled in with color by "the girls," one of whom, Marie, married Johnston in 1943. By that time Johnston had become a supervising animator, and his friend Frank Thomas was rising right beside him. Soon both were numbered among the so-called Nine Old Men who oversaw the work of several others. Going any higher would have taken the pair into film direction, where they did not want to go. "I liked to draw too much," Johnston later explained.

Today, the computer has supplanted the ink-and-paint "girls" and automated the drawing of such special effects as fires, explosions, and reflections. While computers are timesaving aids to the animators, the process of creation has changed very little. The animators still work as they have since about 1940, when animation at Disney became an art. Before that transformation, animated cartoons featured figures that appeared weightless, with no discernible bone or muscle, and stories that were pure plot without characterization.

Audiences were sufficiently intrigued by the medium to accept its apparent limitations, but Walt Disney, a perfectionist, wanted more: "realism," he called it, but realism caricatured. To achieve the effect he sought, Disney arranged for—and required attendance at—evening classes on action analysis, in which live-action film clips were run backward and forward to break motion into its visible parts. Animators learned how to "squash and stretch" their figures to convey motion; a smile was no longer a simple amiable line, but an expression that changed the shape of the face. The artists learned how to

Ollie Johnston, the Disney artist who brought the puppet Pinocchio *(inset)* to life in the 1930s, rides his backyard railroad half a century later. Built in 1951, the elaborate model train inspired Walt Disney to build a similar set for his own home.

draw characters, even villains, that were appealing and to represent gentler emotions. Johnston was among the animators who thrived on the new approach and helped propel it. Until the later 1930s Disney characters seldom touched and then usually to hit one another; Johnston got them to hold hands or, if cats, to twine tails.

As the soundtracks also became more sophisticated, moving away from what Johnston called "silly symphony" tunes, animated characters needed to hold a beat. When an animator sat down to draw, a tape or record of the complete soundtrack had already been prepared. To match the soundtrack, animators listened to it as they acted out events, from fistfights to cat chases. Metronome ticking, Johnston stood before a mirror and danced like Baloo, the zany bear in the 1967 *Jungle Book*.

Under Disney's strong encouragement, that bodily absorption of artists into a kind of parallel cartoon universe pervaded their lives outside the studio as well. "Walt always wanted you to observe everything," Johnston recalls. "If we went out to dinner, I'd watch somebody having an argument at another table," absorbing the action and movement for use in an animated quarrel. Constant observation enriched the animators' lives. "You begin to appreciate things, like trees, flowers, as well as people and animals."

Among the keenest observers was Disney himself, who evidently practiced what he preached. "He'd say, 'You know, I was watching the dog the other day, and here's what he did when he woke up this morning,'" Johnston recalls. "And he'd act out the yawn and the dog

smacking his lips and all that." Walt Disney was always seeking some further, animating detail to make his fantasies more real. "In 40 years, most of us can count on the fingers of one hand the compliments we got," says Johnston. But, he adds, "you didn't mind because you were lifted up to do things you couldn't have ordinarily done. And he gave you this wonderful stuff to work on."

Nor does Johnston, looking back, have many complaints about the hours—15-hour days and six-day weeks toward the end of *Snow White*—or the difficulty of the job. He recalls that drawing Bambi was particularly challenging: "I could barely draw a deer, and here I've got to make people understand what he's thinking." In that case, according to Johnston, Disney's reaction to preliminary sketches of Bambi and his rabbit playmate, Thumper, made it all worthwhile. "Thanks, fellows," he told the animators, tears in his eyes, in a rare accolade. "That stuff is pure gold."

But, by about 1960, the gold had begun to lose some shine. As the public's love affair with animation waned, the studio turned to live-action comedies. Disney died in 1966, shortly after approving—and praising—Johnston's final scene for *Jungle Book*. Johnston retired in 1978, as did Frank Thomas. The pair continued to collaborate in books and speeches devoted to the happy days at Disney, a pursuit both popular and profitable. On a lecture tour of Eastern Europe and Japan that began in 1985, they found that "the Disney name is pure magic," Johnston has said. For him, that came as no surprise: "It was magic to us while we worked there." □

St. Peter's Stones

Roman skill at road building goes back to classical times, but the city's hard-wearing gray basalt cobblestones, known as *sanpietrini,* come from the 17th century. Their evocative name derives from the Italian for "Saint Peter"; the first public area to be paved with the stones was the square that bears his name. Despite the ecclesiastically potent name, the stones have often had a decidedly secular origin; at one time they were paid for by a tax on prostitution.

The streets made from sanpietrini, known as *selciato,* have given rise to a narrow niche in the world of masonry: the *selciaroli,* masters of the Roman cobblestones. The unusual craft is laborious, exacting, and delicate, all at the same time. Many first entered the trade as children. Ercole Parroni, for example, began laying the neatly fitted stones in 1943 at the age of 10, following in his father's trade. "In those days," he recalls, "all Rome's streets were cobbled and there was a lot of work, but much longer hours and harder conditions. I chose to learn this job because I like it, and I do it with passion." But the family passion has evidently cooled. Parroni's two sons followed other muses, one to become a furrier, the other to the Church.

The 59-year-old selciarolo heads a team of selciaroli employed by a local contractor and is known for the swiftness and efficiency of his stone laying. His raw materials are beveled cobblestones, each wider on its upper surface than on the bottom, a shape that allows ◊

them to be set firmly into an elaborately constructed base of mortar, hollow bricks, concrete, and sand. As a specialist, Parroni does not construct the sand bed himself. Kneeling with a piece of rubber tire wrapped around his right knee, he moves along the prepared bed, pushing each stone into place with his left hand and then hammering it in with two carefully placed strokes of a long-headed hammer. "You have to be fit to do this job," he says. "It's quite a strain kneeling on your right knee all day and twisting to take the stones, getting up and down. Arthritis is a problem with this job. But I wouldn't change my work."

Working steadily, Parroni can lay 840 cobblestones an hour in any of several classically ordained patterns—side-by-side, herringbone weaves, or concentric semicircles. As he ignored the passing clamor of German boots and armor half a century ago, Parroni and his co-

workers labor on a calm island of preoccupation in the midst of Rome's raucous torrent of traffic. "You cannot work thinking of other things," he says, focusing on the complexities of an *arco contra-stante,* a pattern of intersecting arcs requiring smaller stones on the sides to make the curve.

Because the shapes and contours of the roads are uneven, the basic patterns adapt to the local terrain. Parroni and his colleagues must sometimes deftly chip the obdurate basalt into a more accommodating shape before laying it into place. After he has set the stones in place and moved on, another worker pounds them into their sand bed with a heavy wooden tamper bound with iron strips, then forces a quick-setting bituminous substance between the stones that glues them into place.

Depending on the size of the road and the demands of the situation, four sizes of stone may be used. For ordinary paving, Parroni's team uses the *cubetto,* or "small cube," a stone that measures more than four and a half inches on a side. Fancier patterns require smaller stones: the sanpietrino itself, which is a little more than three inches wide, or the smaller *selcetto*—literally, "little flint stone"—measuring about two

and a quarter inches. The fourth type is the huge *guida;* used for straight guiding lines, it is nearly 10 inches on each side. The stones of a finished selciato may last for centuries, provided the base has been well prepared.

Such roads, however, also take an eternity to build. Despite Parroni's extraordinary speed, his work crew reckons its progress in a handful of yards per day, while asphalt-laying machines can produce less durable, and less attractive, roadways hundreds of times faster. "Streets paved with cobbles are much more beautiful and they are ecologically pure, too," Parroni explains. "Asphalt causes cancer because it gives off fumes when it's laid and in the summer. Basalt stones do not." But not everyone shares his enthusiasm for the ancient pavement or his hatred of asphalt. Cobblestones are popular with tourists but less so with motorists, who find the bumpy ride tough on machinery. Utility companies that must dig them up to lay their lines are not fond of the sanpietrini either; the cobblestones are difficult to extract and even more challenging to replace. And women in high heels complain that cobblestones ruin their shoes.

With progress working against them, the selciaroli might be close to occupational extinction. They have been preserved, however, by the Roman love of antiquity. Efforts are underway to attract newcomers to the craft—Parroni is one of only 50 or so qualified cobblestone masters in Rome. And, in a bid to appease car-proud commuters, improvements in the bituminous "glue" have helped smooth the once bumpy surface of Rome's beautiful handmade streets. □

Shielded from the Roman sun by a folded-newspaper hat, cobblestone layer Armando Rossi places one *cubetto* while reaching for the next, as a colleague waits to pound the fitted cobblestones into place with a wooden *mazzabecco*.

Seated at his 1978 Hammond Colonade
organ in July 1984, Yankee Stadium
organist and master showman Eddie
Layton (below) smiles from his perch
high above the playing field.

Key Player

Although few know him by name,
Eddie Layton has brought more
baseball fans to their feet at Yankee Stadium than Mickie Mantle,
Roger Maris, and Reggie Jackson
combined. As the ballpark organist, he is a leading member of the
small and shrinking fraternity of
invisible musicians who amuse,
entertain, and rally fans at major-
league-baseball stadiums.

Layton is certainly the dean of
the group, having served as the
New York Yankees' official organist
since 1967. Perched high above
home plate behind a 50,000-watt
Hammond organ which, at full
power, can be heard for miles, Layton plays the national anthem before every other game, noodles
show tunes during lulls, and occa-

sionally throws a curve ball of his
own, playing "White Christmas,"
for example, on scorching days.

The organist is the composer of
the come-from-behind CHAAARGE!
theme that now rallies the faith-
ful at almost every professional
sporting event in the country. Eddie Layton also created another
familiar motif, composed of an
emphasized high note followed by
three ascending notes from below,
that inspires rhythmic, four-beat
hand clapping.

Although evidently a perfect
match for his job, Layton got into
ballpark music by sheer happenstance. He was playing background
music for three CBS soap operas
when the broad-
casting com-
pany pur-
chased the

Yankees and asked him to take on
the baseball-organist role. When he
is not livening up ball games, Layton tours as a soloist for Hammond; his 24 albums of organ music have sold more than two and a
half million copies.

There are very few major-league
ballpark musicians like Layton left
in the United States and few real
organs. Nancy Faust of the Chicago
White Sox, for example, now plays
a synthesizer. At a number of fran-
chises—Oakland and Baltimore
among them—the management
has replaced live musicians with
recordings and rock videos. And at
San Francisco's Candlestick Park,
they play taped organ music, a
pale, plaintive reminder of the day
the stadium's organ was stolen. □

Masters of the Game

By the early 1990s, more than 70 million people in the United States regularly played the chirpy home video games produced by the Japanese firm Nintendo. Although most muddle through on their own, others find the games are more fun with a little guidance—advice duly provided by some 200 games specialists who staff an unusual hot line at the firm's American headquarters in the Seattle suburb of Redmond. Fielding the questions of neophytes and enthusiasts alike, the unseen experts coach callers on how to win, give them encouragement, and occasionally steer them to other Nintendo games.

Nintendo's game counselors, as members of this peculiar profession are known, answer a boggling 100,000 to 150,000 calls per week. Each counselor is aided by a special Nintendo system that contains the solutions to every game problem the company has ever devised. Somehow, even this does not preclude unexpected questions, which sometimes require a callback.

Most callers, of course, are considerably younger than the counselors—and excited to find adults whose work involves playing Nintendo all day. The company admits that its move from a toll-free 800 number to a standard number became necessary because so many youngsters called for guidance, but not on how to play the game—they wanted to get into the business. Explains Tim Dale, "It's pretty exciting for a kid to get hold of somebody who plays games for a living." Dale began as a game play counselor in 1985, then moved up

to assistant game counseling lead and finally to game counseling lead. In his rise to manager, he has mastered hundreds of games.

As for those on the other end of the line, many call the hot line again and again. "I would say there's a certain amount of rapport that goes on with the game counselors," says Dale. "It's nice to call and talk to somebody who knows what you're talking about when you say you just defeated the last guy in *The Legend of Zelda.*" In some cases—especially with beginners who are having difficulties—the

Pseudosundae

Setting photographers' studio tables with dishes that endure long shoots is the job of the food stylist, who gives advertising a kind of cooking that is literally too pretty to eat. When the law permits, stylists often substitute a more resilient substance for the supposed food—replacing the milk in a bowl of cereal with white school glue, for instance, or using vegetable shortening as a stand-in for such ephemeral stuff as ice cream. In the sequence that begins at right and continues overleaf, food stylist Lisa Cherkasky prepares a melt-resistant pseudosundae—mouthwatering to the eye, but not intended for the palate.

Using egg yolks to impart a vanilla coloring, Lisa Cherkasky kneads powdered sugar, vegetable shortening, and corn syrup into a durable surrogate form of ice cream.

Flanked by fellow counselors, Nintendo telephone adviser Mike Rasciner *(far left, foreground)* uses both a Nintendo set and a computer to help customers get hero Link past such perils as Helmasaur King *(left)* in *The Legend of Zelda*.

relationships can become quite friendly. One former staffer recalls fielding a call every day for six months from an elderly woman determined to win at *The Legend of Zelda*.

"On any given game there are common questions that get asked," Nintendo manager Dale says. "In *The Legend of Zelda* it might be how do I get a hammer or one of those bottles. In *Super Mario World* it's how do I get to the second exit in the cheese bridge, or any world, sometimes chocolate island is a pretty common one. Every call is unusual in itself, just because of the nature of the games and the weird language that is spoken between game counselors and game players. There are things said to each other like 'Have you been to the mansion with the eyeball in it' or 'Have you defeated the main boss character,' 'Have you warped from one area to the next?' "

Everyone at the help center has his or her own favorite calls. Mike Rasciner, a graphic artist turned counselor, enjoys queries from adults reluctant to admit that they play Nintendo games. "Parents call in pretending to be asking for their kids," he says. "But I say something like, 'So you're stuck at . . .' and they say yes."

But counselors also get some profoundly satisfying queries. "I was once told that somebody helped a legally blind person through the game *Metal Gear*," Dale recalls, "by simply listening to the noises that the game made and with the assistance of a friend who was also on the other line. I think that some of the most interesting ones are some of the older people who are in their 70s who think Nintendo is the best thing in the world that's happened to them and it gives them a lot of enjoyment. Some of them have even said that it gives them therapeutic results—helping their arthritis or mobility in their fingers. Those calls are always nice." □

n the stylist molds the all-important top op of simulated ice cream into a regular cream scoop, setting aside the remainder he mix just in case.

Using a wooden skewer as a sculptor might to perfect the top scoop's ridges and textural features, Cherkasky prepares the surface for its toppings, then sets the scoop aside.

Cherkasky loads the false dessert into the base of a sundae glass artfully filled with thick chocolate fudge sauce, which she adjusts around the "ice cream."

Playgirl

As chief clothes designer for Mattel Corporation's 33-year-old Barbie and other dolls, Kitty Black Perkins is all but assured an eager market for her miniature dresses, shoes, swimsuits, and bridal gowns. Perkins is the first to admit, however, that working for her 11½-inch-tall client includes some demands that might daunt better-known designers.

Each new outfit she undertakes must be created in a speedy two to five days, for example, and the emphasis is not just on looks but on play value. That means, among other things, that most items of clothing must have more than one use. To guard against certain all-too-likely contingencies, Barbie's clothes must also be saliva-proof and able to resist a five-pound tug.

To keep Barbie's clothes current, Perkins scours department stores, follows fashion magazines, and even attends European couture shows. The only design restriction, she says, is some modesty—"We must make sure she's covered"—and a certain eco-consciousness: Barbie never wears real fur. □

Although Kitty Black Perkins *(below)* designs a host of Barbie work- and play-clothes every year, the perennial best-sellers are such wedding attire as the 1991 Dream Bride gown *(left)*, modeled here by Barbie.

With the finished top scoop pressed firmly in place, an intent Cherkasky applies chocolate sauce to its upper surface, filling in holes and extending drip lines in order to make the chocolate appear more fluid.

Last-minute touches are performed on the set in order to make sure that the lighting is correct. Here, Cherkasky positions colored sprinkles with forceps, having already applied nuts and a whipped topping.

Guided by the photographer, who watches through the camera lens, the stylist inserts a spoon handle—the spoon's bowl has been moved to avoid disturbing the precariously assembled counterfeit sundae.

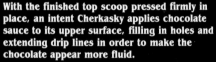

Working with chisels, tongs, and other ice-carving tools *(below)*, Nobuhiko Takayama finishes *Beauty and Space (right)*, an abstract piece commissioned by a design firm in 1992 and carved from ten 300-pound ice blocks.

Cold-Handed

For the Allied troops who occupied postwar Japan, any diversion came as a welcome relief. At first barred from Japanese restaurants, the occupiers took to staging elaborate banquets at the numerous military clubs dotting the conquered nation. Among the refinements most in demand for such occasions were figures—birds, fish, animals, and the like—carved from ice. Without its frozen, ephemeral sculpture, no buffet was considered complete. Originally the clumsy efforts of chefs, the ice figures soon attracted talented sculptors

accustomed to working in wood and stone. Today, crafted by largely anonymous ice masters, such sculptures remain a social fixture in Japan, where displays of glacial swans, eagles, and other beasts are de rigueur at parties and even serve as short-lived set decorations under the hot lights of television.

Nobuhiko Takayama, a stocky, confident man in his 40s, was one of the first Japanese sculptors to

see a good living in this frigid corner of the art world. Born in 1948, he was a youngster during the postwar occupation fad for ice sculptures, but he grew up to carve ice for one of Japan's leading ice-sculpture firms. Takayama originally trained as a conventional sculptor, working with bent metal. His attention later turned to ice, with which, he says, "I can express what I want to show." Takayama joined Tokyo's Kubodera ice-carving firm in 1972, gradually working his way up to the position of managing director. Despite his executive status, however, Takayama continues to work as an ice sculptor, designing the firm's creations himself and helping to execute many of his ideas. Because his medium remains a highly commercial art, Takayama's work reflects his corporate clientele: an Exxon Tiger, a Formula One racecar, and a replica of London Bridge. Takayama prefers his smaller, more modest works. These include small pagoda-like forms known as *goju no tu,* in which he feels that the coolness of the ice expresses the calmness of the pagoda. ◊

Similar to, but more perfect than, its real-life counterpart, the completed pseudosundae stands ready to be photographed, topped by a seemingly intact maraschino cherry.

From behind, the sundae's secrets are revealed: A swab props up the pitted cherry, the chocolate is not layered, and little whipped cream or toppings appear on this side.

Whatever its size, any ice sculpture begins with the production of suitable pieces of ice, usually in the form of 300-pound blocks. The sculpting team at Kubodera shares a building with an ice-making company, which provides the sculptors with their raw materials and insulated studio.

Among the many tricks of the trade is the production of white ice by cooling water close to freezing and then mixing it with snow or shaved ice; ultraclear ice, on the other hand, requires pumping large quantities of air into water and freezing it over one or two days. Sometimes, for huge figures, 300-pound ice blocks are fused. Forms are cut out of the blocks following a kind of blueprint, which at Kubodera is usually prepared by Nobuhiko Takayama. The plan specifies where and how to strike with any of an elaborate set of tools, including flat and triangular chisels and specialized saws. These are wielded in the ice room, a large, frigid space. Sculptors usually wear ski clothes, but the cold is not as bad as it could be. Says Takayama, "You work hard enough to stay warm."

Like other Japanese ice carvers, Takayama sometimes freezes such objects as company logos deep into the ice, suspending an embedded element with threads until the ice is firm enough to support it but still soft enough that the threads can be gently removed. In recent years, he has contemplated taking that idea one step further by somehow presenting a lighted candle inside an ice carving. The problems include a lack of oxygen as well as the danger of melting, but with an inlet to supply air to the candle Takayama thinks he can find a way to achieve the effect.

For Takayama, who also serves as his company's chief salesman to Japanese hotels and wedding halls, the job continues even after a finished ice creation is installed. For one thing, as he points out, "you've got to hang around until the party is over and take out what remains of the carving."

Since Japanese parties generally begin in the evening, waiting for final cleanup can make a long day for Takayama and other carvers, who usually start their carving day at 4:00 or 5:00 a.m. The profession is not for everyone, however. In 1992 Takayama's only son opted to start out in a pharmaceutical laboratory; having observed his father's working hours at firsthand, he wanted no part of ice carving. As for Takayama himself, fatigue and lost family time are more than compensated, he says, by the daily challenge of creation. "It makes me feel good," he admits, "to hear people say nice things about it." Furthermore, in periods of economic decline, he finds it reassuring to have a product that must be continually replaced. □

This elaborately detailed 12-foot-high ice pagoda, known as a *goju no tu*, was one of sculptor Nobuhiko Takayama's largest frozen creations.

Never-Ending Story

When it first opened to traffic in 1864, the Clifton Suspension Bridge that spans England's Avon River near Bristol was considered one of the country's great engineering feats. Suspended 245 feet above the river's high-water mark, the 1,352-foot wrought-iron structure has been open ever since—itself an impressive feat, since the bridge built for horse-and-carriage traffic must now support some three to six million automobiles and light trucks a year. Once completed, however, the Clifton bridge, like all great bridges, came to demand as much attention as a hive. Maintaining the venerable structure has proved to be a full-time vocation for an anonymous but dedicated quartet of bridgemen, led by bridgemaster Ken Williams.

Since the maintenance crew also helps out Williams's toll-keeping staff, actual bridgework must wait until the morning rush hour is over at 9:30 a.m. Much of the time thereafter is spent cleaning up refuse, but from May to September the structure must under-

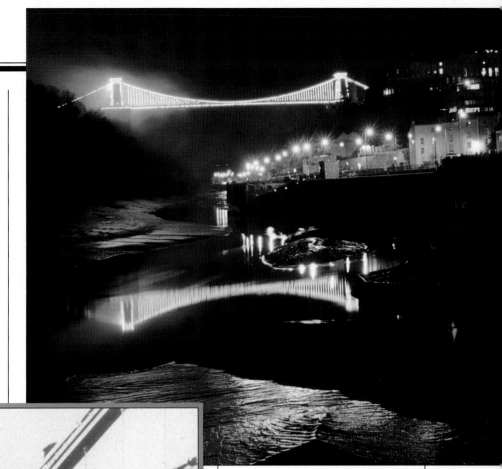

go its annual repainting. Wrought iron is notoriously subject to corrosion, and any sustained exposure of the metal to the elements would spell long-term disaster. Much of the maintenance crew's time is spent cleaning and preparing the surface to be painted with the 250 or so gallons of acrylated rubber paint applied to the bridge most years, weather permitting.

Other tasks abound, each extremely demanding because of the very scale of the big bridge. Keeping such an expanse safely lighted at night, for example, requires a total of 4,000 light bulbs, about 60 of which wink out each week because of normal wear or vandalism. Putting in light bulbs on the elevated portions of the bridge, ◊

Working behind the scenes to make Britain's Clifton Suspension Bridge a nightly festival of light *(above)*, an anonymous maintenance-crew member dangles like a spider from the main cable *(left)* to replace some of the bridge's thousands of light bulbs.

moreover, is a risky business performed only in good weather.

In a stiff wind, the bridge becomes downright exciting. "The wild screams of the wind through the chains, bars, and caps, were audible at a distance, and very loud when close," wrote one turn-of-the-century visitor. "The appearance of the roadway, as we stood under the arches, was like looking along a ship's deck in a breeze, and in walking one needed sea legs; and at the other end where the wind concentrated, everyone,

including a strong dog, was rudely blown across." To keep the lateral motions of the bridge under control, the cross girders at each end of the bridge are reinforced with sway guides—metal tongues installed between rubber-and-steel bearings—that must be inspected and replaced frequently. Since the original guides were imbedded in the deeply buried underpinnings of the bridge, workers had to open a way to the chains for maintenance.

One of the most irritating, and unending, jobs required of the Clif-

ton bridge workers has nothing to do with the bridge itself, but with some of the people who use it. The crew is forever replacing the bridge's tollgate barrier arms, which, with surprising frequency, are ripped away by scofflaw drivers, determined to cross the Avon toll-free. Still, the game is worth the candle. "All of our regular users of the Bridge," remarks bridgemaster Williams, "often pass comment on how well the Bridge looks." When all the work is done, of course, it is time to start again. □

Bully but Uncowed

Since its invention in the 1940s, artificial insemination has revolutionized medicine, zookeeping, and the livestock industry. Nowhere has it had a more pervasive impact

than in the cattle business, in which the vast majority of dairy cows are now inseminated by human technicians wielding precollected samples of bull semen. For

livestock farmers, the advantages of the new technique are many. Risky, costly transportation of bulls and cows is rare now that frozen semen does the traveling,

stored at a cool −320 degrees Fahrenheit. Breeders in remote locations have equal access to the semen of prize bulls all over the world and even to the sperm of bulls now long dead. Because it reduces physical contact among animals, artificial insemination conveys an indirect benefit as well: It curbs the spread of diseases.

Among the spectrum of occupations created by this revolution in animal husbandry, one is as crucial as it is obscure: If bulls are to be bred remotely, they must first be tapped. Joe Maher, who began working for the South Eastern Cattle Breeding Station in County Tipperary, Ireland, in 1959, earns his living just this way. He got into the business, he says, not because of any skill in handling stock, but because of his talents as a laboratory technician. The knack of dealing with large, overexcited animals had to be picked up on the job.

Every morning at around 9:00, about 10 of the facility's 65 bulls are led from their stalls to a nearby yard and tied to widely spaced points on the rim of a circular tethering device. The bulls are accustomed to the routine, and the smell and closeness of their fellows soon make them eager to work. When a given bull appears ready, it is led to a mechanical cow—a French-made iron frame with a cow- or bullhide over it. Maher waits inside the frame and, at the propitious moment, collects the specimen in a warm, rubber-lined tube. Most bulls go along with the mechanical cow, but for some a metal frame does not create the right mood. In those cases, the animal may be encouraged with another bull—a "teaser cow" —with the semen being diverted at

the last second by a handler standing just to the side of the bull. This alternative procedure is not for the faint of heart, Maher points out, since it puts the stockman uncomfortably close to two large, sexually aroused animals.

With the collection process over, the contented bull is returned to his stall, off-duty for a minimum of three to four days. For Maher and the other collectors, however, a long morning of playing cow is just beginning. After each collection, Maher studies the resulting semen under a microscope to determine the ratio of live sperm to dead ones; a machine runs a quick sperm count. If the collection meets the station's criteria, Maher mixes the semen into a solution in a labeled beaker and stores it in a warm water bath. When beakers have been prepared for all of the day's bulls, Maher transfers the beakers into a cold tub to sit for about half an hour—just enough time, he says, to enjoy a mid-morning cup of tea.

After tea, Maher uses a special machine to pour the cooled semen into laboratory straws, each labeled with the donor bull's initials. A good collection from one bull can fill as many as 200 straws, and clients usually need no more than one to inseminate a cow. The straws are returned to the cold tub, and Maher breaks for lunch. In the afternoon, he places the straws over liquid nitrogen in a large stainless-steel vat, where they freeze within 10 minutes. The straws can then be stored in liquid nitrogen indefinitely, since frozen semen remains potent for decades. The day's take securely frozen, and with no more tethered bulls to fool, Maher bicycles home. □

Ringmaster

Held every year just before the deprivations of Lent, Rio's Carnaval parade is a world-famous bedlam of towering floats, booming samba drum corps, and acres of sequined, befeathered flesh. But for all the bustling uproar, the tens of thousands of participants are under the invisible control of a few highly professional specialists known as *carnavalescos,* experts who supervise every aspect of the fantastic explosion of colors and sounds.

The carnavalescos have emerged as the ringmasters over the past 40 years, but the parade itself predates them by half a century. The so-called samba schools—troupes specializing in Afro-Brazilian dances—were founded about 1900; they were constituted as educational associations to get around laws against such performances. Eventually the schools began using the imported tradition of Shrove Tuesday parades as a vehicle for public appearances, combining their dances with satire, fantasy, and sheer ostentatious display.

Despite the growing spectacles put on by the schools, the role of parade organizer was largely amateur until 1959, when Fernando Pamplona, professor of decorative arts, was hired by one of the more innovative and ambitious schools. The experiment was a success, and today parade orchestrators are as professional and commercial in their approach as Brazilian soccer coaches. They also enjoy about the same amount of job security. Like the coaches, they can be abruptly hired or lured away and may be fired just as fast if they do not produce satisfactory results for their samba school. Some 14 ◊

Tricked by a false cow, a prize Hereford bull *(left)* at the South Eastern Cattle Breeding Society in County Tipperary, Ireland, will father whole herds of calves through artificial insemination, using semen collected by agile John McGrath.

Master *carnavalesco* Joâozinho Trinta (below) describes the fabulous float designs he pioneered at his samba school's workshop in 1991—designs now echoed in Brazil's Carnaval by such towering creations as the one at right, entered by a rival school.

schools participate in Rio's main parade competition, which is judged by a city-sponsored commission on such elements as drumming, dancing, float design, theme, and general creativity.

As part of the quest for a parade victory, the carnavalesco performs a host of duties. In addition to coordinating myriad vital but mundane details, the carnavalesco dreams up the floats and costumes and works out the parade organization for the 5,000 or so people who will march for the school.

At least half of all carnavalescos have university degrees, and many are engineers or industrial designers. But none has had a greater impact on the evolving Carnaval than a man with almost no formal education, Joâo Clemente Jorge Trinta, better known as Joâozinho Trinta. A native of the hardscrabble northern state of Maranhâo, Trinta grew up poor; his father died when the boy was two, and his mother got a job as a minimum-wage factory worker to support the family.

Eager to escape rural poverty, Trinta first tried to join the theater company in the state capital, then dreamed of becoming a classical ballet dancer. Given his stature—he stands just under five feet tall—neither vision materialized. Instead, he gravitated in 1956 to Rio, where he made

decorations for several of the extravagant balls that welcome Carnaval season. That experience became the basis of his knack for presenting the samba schools.

In 1974 Trinta became the first director to build towering floats so high—some exceeded 30 feet— that they were better seen by television cameras than by wealthy spectators in the parade-side bleachers, a step that thrust the parade decisively into the TV age. Trinta was also the first to encourage the displays of male and female nudity that have become hallmarks of the event.

Trinta won the Rio parade championship seven times in the 1970s and early 1980s, each victory with a more spectacular display than the last. In 1991 his fantasy for the suburban school of Beija-

Flor—Portugese for "hummingbird"—was entitled Alice in the Brazil of Wonders and was loosely inspired by *Alice in Wonderland*. It featured 4,000 musicians and dancers, 11 floats, and uncounted tons of ribbons, feathers, sequins, mylar, and other gaudy materials. An apparent attack on the privileged classes of Brazil, it ended with a mass decapitation scene, an echo of the Queen of Hearts' cry, "Off with their heads!"

The child of poverty, Trinta has an ambivalent attitude toward Carnaval's conspicuous luxury in a country where huge numbers of people live in misery. Noted for his aphorisms, Trinta contends, "They are poor who like luxury. One who likes misery is intellectual." His spartan lifestyle and use of inexpensive materials for the parade displays bear out that view, but one of his most telling gestures of sympathy for the deprived has been to create and finance a samba school for Rio's thousands of abandoned children—the poorest of the poor, and perhaps the most in need of a little luxury, even the ephemeral kind of Carnaval. □

Six-year-old Hamidullah Nuriddin selected four new Crayola colors and one old tint (lemon yellow) to sketch his *Mobile Mosque (right),* following the preference anticipated by Crayola crayon designer Janden Richards *(below).* Nostalgic adults, however, missed the eight discontinued hues.

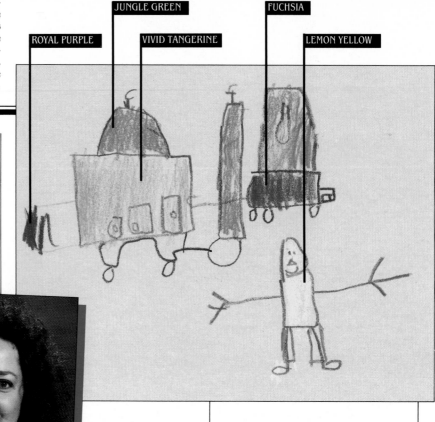

ROYAL PURPLE · JUNGLE GREEN · VIVID TANGERINE · FUCHSIA · LEMON YELLOW

Color Wheel

As art director for Crayola Products, commercial artist Janden Richards once occupied a position almost classic in its obscurity. Yet in 1990 her behind-the-scenes decisions stirred up many American households in a way few more prominent professionals are likely to do. Under instructions, Richards had revamped the company's crayon line.

As the unquestioned king of the world crayon market, Crayola produces two billion crayons annually. But managers, never complacent about market share, wanted to be sure the company kept its edge. One way to do it, they decided, was to make Crayola's crayon palette match the bold hues of Saturday-morning television and other eye-stunning children's products. The art director was told to change Crayola's spectrum.

Richards began the great change by working with Crayola's market researchers to question youngsters intensively about their preferences. She then chose new colors, in part by analyzing the old ones and finding gaps in the color spectrum: A new color named jungle green, for example, provided a truer green than any in the existing assortment. In the end, Richards created 8 new colors for the company to add to its standard 64 hues: not only jungle green, but also dandelion, wild strawberry, vivid tangerine, fuchsia, teal blue, royal purple, and cerulean. To make way for the bright newcomers, however, some old standbys had to go: green blue, orange red, orange yellow, violet blue, maize, lemon yellow, blue gray, and raw umber.

For her primary customers, Richards had done the job right. Most children loved the change. Among adults, however, Crayola's spectrum shift was the occasion for an upwelling of outrage. Thousands of former customers wrote in anguish. Why not change the colors of the American flag to "Wild Strawberry, Blinding White, and Teal Blue," inquired one letter, which also asked, "Are toddlers now to be the decision-makers in all matters of esthetics?"

A saddened lemon-yellow enthusiast wrote that she had at first assumed the news story about the color change had to be a joke: "To me and many of my friends, this color was much more vibrant and brighter compared to the plain, ordinary yellow." Still others pointed out that eliminating the color maize was an affront to that grain's important role in early American history. Another correspondent accepted the change but asked if she could buy a box of raw umber crayons to sustain her through that color's termination.

If anything, the adults' letters confirmed the generation gap Crayola's marketers had suspected. The pleas, however, did not go entirely unanswered; the company eventually responded to its former customers by issuing a special, limited edition tin that included all 64 current colors plus the old standbys. "We were tampering with their childhoods," Richards explained. "We had to do something to let adults know we understood." □

Seafood Delight

Chefs may be kings of the kitchen, but only one obscure branch of the profession routinely wields life-or-death power. Japan's fugu chefs owe that distinction to the fugu, or blowfish, a tough-skinned, inflatable bottom feeder that weighs as much as 30 pounds and is among the most poisonous animals in the ocean. There are about 100 species of the fugu, and each is rich in the nerve poison called tetrodotoxin, 275 times more toxic than cyanide. An unprepared fugu is one of nature's deadliest meals; a medium-size specimen can kill 30 people. Biting into fugu au naturel causes numbness, spreading paralysis, slow loss of speech, and finally, of breath and life—during all of which the victim is said to be fully aware. There is no antidote.

But not everyone dies from eating blowfish, as this traditional Japanese verse testifies: "Last night he and I ate fugu; Today I help carry his coffin." In fact, raw fugu is a Japanese gourmand's delight when properly prepared. The meat induces a numbing sensation on the lips, toes, and fingers—the sensations that precede death, scaled down—that fugu fanciers rate highly, and the very presence of danger evidently lends added flavor to the food. The trick is all in the prep-

aration, which involves removing the most toxic parts of the fish—liver, intestines, kidneys, eyes, and, in a female fish, ovaries—and carefully washing the fillets that remain. In all, 30 separate steps are required, which qualified chefs perform in 20 minutes.

But mistakes happen. A 1984 study estimated that in the previous decade 200 people had died in Japan of fugu poisoning. Perhaps the most famous was kabuki actor Mitsugoro Bando VIII, a "living national treasure" who died in 1975. He had entreated his chef to serve him a minute portion of the toxic fugu liver, a forbidden pleasure considered the height of exotic dining by some. In a fatal case of overeating, Bando had four small servings. The chef who served him was given a suspended sentence of eight years in prison for "professional negligence." Later laws have provided stiffer penalties.

Because of the popularity of the deadly dish, however, fugu chefs are surprisingly numerous; 10,000 are licensed to prepare the dish in Tokyo alone. To become a fugu chef, aspirants must apprentice for two years, then face a two-hour examination that tests detailed knowledge of local food ordinances and practical skills: Applicants must clean and dissect a fugu, identify all its parts, and prepare an elaborately decorated plate of its flesh within the requisite 20 minutes. As many as 50 percent of the candidates fail—a comforting statistic, under the circumstances. □

Innocuous in appearance, the potentially deadly fugu *(above)* must be carefully gutted by trained cooks *(left)*, seen butchering the fish at a Tokyo restaurant that specializes in the toxic treat.

Hard Rock

Every day, diamonds sparkle on millions of hands, wrists, ankles, ears, and throats, mineral emblems of love, lust, and wealth. But these lumps of tightly packed pure carbon are rather ordinary stones when first taken from the earth—their brilliance must be added by the cutting and the polishing that turn a rock into a dazzling prism for light. This is the secretive province of the diamond cutter, men and women who labor in a dingy, clannish collection of fiercely independent sweatshops from Bangkok to Manhattan.

Imparting dazzle to the world's hardest substance is a tiresome, nerve-wracking process: One slip can turn a precious stone into a shattered curiosity. Perhaps no step is riskier than the first, in which diamond cutters break the rough, rocklike natural diamond into at least two parts. The clean plane of the break then forms a top surface, or "table," for each of the jewels to be cut from the stone. Since diamonds vary in hardness, a saw dipped in diamond dust can cut through most materials, albeit very, very slowly. But for big diamonds, or those ill suited to sawing, cutters rely on cleaving—the Zen-like application of a single blow to split a diamond along a precisely determined line.

Traditionally known as a personal science, cleaving is high drama on a tiny stage. In principle, the process is simple: The cutter uses an especially hard diamond to scratch a thin line on the uncut stone, then places a small wedge in the incision and taps it sharply with a mallet. The diamond's rigid crystalline structure allows the blow to split the gem along its internal lattices, or grain. But a blow aimed wrongly or struck with the wrong force can shatter a diamond or fill it with internal cracks. Given those hazards, cleavers sometimes spend weeks or months studying the grain of a rough stone in strong light, trying to find the path of least resistance that will also preserve the maximum bulk. Sometimes, if the stone is big enough, the cleaver will cut tiny windows into the surface of the diamond to get a clearer view. In recent years, x-rays have come

Although many diamonds are still cleaved with a single daring mallet stroke *(center)*, this 890-carat stone *(far left)*, one of the largest rough diamonds ever found, was cut with a saw, then finished into a 407-carat gem *(near left)*, the world's biggest "fancy-colored" diamond.

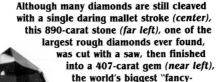

into widespread use for examining the grain of bigger stones.

Despite all the preparation, the tension of the actual moment of cleaving can become all but unbearable. The cleaver of the 3,106-carat Cullinan diamond, the largest in the world, was Joseph Asscher of Amsterdam, who had two doctors on hand when he picked up his mallet and wedge in 1908. Asscher had previously suffered a heart attack and was taking no chances. When he took his first blow, the metal wedge shattered. Asscher tried again. This time the diamond split apart as planned,

and according to legend at least, the relieved cutter fainted—a tale his family denies. Similarly, the cleaver of the 726-carat Presidente Vargas diamond is said to have lost six pounds when he turned to the task in 1941 and took three blows to split the rough stone.

Although cleaving a large diamond is one extreme of the cutter's art, the cutting and polishing of even ordinary stones requires constant expert observation, a fact that makes diamond finishing too individualized a process for giant enterprises. It is ideally suited to a myriad of tiny entrepreneurial shops that seek their profit through the thrifty conversion of rough diamonds into gems by cutting, grinding, and polishing. Not a great deal of space is necessary—just plenty of strong light.

In Manhattan's Diamond District, one of the world's top centers of the craft, millions of dol-

lars' worth of stones pour out every day from a two-block midtown area, where more than 1,500 firms carry on a clamorous business. There, as in other diamond districts, family ties run deep. Educating a newcomer takes a minimum of three months and involves the potential destruction of some of the world's most expensive training aids. Kin are also considered less likely to practice such thievish tricks as "stone-growing," in which a grinder or polisher substitutes a slightly smaller cut stone for the owner's original item.

Medieval artisans in a high-technology age, diamond cutters are continually offered mechanized alternatives—so far none has matched the skill of a master cutter. Recently, lasers have been found to cut through diamond without the burring effect left by saws, but the process is expensive, and weight loss from lasers is still marginally higher than from cleaving. The technique remains largely restricted to stones with highly distorted grains, where no clear cutting path can be established.

It would seem, in fact, that nothing threatens the diamond cutter's discreet trade—except, perhaps, a sudden change in jewelry fashion. It has happened before: During the Middle Ages, the gem lost its previous reputation for magic and fell momentarily out of favor. Only the invention of the modern, 58-faceted brilliant cut, which greatly amplifies diamantine glitter, saved the stone. Thus, among a diamond cutter's nightmares, a catastrophically shattered stone may rank second to changes in the minerals of courtship. □

Sex Objects

Profits in the billion-dollar chicken-and-egg business depend, in part, on the simple act of separating infant hens from baby roosters as soon after birth as possible. Only the females of the egg-producing breeds are of commercial value, and even male and female chicks bred for meat must be raised on different diets. Yet the gender of newborn fowl is not easy to determine at a glance; at this stage of life, the sexual organs of both genders are tucked underneath the rib cage well out of sight. Determining which chicks are male and which are female is thus a job for the experts. Most hatcheries place the tasks in the hands of a little-known group of subcontractors: highly accurate, lightning-fast professionals aptly known as chick sexers.

The traditional method of chick sexing focuses on subtle differences in feather growth, since female chicks grow feathers more rapidly and so have more of the stiffer primary feathers. Beginning sexers take about two weeks to learn how to differentiate the feather formations; from then on, most score an accuracy rate of about 99 percent. An experienced wing examiner keeps up that rate while judging about 2,000 birds an hour. The disadvantage is that chickens thus sexed must be continually bred to emphasize the difference in feather development, sometimes in lieu of more valuable characteristics.

In 1924 Japanese researchers developed an alternative, somewhat more difficult, approach—vent sexing. This procedure, still catching on in the United States, involves rapidly examining the interior of a chick's anus for variations in texture and formation. The differences between the genders are marked, but by no means obvious to the uninitiated. Because unskilled examiners could injure their subjects, vent sexing requires more training than the feather method.

All told, there are no more than 200 to 300 vent sexers at work in the United States, and they are paid well for their odd but essential skill. According to one industry contracting firm, a top sexer can earn as much as $65,000 a year for contemplating the behinds of baby chickens. □

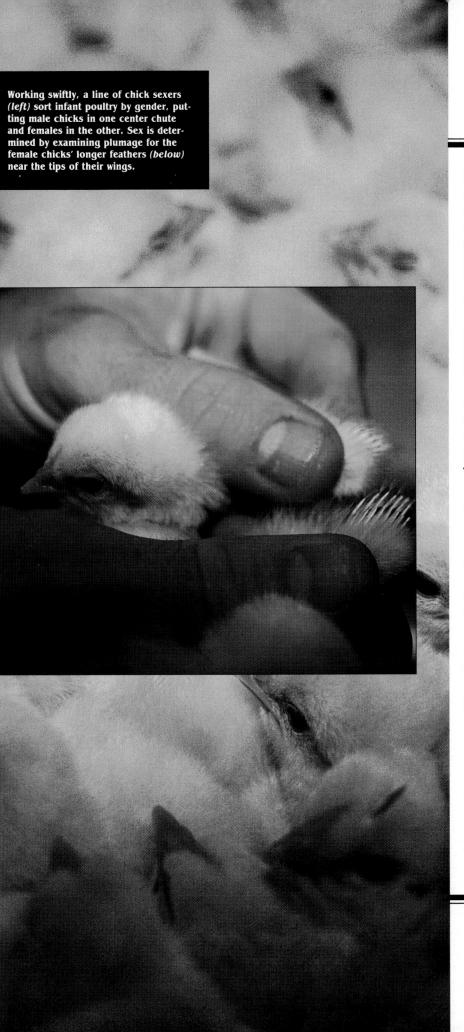

Working swiftly, a line of chick sexers *(left)* sort infant poultry by gender, putting male chicks in one center chute and females in the other. Sex is determined by examining plumage for the female chicks' longer feathers *(below)* near the tips of their wings.

She the Jury

Between 1974 and 1992, the year of her death, a little-known psychologist, Cathy Ellis Bennett, created a new, and controversial, branch of the legal arts. She performed a behind-the-scenes service now considered essential at major trials: professional jury consultant.

The process of jury selection Bennett helped to revolutionize is hardly new. Lawyers for both defense and prosecution in criminal trials have long had the right to eliminate potential jurors on several grounds, including those of bias. The problem with that system, according to Bennett and many defense attorneys, is that the way jurors are usually screened tends to hide biases, not reveal them. "We all have some bias and prejudice," she commented in 1982. "The problem is, no one is going to get up in a courtroom, particularly if a judge is present, and admit that he or she is prejudiced."

Given the awe-inspiring presence of the judge and, often, of the press, how can lawyers coax potential jurors into revealing their true feelings? Bennett started to find the answers in her first case, that of American Indian activist Russell Means, who was accused of murder after a highly publicized shootout with FBI agents at Wounded Knee. Heated pretrial publicity, combined with the defendant's race, made the task of finding an open-minded jury more difficult.

Bennett's contribution was to add to the attorney's questioning a set of interrogative techniques common in clinical psychology. These appear far more likely than legal questioning to cause jurors to expose their own feelings and ◊

Seated beside William Kennedy Smith during jury selection for his 1991 sexual-assault trial, consultant Cathy Bennett *(right)* passed notes to Smith's attorney suggesting ways to detect the hidden biases of prospective jurors.

opinions. Instead of asking such "close-ended" lawyerly questions as "Does anybody here feel any prejudice against Indian people?" she encouraged Means's attorney to ask open-ended questions that required more self-revelation, such as what the juror's own experience had been with American Indians.

One potential juror answered that question, as attorney John Ackerman later recalled, by saying, "When it got real cold, the Indians would come across the border from Canada and they'd come onto our farm and we could tell they were real cold, and so my Dad would let 'em stand out in the shed." Bennett passed Ackerman another question: "What would you have done if they had been white people?" And then, says Ackerman, the woman "said 'My God, I am prejudiced,' and began to cry." That dramatic answer eliminated the potential juror without expending a precious peremptory challenge, which attorneys can use to dismiss a juror without cause.

Because this kind of jury selection smacks of selective engineering designed to assemble juries likely to favor one side or the other, it remains controversial—particularly to the side without a jury consultant. To Bennett, that criticism was nonsense; every jury, she believed, has an authoritarian, antidefense leaning. "The best you can hope for," she commented, "is to get at least a few people on the jury who are open-minded and not prosecution-prone."

The daughter of an air-force master sergeant, Bennett grew up as a self-described flag-waving patriot, and that early idealism carried through into her approach to her work with jury selection. "I only take cases I believe in," she once said. "I have to feel that this person is in really bad trouble, that the publicity has really done a job on them." To her, a client's guilt or innocence was not the point; it was enough if she felt that the accused was not going to get a fair trial without her help.

That attitude led Bennett into a number of high-profile cases, in which she was often retained by the defense to help weed out those potential jurors who had already decided the case based on television and newspaper accounts. In 1984, for example, she helped choose the jury in the trial of former auto-industry executive John DeLorean, who was filmed by FBI agents making a purchase of cocaine. DeLorean was acquitted despite the videotape evidence; Bennett got much of the credit.

Eight years later, terminally ill with cancer, Bennett scored her last legal triumph, one perhaps even more controversial than the DeLorean verdict. Concerned about massive media coverage of the William Kennedy Smith rape case, Bennett dropped out of hospital-based cancer therapy to help Smith's lawyers select 6 jurors out of a panel of 100, a process that took months. Among other matters, her questions probed their attitudes toward the Kennedy family. The jury she helped choose acquitted Smith on December 11, 1991, just six months before her death at the age of 41.

Ironically, Bennett's successes at the bar were all savored second-hand. She passed her penetrating questions as notes to the defense attorneys and never asked a single one herself. While dedicated to justice, she had not bothered to become a lawyer. □

Breakaways

Before the women of striptease can take it off, they have to put it on. During the heyday of the bump-and-grind circuit, the sequins, feathers, baubles, beads, and boas striptease artists preferred were those sewn into the costumes of Rex Huntington, in his day the preeminent designer of ecdysiastical fashion in the United States.

Although few outside the business know of Huntington or his accomplishments, for more than six decades he created exotic fantasies for the likes of Chesty Morgan, Trudine the Shimmy Queen, and Tempest Storm. Huntington, who produced an occasional outré outfit until his death in 1992, was known for the pains he took to flatter the good points, and underemphasize the bad, of each client.

"I made the girls look good," he told an interviewer, in part by taking away inches on hips, through flattering placement of fringes and the like, and putting them back on busts. He also had considerable imaginative flair. "He would always give you a new way of doing your act," recalls Ann Perri, known as the Jane Russell of burlesque. "He would give you a couple of different ways to take off your clothes."

For example, stripper Dixie Evans—who was herself known as the Marilyn Monroe of burlesque—once commissioned Huntington to create a "flipper," a piece of weighted material sewn onto the back of the G-string that could be flipped upward with an appropriate bump. Huntington sewed a mir- ◊

Reliving glory days in 1991 with her old friend Rex Huntington, retired stripper Joan Torino models an elaborate burlesque outfit Huntington designed for her in the early 1950s.

ror and rhinestones on the underside, so that during her rendition of the song "I've Got My Eyes on You," Evans could raise the flipper to reflect the eyes of customers in the first row.

The grandson of a milliner, Huntington was born in Richmond, Indiana, in 1907. He was seven when he made his first costume, a pair of cowboy pants. After a brief stint as a Detroit autoworker, he found employment dancing and singing in stage choruses and experienced an epiphany of sorts when he glimpsed the spangles and rhinestones in the costume shop at Detroit's Hollywood Theater.

Eventually he became a head of wardrobe and began making "strips"—skirts with an easily undone hook-and-eye fastening—for burlesque artists on the side. His taste for the spectacular and his eye for the practical soon made him a favorite among the ladies who disrobe, and in due course he opened a specialty shop.

A stripper's talent lies in stretching a relatively simple act over a relatively long interval of time, and Huntington was a master of constructing cos-

tumes that took as long as 20 minutes to disappear. They might consist of a hat, a cape, and a dress that had more than one element, as well as a negligee, gloves, a garter belt, stockings, more than one bra, and, of course, the all-important G-string. Some retired strippers still treasure Huntington's fabled garments.

Always obscure, Huntington's special abilities are less needed now; the glamour days of striptease are over, done in by mass-produced pornography and the casual nudity of the Age of Aquarius. With fancy-undress costumes virtually a thing of the past, the octogenarian designer noted regretfully that ladies taking off their clothes are hardly worth seeing anymore. □

In her act, Joan Torino sang two slow songs, then a fast one, as she removed this Huntington costume, taking about 20 minutes to discard cape, six separate skirt panels, boa, and underlying teddy—all, in fact, but the bare essentials *(top)*.

As Angelica Huston, Woody Allen, Diane Keaton, and Alan Alda play a New York restaurant scene for the cameras, script supervisor Kay Chapin *(standing)* calmly keeps track of the scores of elements that must stay consistent from take to take.

Scene Healer

By definition, everyone involved in making a motion picture works behind the scenes except the actors. But there is an unseen hand in every film that, in a way that directors, editors, and producers cannot, makes the crucial difference between cinematic coherence—and chaos. While the finished product may not show it on the screen, most movies are jigsaw puzzles, pieced together from ex-

tremely short scenes shot wildly out of sequence. Weeks, and considerable distances, may intervene between shots intended to follow one another in the final product, and individual scenes are filmed over and over again with subtle variations. When editors begin to assemble the pieces of the puzzle into a finished film, the possibilities for visual slip-ups are enormous. The script supervisor—in England, the continuity supervisor—removes much of that risk.

The essence of the script supervisor's role is to ensure that there is visual continuity from scene to scene—and there are hundreds of them in a feature film. A heroine seen entering a room in one dress, for example, must be wearing the same garment when she sits down; a character who empties a gun in one action sequence must reload it on-screen before firing again.

Kay Chapin, a script supervisor since 1963, describes her job as "keeping a written record of ◊

every shot photographed, so that the film editor knows what the director's intentions are." Chapin also prepares a master script for the editor, indicating the innumerable details of timing, action, and dialogue that are not included in the original shooting script—a kind of blueprint for the director and the film editor.

Her credits are impressive. In 1992 Chapin completed work on *Age of Innocence,* director Martin Scorcese's adaptation of the Edith Wharton novel set in New York in the late 19th century. She has worked on 18 Woody Allen films and on *Big* and *Prince of Tides,* among many others. At 60 she began work on a project provisionally titled *Manhattan Murder Mystery,* a 1993 release by Allen.

Work as a script supervisor, Chapin notes, varies greatly from one director to another. Some, like Allen, prefer that actors improvise, to produce a more spontaneous and conversational style. Others, she says, want the script followed to the letter but like to shoot multiple versions of each scene. Any filmic method, however, may open the way to continuity disaster.

So many details must match from shot to shot, in fact, that perfection remains a distant goal for Chapin and her several hundred colleagues. Although script supervisors take copious notes, record scenes photographically, and compile endless lists, minor errors almost always creep in during the film edit. These flaws, in turn, have created a kind of substratum of employment for freelance writer Bill Givens, whose specialty is finding flubs, as they are called. A kind of professional nemesis for filmdom's harried script supervisors, Givens has assigned himself the task of detecting movie flubs, a lucrative vocation that has resulted in *Film Flubs,* published in 1990, and the 1991 book *Son of Film Flubs,* which describe the visual and research glitches he and a small army of contributors have detected in feature films. In one shot of *The Wizard of Oz,* for example, the Tinman chopped down a tree with an ax that was not in his hand a moment before; actress Katherine Ross mysteriously moved between the handlebars and crossbar of a bicycle while Paul Newman pedaled her around the yard in *Butch Cassidy and the Sundance Kid; Pretty Woman* star Julia Roberts picked up a croissant in one shot but bit into a pancake in the next. Givens's list is a long one, compiled with less malice than glee, and few films are not on it. Art, as script supervisors know better than most, must have its imperfections. □

THE GOOD, THE BAD, AND THE UGLY

Like beauty, the quality of an occupation is often in the eye of the beholder. Some jobs seem to be the stuff that dreams are made of, splendid visions of occupational happiness in which courage, intelligence, power, fortitude, and profit are happily combined. Other professions, to outsiders at least, seem mere necessary evils, dirty jobs that someone has to do. But such simplistic classifying ignores the quicksilver chemistry of the human elements involved—the effects of pride, bravery, a taste for glory, even naked greed. The best jobs are never all they seem. Millionaire athletes live in the shadow of dis-

abling injury, scientists who enjoy their work too much may seem unserious, and the most cosseted general must send troops off to die.

Conversely, the hardest, dirtiest work often contains a small but incomparably tasty kernel of satisfaction for the right incumbent. People may work long days and nights in grease and grime, in stealthy jobs that draw the opprobrium of their fellows, often propelled by base motives. Yet these workers, like their more obviously fortunate brethren, are not immune to a profound sense of achievement from a job well done—from being the best at anything, even something mean.

Man of the *Times*

When the 1841 general election in Ireland turned into a slugfest, 21-year-old William Howard Russell, a reporter for the *Times* of London, thought he detected a way to make the story exciting. Dropping into the local hospital, he found it busy bandaging the electorate. Russell filed his report: "With countenances crushed and bruised out of all the lineaments of humanity and bathed in blood are lying a number of poor fellows, some of whom it is to be feared are fast hastening to another world."

It was a promising start for the man who would become the first professional war correspondent. Over the next 50 years, "Mr. Russell of the *Times*," as he liked to refer to himself, came to personify the most romantic ideal of war reportage—an ideal that persists today. Russell turned up in some of the 19th century's hottest spots, and his eyewitness reports shaped and informed public affairs. Such was his eventual reputation that prime ministers and kings took him into their confidence. He was a privileged guest at the Lincoln White House, and he quarreled with Prussian chancellor Otto von Bismarck. Yet Russell, whose strength was not his writing style but his accuracy and keen eye for detail, professed no enthusiasm for war. He was simply a newspaper reporter, Russell said, whose job "is to see what is done, and to describe it to the best of his ability."

Although he reported on armed conflict in Schleswig-Holstein in 1850, Russell made his reputation as a reporter during the Crimean War. The fighting there, one of a long series of conflicts between Russia and Turkey, broke out after Russian forces moved into Moldavia and Wallachia, in modern-day Romania. While the quarrel was an obscure one, the British and French were glad to join any war against the czar. Britain sent its army to join French forces attacking Russia's Crimean peninsula in 1854. The *Times* sent Russell.

Traditionally, the British press had relied mainly on official military dispatches for its reports, but two years earlier the death of the duke of Wellington, a firm opponent of battlefield reporting, had allowed journalists to get closer to the front. What Russell discovered from this new vantage point was a scandal, which he reported in exhaustive detail: bungling by the generals, grossly inadequate medical facilities, anachronistic regulations, red-tape rigidity.

He also reported British bravery, such as that displayed at the successful October 1854 defense of the British-held port city of Balaklava. Movingly, Russell wrote about the "thin red streak topped with a line of steel" of British infantry that was the only obstacle between the advancing Russians and the city. Condensed into the "thin red line," the phrase became a patriotic cliché.

The same day Russell watched the thin red line, however, he also witnessed the infamous charge of the Light Cavalry Brigade. In that bungled maneuver, an entire British brigade was ordered, apparently by mistake, to charge into the wrong flank of the Russian forces attacking Balaklava and galloped into a barrage of infantry fire and large guns. In less than 25 minutes, 247 members of the brigade were dead. Russell's appalled description of the slaughter probably inspired Alfred, Lord Tennyson, to write his famous poem "The Charge of the Light Brigade." Russell's Crimean reporting had an equally dramatic effect on British politics: In January 1855 he became the first British journalist to cause a government's downfall.

When the war ended late in 1855, Russell returned home, arguably its only hero. Prime Minister Henry Palmerston invited him to breakfast and asked his advice in running the army, actor Charles Kean offered him a box at his theater whenever he wanted, and Russell's alma mater, Dublin's Trinity College, gave him an honorary doctorate. Russell began work on a book based on his Crimean reports and went on the lecture circuit.

But for Russell the home front was in some respects as stressful as the trenches. His wife, Mary, was given to nervous disorders complicated by several difficult pregnancies; finally a permanent invalid, she would die in a nursing home in 1867. Russell doted on his children, but from a distance. He was chronically short of cash, and he suffered constantly from the effects of overindulging in food and drink at the clubs he frequented with such friends as novelists Charles Dickens and William Makepeace Thackeray. When the *Times* issued its next call to arms, Russell did not hesitate to respond.

The occasion was the Sepoy Rebellion in India, a violent revolt against British authority, rife with stories of atrocities against British women and children. Russell arrived in India in early 1858, in time to observe the recapture of

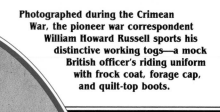

Photographed during the Crimean War, the pioneer war correspondent William Howard Russell sports his distinctive working togs—a mock British officer's riding uniform with frock coat, forage cap, and quilt-top boots.

the North did not prevent him from reporting honestly the disorderly Union retreat at Bull Run, the war's first engagement. Russell was immediately transformed from the Union's honored guest into *persona non grata*, and his case was not helped by the *Times*'s support of the Confederacy. After little more than a year, during which he was regularly threatened with death and denied access to the front, "Bull Run Russell," as he had become known in the United States, went home.

The correspondent continued to cover European conflicts and the increasingly powerful weapons being employed. But just as the technology of warfare was changing, so were the means of covering wars. The invention of the telegraph made speed more important than accuracy or depth, and for the first time ever, other newspapers were offering the *Times* serious competition at the front. Suddenly the field was crowded with war correspondents, younger and quicker on their feet than the man who had more or less perfected their profession.

Russell was also becoming frail from his long service at the front. Over the years, he had come re-

peatedly under enemy fire, been permanently lamed, and fallen ill with various fevers. Nor did he perceive much gratitude from his employer. "I am bound to say that the *Times* seems to have very little feeling of what I go through, very little indeed," he confided to his diary after an attack by insurgents in India. For its part, the *Times* complained about his expenses.

During the Zulu War of 1879, the *Times* changed chief editors and sent other correspondents to South Africa. Undaunted, Russell, now near 60, went into the field for the rival *Daily Telegraph*. Crossing a ford during a sudden storm, Russell was trapped under his horse and almost drowned. It would be his last campaign.

The intrepid correspondent was welcomed home by a bill from the tax collector. "I have all the risks of a soldier and none of his honors," he grumbled. In the years to come, however, the risks receded and the honors multiplied. Although Russell continued to travel, it was generally as an escort to aristocrats. In 1884 he married Italian countess Antoinette Malvez, a financially secure woman 27 years his junior. Then, in a final acknowledgment of his place in history, Russell received a knighthood in 1895, 12 years before his death at age 86. In 1909 a bronze torso of Russell, wearing his trademark campaign cloak and writing in a notebook, was unveiled in the crypt of St. Paul's in London. It was inscribed: "The first and greatest of war correspondents." He had set the tone that placed the journalism of battle firmly into the fantasies of young men and women who wanted adventure as much as they wanted to write. □

the city of Lucknow, where 1,500 British troops and civilians had been under siege. This time he had no quarrel with the support the army received, but he was shocked by contemptuous white attitudes toward Indians and by the brutality of British soldiers and their Sikh allies in suppressing the rebels. In reports to the *Times*, Russell tempered the stories of atrocities and argued for clemency, predicting that unless the British changed their ways their power over India would be fleeting.

Russell brought his antipathy to racial inequality with him in February 1861, when he arrived in the United States to cover the impending Civil War. But his support for

Her Deepness

Scuba-diving 45 feet under the surface of the Atlantic Ocean with a *New York Times Magazine* reporter who had come to interview her, Sylvia Earle leaned back, lazily crossing one leg over another. In the idyllic moments that followed, she watched happily as schools of gorgeous tropical fish swam past. Gliding along the ocean floor, she inspected diminutive starfish, translucent strings of conch eggs, and the bloom of a sea flower, stopped to untangle fishline from undersea plants, and—reluctantly—returned to the atmosphere.

Perhaps the world's paradigm of a celebrated oceanographer, Earle appears to be happiest submerged. By 1991, at the age of 55, she had spent some 6,000 hours—roughly two-thirds of a year of her life—underwater. As a scientist, she specializes in the study of algae, primitive, plantlike organisms that include 300-foot-long kelp as well as microscopic spores. She has pressed and cataloged some 20,000 specimens over the years,

attempting among other things to form a complete record of undersea plant life in the Gulf of Mexico. Earle is best known, however, for her record-setting deep dives, which have continually pushed the limits of diving technology and earned her a royal-sounding sobriquet: Her Deepness. It is a career something like hers that students must envision as they dream of becoming marine biologists.

Even as a young girl, Earle was interested in nature, and when her family moved from New Jersey to Florida, she spent hundreds of hours examining the plants and animals in the nearby Gulf of Mexico. In 1953, as a 17-year-old college freshman, she began to dive, using a traditional hard-hat helmet. Within the next few years, the general availability of scuba equipment revolutionized the study of marine biology—and opened new worlds to Earle. By then a Duke University graduate student, she became one of the first female researchers to explore freely underwater. She went on to identify a number of new organisms and to

discover such previously unsuspected geologic features as undersea "dunes" off the Bahamas.

Earle had married twice, had three children, and racked up many more hours underwater by 1970, when she led an all-female mission for Tektite, a government-sponsored project in which teams of scientists lived in an underwater habitat 50 feet down, off the coast of the Caribbean island of St. John. For two glorious weeks Earle and four female colleagues inhabited and explored the deep. They resurfaced to a shower of modest fame that included a Chicago ticker-tape parade and the media moniker "aquababes."

The fanfare faded, but the expedition's impact on Earle endured. "In a very fundamental way, I'm changed forever because I lived underwater for two weeks," Earle later said of the experience. "I learned to recognize an individual animal not merely as an eel or a fish, but as that eel or that fish who lives under that rock," she said, adding, "I wouldn't deliberately eat a grouper any more

than I'd eat a cocker spaniel."

In the years that followed, Earle continued to mix research projects for a variety of institutions with more publicized deep-diving feats. In 1979 came the dive for which she is best known. It took her 1,250 feet—the height of the Empire State Building—below the surface of the Pacific Ocean near Hawaii, deeper than anyone had previously gone outside a submersible. For the occasion, Earle wore a so-called Jim suit, a rigid, half-ton contraption named after pioneer diver Jim Jarratt, for whom the first such device was developed in the 1930s. Earle descended strapped to the outside of a small submarine, then, protected by the Jim suit from the water's bone-crushing pressure of 600 pounds per square inch, stepped off onto the seafloor, which was illuminated by the sub's lights.

Free to retract her hands inside the suit torso in order to write notes, an enraptured Earle strolled about, writing lyrically of luminous green-eyed sharks, crabs swaying on the branches of a pink sea fan, and "sparks of living light, blue-green flashes of small transparent creatures brushing against my faceplate." Two and a half hours later, Earle was transported back to the top. Climbing out of her suit, she asked, "So when do I get to go deeper?"

The answer came in 1985, when Earle took a submersible 3,000 feet down in the Pacific; the vehicle was supplied by Deep Ocean Engineering, a company she co-founded in the early 1980s to build submersibles and underwater robots for research and commercial use. Her ultimate goal, and the company's biggest project, is a submersible that can descend 35,800 feet, the greatest known ocean depth, and stay there for a useful period of time. "We want to have working access to the sea, not just touch bottom and return," Earle explains.

Earle has been stung by a poisonous lionfish and been forced to karate-kick overly friendly sharks, but the greatest risks of her seemingly ideal occupation may be from psychic injuries ashore. While she has raised three children, her personal life has included three broken marriages, which she regards as a casualty of her dedication to her work. And since 1970, when Earle became front-page news as an aquababe, she has been criticized by her peers as a popularizer. "Real scientists were supposed to spend their lives in a lab," she notes. "I still get it from scientists who think I am a lightweight scientifically." She does her share of conventional research preparing her algae catalogs, Earle maintains, but "I prefer using the ocean as a lab."

In October 1990 Earle embarked on an adventure of another sort, becoming chief scientist of the National Oceanic and Atmospheric Administration. But her views on conservation and exploration differed from those of the White House, and little more than a year later she was forced to admit that the disagreements were insurmountable. Earle resigned in January 1992, noting diplomatically that she could be "even more effective if I am on the loose." There was also another concern, which could probably have been foreseen: "I am suffering from dry rot," Earle added. "I want to spend more time underwater." □

The Whole Shebang

In the summer of 1942, U.S. Army major general Dwight David Eisenhower was named to head U.S. forces in Europe, arguably the most coveted command in the history of warfare. Gleefully articulating the ultimate career goal of every officer, Eisenhower wrote his wife, Mamie, "I'm going to command the whole shebang!"

Ironically, until the outbreak of World War II, the career of Dwight David Eisenhower had been going nowhere, slowly. A poor boy from the cow town of Abilene, Kansas, Ike—from his surname—had become a West Point cadet in 1911 because the academy offered a free education. His pacifist mother is said to have cried when she learned of his acceptance there. In October 1918 he received his embarkation orders to Europe, but World War I ended before his ship even sailed. In the peace that followed, he developed into an efficient and dedicated staff officer, but at a succession of army posts he was more sought after as a football coach than as a great strategist. For 25 years, during which he married and had two sons—one died in childhood—his knowledge of the battlefield remained purely academic. In 1940 a resigned Eisenhower told his son that the chances for a general's star "were nil," adding, "Of course, in an emergency, anything can happen—but we're talking about a career, John, not miracles."

Even before Japan's December 1941 attack on Pearl Harbor, however, the tempo of military promotions began to accelerate in ◊

At ease in scuba gear on the ocean floor *(left)*, oceanographer Sylvia Earle encounters a large grouper with no apparent fear of human beings, but considerable curiosity.

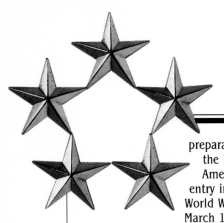

preparation for the likely American entry into World War II. In March 1941 Eisenhower became a full colonel, moving up the ladder to brigadier general in September of that year. "When they get clear down to my place on the list, they are passing out stars with considerable abandon," he wrote to Brigadier General Leonard Gerow, an army friend of long standing. In the years to come, he and his fellow graduates of 1915 would become "the class the stars fell on." Of the 164 graduates, 59 reached the rank of general, earning a total of 111 stars.

When war broke out in December, Brigadier General Eisenhower immediately applied for a field command, but his talent for administration landed him instead in Washington, D.C., assigned to readying the nation for war under General George C. Marshall. As the army exploded in size, adopted new weapons systems, and radically changed the way it was organized and operated, Ike worked 18 hours a day, meanwhile helping to allocate manpower and matériel for the two-front war.

When General Marshall sent him to London in 1942 to review American involvement in the war, Eisenhower *(right)* secured the command of U.S. forces in Europe. In his new role, Ike was looked after by a large and devoted family of attendants that included a personal assistant, a valet, a cook, two drivers, and two stenographers. It was the beginning of a curiously domestic existence at the apex of the military pyramid. In the years ahead, the general's aides were

reported changing his razor blades, putting toothpaste on his toothbrush, dialing telephone numbers for him, and writing to his wife and his mother about his health.

The supportive staff was surely welcome relief to Eisenhower from a series of responsibilities that were at times close to unbearable. In his own letters home to wife Mamie, Eisenhower poured out his heart, griping about everything from the weather and the food to the constant politicking he had to do. "In a place like this the commanding general must be a bit of a diplomat—lawyer—promoter—salesman—social hound—liar (at least to get out of social affairs)—mountebank—actor—Simon Legree—humanitarian—orator—and incidentally . . . a soldier," Ike

wrote her in August 1942. "Soldiering is no longer a simple thing of shouting 'Turn boys turn!' "

Given the third star of a lieutenant general, Eisenhower had to perform a new role as a high-wire artist in the most delicate of balancing acts, answering to the often differing interests of Britain and the United States. But the job did give him a chance at field command in the Allies' first joint enterprise, Operation Torch, an effort to drive the enemy out of North Africa launched in November 1942. "I simply must have a grandchild," he wrote in his diary just before the attack, "or I'll never have the fun of telling this when I'm fishing gray bearded, on the banks of a quiet bayou in the deep South." Eisenhower initially directed the invasion from the Rock of Gibraltar, then moved into the field, taking his first real battle command in March. Though the campaign proved longer and costlier than projected, it was victorious and won Ike a fourth star.

Torch was only a prelude to greater challenges: the invasion of Sicily and Italy later in 1943, and finally, the invasion of France with Operation Overlord in 1944.

The greatest adventure of Eisenhower's life, Overlord brought its share of headaches, including personality clashes with strong-willed generals who had far more combat experience—but fewer stars.

As he planned the invasion, Eisenhower chose the generals, dictated the commitment of landing craft and air power, and most important, named the date. Initially D-day was planned for May, but moving the forces into place by that month proved impossible. It was then set for June 5, 1944. A forecast of bad weather led Eisenhower, at his advance command post on the English coast, to postpone it a day. Further delay would require the invasion to be postponed by another month, until the tides were favorable again—yet going ahead with an invasion in a

storm could be fatal. Eying the rain, Eisenhower gambled on the invasion—and won. The attack on June 6 was hugely successful.

Soon the Allies began the drive to Berlin, with Eisenhower assuming direct command of the ground forces in September. Less than a year later, after a promotion to five-star general, Eisenhower accepted Germany's unconditional surrender, which he reported to Washington in a characteristically understated cable: "The mission of this Allied force was fulfilled at 0241 local time, May 7, 1945."

By then, Eisenhower had become a world-class celebrity; with the deaths of Hitler and Roosevelt, he was one of the best-known men in

the world, just behind Stalin and Churchill. "General, there is nothing that you may want that I won't try to help you get," said Harry Truman, en route in July to the Potsdam Conference. Truman, who had become president three months earlier, added, "That definitely and specifically includes the presidency in 1948." Eisenhower reportedly laughed at the idea.

Seven years later, in 1952, Ike was elected president, serving two terms. But the job of running what really was the whole shebang turned out to be something of an anticlimax. Nothing in peacetime ever matched the exhilaration of war for the man who, forever after, was known as the General. □

Brother Rat

It was called, locally, the Big Dig: the construction of a network of tunnels and roads beneath the city of Boston. Not everyone was sure the massive undertaking was wise in such an old seaport, and not just because it might undermine the city's historic buildings. According to a number of municipal officials, the project would evict tens of thousands of rats from their age-old homes along the waterfront and elsewhere, sending the disease-bearing rodents scurrying throughout the city. Once enunciated, the displaced-rat problem seemed to grow worse. Soon, alarmed citizens were hearing that Boston rats outnumbered human Bostonians two to one and lived substantially longer.

Fortunately, those fears were

overblown: The best estimate is that there are between 15 and 40 people in Boston for every rat, and city rats live only six months or so. Yet the potential for rodent problems was serious enough that in 1988, as the Big Dig neared groundbreaking, the city hired biologist Bruce Colvin. He was to handle several environmental effects of the construction—in particular, the spread of rats.

As senior scientist on the immense building project, which will in time put Boston's busiest highway underground and add a third tunnel beneath the harbor, Colvin sticks his nose into areas that most people take pains to avoid. Much of his work involves learning about the city's existing rat population in the targeted construction areas. He and his staff leave rodenticide in some areas, for example,

and measure the amount consumed each day for several days as a way of gauging the rat population. To get another estimate, they conduct rat surveys, walking along the construction route and back alleys to look for burrows and droppings. A third type of study involves trapping rats to test which poisons would be most effective against the Boston rat population.

Although not work for just anyone, this is the stuff dreams are made of for Colvin, who long ago developed an abiding fascination with small wild animals. As a very young boy growing up in a Boston suburb, he spent hours trying to lure local wildlife into a box with a stick and a string. One day, he says, he decided "the heck with this little box thing" and, using a loaf of bread as bait, ◊

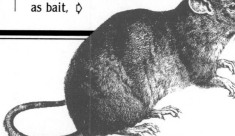

turned the family garage into a private menagerie of birds and mammals. It worked nicely until his father tried to put the car away and was rushed by three squirrels, putting an end for a time to the younger Colvin's zoological endeavor.

As a zoology major at Ohio State—where he kept a trained pet rat named Sheldon—Colvin zeroed in on rodents. He found rats especially compelling because "they've adapted so well to man's environment worldwide," he says. Their short lives and high reproductive rates also make them easy to study. In graduate school at Cleveland's John Carroll University, he was forced to diversify, however. His master's thesis in biology focused on barn owls—namely, their appetite for rats, and its consequences.

Part of the project, which tracked how much rat poison is passed on to owls, required trapping the birds to attach radio transmitters to them. Colvin (below) recalls that the chore required him to lie still in the barn throughout the night, while rats nibbled at him. The good news, Colvin says, was that he found that barn owls forage far afield, never tasting the chemical-laden rats in their own barns. Fortunately for Colvin, the rat nibbles proved harmless, too. "There's a long list of things that have bitten or grabbed me, from snakes to owls to rats," says Colvin, who still spends most of his vacations studying owls. "To most people, if they get bitten by a rat, it would be a notable point in their life. To a biologist, it's just part of the territory."

After getting his doctorate at Ohio's Bowling Green University, Colvin traveled and did additional research, including a study of the role of rats in Malaysian and Philippine agriculture, before getting his job in Boston, which he happily describes as one-of-a-kind. "This is the only construction project in the world that has a rodent

control project, and a rodent control expert on board," he says. Whereas most cities worry about displaced rats only after a construction project is completed, Boston will not allow construction to begin until Colvin certifies an area as rodent-free. Before construction starts, they also supervise the distribution of poison at nearby sewers and utility tunnels.

Since the group's intention is not just to kill the rats already there, but to keep more from arriving, Colvin also makes sure that each site is clear of such potential rat hostelries as weeds and junk piles. Explaining where rats might hide and how they behave is part of his larger job of community education, a key element in rat control. As the construction project continues, he holds neighborhood meetings to discuss garbage disposal and assure residents that the dying rats will not litter the ground in biblical multitudes. To emphasize the need for sanitation, he sweeps the streets on special cleanup days in neighborhoods along the construction route. "I'm dealing with a tremendous mosaic of issues," he says. "It's not just, 'Kill that rat.' "

Although rat killing is clearly the bottom line of his project, Colvin cannot help feeling sympathy for the opposition. Between the tendency of rats to eat one another's children and the arsenal of pesticides a rodent control officer can deploy, "it's a tough world" he says, "for a rat." □

In brilliant fuchsia shirt and spotless white trousers, 86-year-old knacker Cy Osmer stands outside the tanning shed atop his Vermont mountain in September 1992, with fragments of carcasses nearby.

A Man of Parts

Not much goes to waste when Cy Osmer is on the job. Osmer carts away dead livestock from farms, fields, and stables—if the animal is on its last legs, he handily dispatches it with a bullet between the eyes—and turns the remains into salable parts. First he separates each carcass into hide, meat, fat, bones, hooves, and innards. He prepares some items before selling them, tanning the hides into leather, for instance, or rendering the animal fat into tallow, which is used by soap-making firms. The rest is sold to companies that make animal odds and ends into dog food and bone-meal fertilizers. For all of this, he pockets as much as $100 a week. "Maybe more," says Osmer, a gnarled Vermonter and a man of few words. "Sometimes less. It depends."

Accompanied by his dog Jughead, Osmer is one of the less touted but essential aspects of the landscape of rural New England, where he and a handful of other men are known as Four-D—for "down, disabled, diseased, and dead"—Animal Handlers. Often portrayed as a kind of angel of death for nonhumans, the figure of the knacker has cast its sinister shadow over the agricultural landscape for centuries. In fact, the knacker—the word comes from Old Norse *hnakkr*, or "saddle," presumably because the work produces leather—is the necessary creation of any society that employs animals; without such harvests, farmers would have to burn or bury their dead livestock or haul them to a landfill. In some states, including Vermont, dead animals can be left to decay in the woods, a practice not much appreciated by hikers and cross-country skiers.

Osmer has been knackering since childhood. Born in 1906, the first of seven children, he began to teach himself the trade at the age of eight, when he needed meat to feed the foxes and foxhounds he was raising. Soon he was killing and carving up livestock for resale, and he subsequently came to earn more than the rest of his family combined. Over the decades, he raised hogs, worked at horse-meat butchering and rendering plants, and made some shrewd purchases of land. But he never stopped knackering, and his mountain has become everything a knacker's yard should be. Between pickups by clients, his land is strewn with fresh corpses and weathered rib cages, 55-gallon drums with animal parts, and a shed filled with salted animal skins.

By some accounts, Osmer owns most of the mountain—which is about five miles from the village of Woodstock, a tourist favorite—and has been offered as much as $1 million for his land. But the knacker, who lives in a trailer without telephone or television and drives a pickup that he bought new for $20,000 cash, does not want much else that money can buy. "I got enough," Cy Osmer says. "And I don't give it away, either."

Despite his reputed wealth, as a knacker Osmer is among the last of a dying breed. The declining number of local dairy farms has sharply reduced demand for the knacker's services, and demand for his products is down. The price of dog meat and bone meal has been cut in half, and inexpensive vegetable oils have driven down the price of tallow. A rendering plant that used to pay Osmer $20 a barrel for fat now charges him to cart the stuff away. Nor is anybody waiting to step into Osmer's boots. "I haven't trained anyone, except maybe my nephew," he says, "and he don't like the work." □

East River Archaeology

While other children watched baseball or cartoons on television, Ray Nalpant never missed a show with underwater explorer Jacques Cousteau; he cannot remember when he did not want to dive for a living. But, while destined to dive, Nalpant was evidently not intended to share the bright, vital oceans illuminated by Cousteau. Instead, officer Nalpant gropes about in New York City's murky waters for putrefied bodies, murder weapons, stolen cars, and bombs. Since 1987 he has followed one of the saddest professions on earth as part of the 24-member New York Scuba Unit, among the nation's oldest and busiest police underwater-recovery teams.

Recovery, not rescue, is the operative word. Since he joined the unit, Nalpant has saved only one life. He and another diver riding in a patrol boat saw a car, taillights still on, splash into the East River, and they were able to rescue the occupant. As a rule, the survivors have been rescued by the time Nalpant reaches the scene, dressed in his impermeable crimson dry suit

and full face mask to keep out the filthy water, and equipped with a knife, a screwdriver, and a flashlight to give him slight visibility down in the turbid waters. When a USAir flight crashed at New York's LaGuardia Airport in March 1992, for example, Nalpant's duty was, as he puts it, "to unscramble the bodies" in chest-deep water. While he worked, he recalls, the victims' wallets floated by in the frigid March water, opened to pictures of smiling families. His memory teems with such images.

Extracting murder victims from the river may be somewhat less emotionally devastating, but the task is often much uglier. Bodies

have been found handcuffed to cinder blocks, packed in suitcases, even chopped up in small pieces. In the Bronx, Nalpant recovered a footless, handless body that had apparently been flushed back and forth in the sewers for months. "We assumed he was murdered and dumped into a manhole in the street," says the diver.

So-called evidence dives focus on less grisly items, such as firearms, and require meticulous foot-by-foot searches of the murky river bottom. "Evidence searches are like archaeological digs," Nalpant told one interviewer. "It can take weeks to find a significant item." When they investigate an area, Nalpant and his colleagues drop a pink buoy to let ships in the area know there are divers in the water and lay a 75-foot plastic line on the river bottom. They search along the line, then move the line a foot or so farther out, following the direction of the current. They search until the area has been covered or the desired item found.

The submerged rope, fastened at either end with 10-pound grapnel anchors, is the divers' only known reference point in the abiding murk, which must be navigated mainly by touch. "I feel for a car, I feel for the door, for the way to break in," explains Nalpant. "I can do anything by feel." Once found, a piece of evidence is sealed in a water-filled container for protection against the air and for fingerprinting. Nalpant says fingerprints can be detected on such objects.

Working 12-hour shifts, Nalpant spends most of his time searching along the 576 miles of New York City waterfront. On any given shift, three members of his six-person unit work from a 52-foot police boat, while two stand by for dives best approached by helicopter; the sixth assignment is flexible. All six divers work in waters that are as dangerous as some neighborhoods. Tidal currents in the East River, for example, are powerful enough to sweep a diver far off course, and the lack of visibility can be disorienting. More than once, Nalpant has concluded a search and started to ascend, only to hit his head on the bottom of a hull. If the ship is 500 feet long, and he is almost out of his alloted 40 minutes of pressurized air, he has little time to maneuver. Nalpant usually dives back to the bottom to reorient himself by feeling the current,

then tries the ascent again.

Such dangers are perhaps less draining than the burdens police diving can place on the human spirit, even one as resilient as that of the matter-of-fact Nalpant. Among the many tragedies locked in Nalpant's memory is the first time he recovered a drowned body, in a narrow but treacherous stretch of water known as Coney Island Creek. Some children had been playing there; one boy got in over his head, and a passerby jumped in to save him. Both drowned. By the time Nalpant was called in only the child's body had been found by the original emergency crew.

While the would-be rescuer's wife stood by in tears, Nalpant dove in and brought out a man's body. He was about to leave when a family friend called to the scene pointed out that the corpse was not the woman's husband. Nalpant had to dive again, scraping the bottom until he found the husband. Later investigation showed that the first body had been that of a homeless man who had jumped in to save the boy and his doomed rescuer and had followed them both to his death. For Nalpant, the incident was particularly distressing because of the wife's presence; since then, he has kept his distance from relatives of the drowned because it is just too hard to face them.

Although he does not relish the underwater search for the dead, Nalpant still loves to dive. "When I'm down there, it's very much like the freedom of flight, going up and down as you wish," he says. And so, at least once a year, he finds a place where the water is clean, clear, and full of life, dons his scuba gear, and goes diving. □

Tale Bones

The victim's skull had been bludgeoned inward, the bones so extensively fractured that the examining pathologist could not tell what kind of blunt instrument had been used. To describe the probable murder weapon required a doctor with a narrower, and perhaps grislier, specialty—a forensic anthropologist. The pathologist called on William Maples, a highly skilled reader of the bones of the dead.

The work is not for the squeamish. "I can clean the skull, reconstruct it so the pieces fit together and find out the shape and type of weapon," explains Maples cheerfully. He recalls having to visit a series of hardware stores to locate a screwdriver that matched a victim's head wounds. An anthropology professor at the University of Florida at Gainesville, Maples is often called in as an expert in cases of violent crime, including the five serial murders for which his town became notorious in 1990.

Forensic anthropology, the peculiar science of interpreting the subtle messages left in human bones and even cremated remains, began in the late 1800s with the calipers and micrometers ⟩

devised by French criminologist Alphonse Bertillon. Similar instruments are used today, but they are backed up by modern technology: computer databases of bone measurements, x-ray analysis to determine age and the presence of metal, and high-resolution video that allows experts to compare digitized images of a skull with photographs of the living individual.

Getting to the bones, however, can take some doing, especially when they are embedded in a fresh corpse. In such cases, Maples macerates them, or removes their tissue. A macabre undertaking, maceration does the least damage when carried out at "a slow simmer" in plain water, he explains with the offhandedness of a chef. "Usually three to five days are required for more-or-less fresh bodies, with intact spinal columns, hands, feet, and

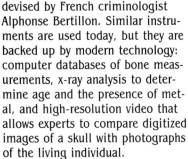

so on," Maples says. Pressure cookers and chemicals strip the bones faster but may damage them—and blur the stories they have to tell. Boiling bones is not for everyone, but Maples makes the best of it, giving his lectures waggish titles such as "Confessions of a Serial Macerator."

But the result is deadly serious. Properly cleaned bones read by a forensic anthropologist are a skeletal biography of the deceased. Interpreted by the right expert, such remains can identify not only a dead person's age, sex, race, and stature, but also the habits, occupation, injuries, and diseases of the departed. Forensic anthropology can even reveal

whether a corpse is that of a right- or left-hander; bones in the favored arm and hand usually appear bigger as a result of more frequent muscle action on that side.

Such detective skills are not just useful in solving crimes. Maples and others in his profession are often called upon to identify anonymous buried remains and the fragmented, charred remnants of people caught in fires and airplane crashes. From time to time, they are brought in to resolve disputes over disinterred historical figures as well; Maples has worked on the disinterred remains of U.S. president Zachary Taylor and the family of Czar Nicholas II of Russia. Always, from Maples's point of view, the answer is in the bones. "When an anthropologist is asked what bones are needed to be sent for analysis," Maples has written, "the answer should be 'all of them.' "

Bones were all Maples had to work with in 1984, when he helped the Peruvian government lay to rest the body of Francisco Pizarro, the brutal conqueror of the Incan empire. Pizarro, who had executed his former partner Diego de Almagro in 1539, was killed in revenge by some of de Almagro's followers two years later. For a century, Peruvians had believed that a mummified body interred in the Cathedral of Lima was the Spaniard. But in 1977 workers turned up two boxes under the altar. One held an assortment of human bones; the other, containing a skull, came with an inscription indicating it held Pizarro's head. Had the nation been venerating the wrong corpse? To get the answer, Maples

Performing in 1992, whale trainer Chuck Tompkins and his 7,000-pound partner Shamu surface with a smile.

and other scientists used x-ray machines and microscopes to examine the bones for the faint remaining traces of old wounds. The results showed multiple wounds that matched neatly the historical accounts of Pizarro's death: a stabbing in the throat that brought him instantly to his knees and was followed with other blows. There was also evidence that he had been stabbed through the eye, the heart, and the liver—a likely pattern for a ritual killing and good evidence that the label on the smaller box correctly identified the remains as those of Pizarro. In January 1985, on the 450th anniversary of the founding of Lima, the bones were put on display in the cathedral and the previous body was removed.

In his detailed scholarly paper on the matter, published in the *Journal of Forensic Sciences* in 1989, Maples duly worked through the likely "wounds to the skeletal remains" that he had found, detailing each cut and thrust under such subheadings as "Neck," "Trunk," "Extremities," "Mandible," and "Cranium" and commenting on the "osteophyte development" and "anterior wedging" of various aspects of the remains.

In the end his enthusiasm for the work burst through the conventions of scholarly prose. Describing the final moments of the man whose bones he had examined, Maples wrote, "After a bitter fight, many or all of the assassins plunged their weapons into the dead or dying man. The skeleton of Pizarro," he concluded, "brought to mind scenes from Shakespeare's *Julius Caesar* or Agatha Christie's *Murder on the Orient Express*"— murders that, like Pizarro's, were the work of many hands. □

Dances with Whales

Despite its size and name, the immense black-and-white killer whale seems as friendly as a puppy when it splashes up to Chuck Tompkins, who scratches its back and its pectoral flipper, then climbs on board. The giant mammal darts through the water at 25 miles per hour. Moments later, the aquatic duo execute the so-called hydro hop, in which Tompkins lies rigid in the water and allows his partner to scoop him up on its vast nose as the whale leaps up 30 feet before crashing back into the water, propelling its passenger in a neat dive to one side. The crowd of 5,000 in Shamu Stadium invariably goes wild, with excitement—and envy. Who would not want to frolic with one of the planet's largest predators and be paid for doing it?

Tompkins has been cavorting with whales ever since he joined Sea World, a marine-life park in Orlando, Florida, as a 21-year-old assistant trainer in 1977, and he admits that the job is an enviable one. "There's a feeling of absolute satisfaction," he says, "when you can build up a relationship with an animal this big." As curator of animal training, Tompkins also has charge of the park's sea lions, bottle-nosed dolphins, and black "pseudorca" whales, as well as the 35 or so human trainers who work in the park. But his chief official responsibility—and unofficial favorite—is the park's quintet of killer whales. Tompkins checks on them daily and spends one day each week with them in the water. "If I didn't do that, I'd lose that bond," he says. "Some of these killer whales, I've worked with them for eleven or twelve years."

Like any meaningful relationship, a bond with a whale takes time and effort to forge. Every day, Sea World's trainers put the orcas through an exercise program of swimming and other routines that is meant to keep them as fit as ◊

Searching for clues in the renowned forensic laboratory he founded at the University of Florida at Gainesville, William Maples (*left*) examines a recent homicide victim's jaw and facial bones.

they might be in the free ocean. The workout is followed by playtime. Sometimes the whales toss around 55-gallon barrels as if they were beachballs, or the trainers may playfully squirt water in the whales' mouths from a hose. Then there are getting-to-know-you sessions, in which a trainer rubs down a whale, scratches its tail fluke, and strokes its dorsal fin.

At times, the job involves long hours: round-the-clock watches of whales acclimating to a new environment or about to bear young. "We have to be there all the time for them," declares Tompkins. The trainers' commitment to the whales produces other drawbacks, too. Because the whales like it that way, the water is kept at 53 degrees Fahrenheit, bone chilling even in a wet suit. The trainers' ears and sinuses also take a beating from rapid 40-foot dives and ascents. But Tompkins and his co-workers do not flinch from such discomfort. "Most of us are half-fish," he says.

The whales spend considerable time with the Sea World trainers, not only learning their parts in shows, but learning how to play a role in the park's extensive marine-research projects. The females are taught to urinate into a cup and, when pregnant, will lumber over for milk suctioning; the whales also comply with the taking of monthly blood samples. As for the performing arts, the creatures are taught to spin and breach, just as they would in the wild—but in response to hand signals. The trainers use only positive reinforcement. If the whales misbehave, "we ignore it," says Tompkins, "and go on to the next behavior." From the whale's perspective, Tompkins says,

"the sight of little people in red wetsuits jumping up and down and waving their arms must be something to see."

Indeed, learning to coexist with humans is an essential lesson for the killer whales, who would seldom encounter a human in their ocean home. Although killer whales in the wild feed voraciously on seals, aquatic birds, fish, and even other kinds of whales, they are believed to leave human beings alone. Despite their presumed good intentions, however, their sheer size—as much as 27 feet and 12,000 pounds in the male, 24 feet and 8,000 pounds in the female—makes killer whales a hazard to anyone within a flip of their massive flukes. Tompkins says that when humans are in the water, the trainers encourage the whales to be "very relaxed, very comfortable and very slow moving, and to treat us like delicate flowers."

But occasional near misses are inevitable. In 1979 Tompkins narrowly escaped being crushed during a maneuver called the human hurdle. He was training a whale to leap over him as he lay at the bottom of the pool when suddenly the animal seemed to stop in midair. "This 7,000-pound whale is going to drop right on top of me," he recalls thinking. Although Tompkins does not know how the whale did it, the great beast saw and solved the problem. With only a foot of its tail in the water, it wrenched its body sideways as it plopped into the water, missing him entirely. "It shows that these animals are more agile than you can imagine," he says now, "and that my relationship was good enough that it didn't want to land on top of me." □

Fisherman's Whiff

In its job of monitoring the safety of foods and other products, the U.S. Food and Drug Administration has many resources to deploy, from analytic chemists to undercover operatives. To study the freshness of fish, however, the FDA needs to go no further than that useful appendage the human nose.

Although the essence of the job comes naturally, fish smelling requires a certain amount of instruction. Training inspectors and even fish processors and retailers how to tell when a fish has been too long out of water—a condition less obvious than it seems—is the job of James D. Barnett, an FDA fish smeller, or organoleptic specialist. Barnett, who is based in Washington State but spends about four months a year conducting fish-smelling courses around the country, notes that visual inspection and chemical analysis can aid in detecting bad fish. But for both the FDA and Barnett, the nose is the final arbiter. A fish must *smell* like rotten fish before the FDA will eject it from the marketplace.

To show his students just what decomposed fish smells like, Barnett travels with packets of the three classes of fish recognized by the FDA. Class #1 is not necessarily odorless, but the smell is not suspect. Shrimp pulled out of the Gulf of Mexico, for example, typically smell of iodine whether fresh or stale. Class #2, which marks the beginning of decomposition, gives off a whiff that is unambiguous to the experienced sniffer. Shrimp in this category may smell "putrid-sour," says Barnett, while canned tuna or salmon may have a fermented odor reminiscent of overripe pineapple. The smell of class #3 would knock most people flatter than a flounder. To prepare his traveling samples, Barnett starts with fresh fish and subjects it to what experts call "time/temperature abuses"—leaving it unrefrigerated for an extended period of time.

Barnett then takes the results in large freezer "totes" to the workshops he conducts, generally held in local hotels. There his training materials are often the source of management complaints. "It's okay, normally, until you bring out the bad stuff," Barnett explains. "Then they say, 'Just what are you doing in there?' " Barnett has had his totes leak but cannot match the experience of a predecessor who once had to store his samples in his hotel-room bathtub. When the man checked out, two women were at the front desk, complaining about the noxious odors coming through their vent.

When possible, Barnett customizes his packets to the region where he is conducting training—mahi-mahi on the West Coast, for example, or catfish in New Orleans. But wherever they are, the workshops are hands-on, nose-down undertakings. Barnett will not use plastic gloves to handle the fish because they interfere with his sense of smell. As for the smelling itself, inhaling deeply is discouraged, for fear of hyperventilation. Instead, Barnett teaches his students to take quick, short sniffs.

Such fish-smelling expertise was not the original career goal of Barnett, who trained to be an entomologist. A 1970 graduate of Mississippi State University, he worked in jobs involving pesticides and plant control before the FDA hired him in 1974 to do microanalysis of contaminated food. After only a year in that lab, Barnett's knack for precision smelling led to an FDA job sniffing fish in New York, followed by a 10-year stint as the agency's fish smeller in New Orleans, where he also served as a regional teataster (pages 44-45). That dual role came to an end in 1990, when Barnett assumed the position of national organoleptic specialist and became a nationwide trainer in the fish-odor field.

Although the position brings the distinction of being a leading expert in a vital field, it has its disadvantages. Barnett at times acquires a class #3 fragrance of his own. "Some days I go home, and my family doesn't want to get around me too much," he admits. He also takes more of the job home than just odor. Whenever he passes a fish market, he goes in to sniff their product. As a connoisseur of seafood, "I'm always interested," Barnett explains. "This job is basically one where you're never really on vacation." One is always on the scent of something. □

Visiting a restaurant fish auction during a training trip to Honolulu, FDA organoleptic specialist Jim Barnett checks the texture and odor of a moonfish, or opah, taken from Hawaiian waters.

Desert Heat

The end of the Gulf War in March 1991 left Kuwait under a black cloud of toxic smoke from 647 burning oil wells, set ablaze by retreating Iraqi troops. A potentially serious health hazard and an obvious environmental threat, the fires were also almost unimaginably costly. Each day six million barrels of crude went up in flames, about 10 percent of the world's daily oil consumption. The smoke was worth $1,000 per second.

This petroleum inferno was also a beacon for an elite among the world's firefighters—the grimy but heroic figures who have extinguished the great oil- and gas-well conflagrations of the century, from the Sahara's GT2 to Mexico's Ixtoc-1. None of them had ever seen a fire of this magnitude. "You half expect to see little guys with pitchforks and tails coming out of the ground," one oil-field engineer told the press. Even the legendary Red Adair, perhaps the world's most famous oil-well quencher, was stunned: "I've never seen anything like this before in my life." As firefighting crews poured into Kuwait, experts predicted that two years would pass before all the fires were extinguished. Four companies—Red Adair Company, Wild Well Control, and Boots & Coots from the United States, and Safety Boss of Canada—were the first into Kuwait. Their firefighters earned $400 to $2,000 a day, depending on their experience and the risks they ran. Though drawn by the money, the teams were also attracted by the prospect of achieving the seemingly impossible— slaying the frightening dragon of a burning well.

The dousers faced a task remarkable for its discomfort. Most noticeable from a distance was the smoke. Thick and foul, it spawned an endless night and gave workers headaches and clogged their nasal passages; some found themselves still coughing up black soot after weeks away from Kuwait on home leave. "It feels like somebody is standing on your chest all the time," observed a Boots & Coots crew chief. Nearer to the wells, heat became the main problem. The 4,000-degree-Fahrenheit fires turned the sand nearby to molten glass. Even at some distance, the ground was hot enough to blister a kneeling man's legs. Clothes were hot against the skin, and metal zippers, heated to hundreds of degrees, could inflict painful burns. Noise levels around the wells, where burning oil was roaring out of the ground at some 800 miles per hour, were nerve-shatteringly high. And there was something deadly hidden in the sand: Many of the wells were surrounded by unexploded land mines *(pages 36-38).* "Every day I'm in that field," one oil-field hand said, "I find three or four new ways to die."

Firefighters used corrugated-tin shelters to approach the wells through the searing heat. Once close to the blaze, they tried several techniques against the flames. The American companies' preferred choice was to pour on water, knocking the temperature down until the oil could no longer ignite. Pumping from reservoirs filled with up to a million gallons of seawater, they hit the fire with four simultaneous streams of water. Usually about a half-hour passed before the well cooled enough to keep from relighting.

The Canadians favored a similar system that relied on fire trucks with water cannons and mobile water tanks. They sometimes used potassium bicarbonate, a dry chemical that robbed the fires of the oxygen that sustained them.

When such methods failed, American firefighters sometimes turned to explosives. They packed about 200 pounds of dynamite into a metal drum wrapped with insulation and soaked with water, then maneuvered it over the wellhead at the end of a 75-foot metal boom attached to a bulldozer, while streams of water cooled the charge and the boom operator. The blast consumed the oxygen around the wellhead, leaving none to maintain the fire. Several teams pumped nitrogen around the flames to displace oxygen, and a Hungarian crew pumped water through two jet engines to blow the fires out with a high-velocity mist.

Putting out the fire in blistering heat was only the first part of the job, however. Even with the flames extinguished, a five-story fountain of oil still roared from the shattered wellheads at pressures as great as 5,000 pounds per square inch. "People think putting out the fire is the hard part," veteran oil-field firefighter Edward "Coots" Matthews told one reporter, "but shutting in the well, that's the dangerous thing." As blowout specialists, working in crews of four to six, moved in to cap each extinguished well, the oil torrents fell in a dark rain that soaked them. The gases in the oily air posed a continuing threat as well: The smallest spark could ignite a flashback, turning the oil-soaked area around the well into a lake of fire.

Often wading waist-deep in oil,

The raging fire extinguished, two oil-field workers are transformed into animated bronzes by a fountain of spewing oil as they try to cap one of Kuwait's many damaged wellheads in the aftermath of the 1991 Gulf War.

crew member at the water cannon quickly doused the fire, but not before Matson suffered second-degree burns over 25 percent of his body. He was one of only seven men severely burned during the firefighting effort, which involved 10,000 workers from 34 countries. Two other firefighters died, neither while actually battling the flames.

The last fire was extinguished on November 6, 1991, after only eight months of grueling work, rather than the two years originally estimated. The final battle of the firefighting war was fought by Safety Boss of Canada, at the last burning well 10 miles from the Iraqi border. As the crew moved in on the blaze, a more sedate crowd gathered in the Burgan oil field, about 80 miles south. There, 20 minutes after the Canadians had snuffed the final fire, the emir of Kuwait, Sheik Jabir al-Ahmad al Sabah, ceremonially closed a hydraulic valve, bringing to an official end the inferno that had raged across his desert kingdom. □

the blowout crews had to cut the top off the well pipe, install a blowout preventer, and then close the valve to shut off the oil. To protect them from flashbacks, workers had water cannons trained on them at all times. That precau-

tion paid off in July 1991 when a flashback caught Dwight Matson. The 28-year-old Canadian was in an oil-filled hole trying to twist free a scorched bolt on the wellhead when the fire relit. Matson vaulted out of the hole, his back on fire; a

Probing the Envelope

"Why break your Aeroplane yourself when we do it for you?" asked a small advertisement in a British aviation journal in 1911. Its appearance marked the debut of the professional test pilot; an aviator who, as the ad succinctly promised, "takes the risks of testing experimental machines." Whether it was because aircraft designers still preferred to test their planes themselves—the Wright brothers, for example, had been their own test pilots—or because they had learned that the would-be test flier had acquired his pilot's license only two weeks before, there was no immediate response to his ad. But within a year, young Wilfred Parke, the man behind the ad, was testing new planes, discovering how they flew, and what to do when they fell—it was Parke who established that opposite rudder stopped the deadly spiral of a tailspin. Two years and some 2,000 flights later, one of those planes killed him.

Parke's short, brave career was an apt beginning for a profession that has claimed its share of lives, yet remains an envied occupation high on the aviation totem pole. Put simply,

there are pilots, and there are test pilots. Even the development of computers that can design and analyze aircraft performance has not dimmed the test pilot's aura. At some point, he or she must take the machine into the atmosphere and explore its dynamic limits—and beyond.

The risks still inherent in such work are a large part of the attraction for people such as Edward T. Schneider, a veteran test pilot employed at the NASA Ames Dryden Flight Research Facility at Edwards Air Force Base, California. It is still a joy to be on the cutting edge of aviation technology, says Schneider, and it is great to fly every day.

Best of all, he says, is "being able to do new things and things that are risky. Risky, but not scary," he quickly adds, to distinguish between the ability to recognize danger and the fear of it.

Like most test pilots, Schneider got his training in the military; he became a naval aviator in 1969, when he was 21. His last navy posting, in 1982, was to NASA. When one of the civilian test pilots in the office was killed in a training accident, Schneider got the job. As a research test pilot, Schneider spends most of his time testing modifications to existing aircraft. For example, when NASA engineers experimented with a new wing design to reduce drag, and thus improve fuel efficiency, it was Schneider's job to put the redesign through its airborne paces, pushing the plane to the limits of its performance parameters—the envelope, as it is called. In the course of business, Schneider brought the plane to a carefully predetermined combination of attitudes and air speeds, turning and maneuvering to find out whether, as he puts it, "anything bad" would happen. Schneider has also tested modifications aimed at improving the maneuverability of the U.S. Navy's F-18

Hornet at speeds as low as 80 or 90 knots—ordinarily, the fighter is not flown below 120 knots. In this case, pushing the envelope means trying to fly the plane ever more slowly, into a regime where many aircraft suddenly stall and spin out of control. In a planned total of 45 flights, Schneider has been deliberately forcing the jet into spins and then out of them. If he fails, of course, "it's going to spin right down to the ground."

A test flight on one project or another every morning, lasting from an hour to an hour and a half, gives Schneider the daily ration of flight that keeps his job compelling. For the rest of the day, though, he is grounded. Part of the time is spent preparing for and reporting on each flight. In the afternoons he may spend hours in a ground-based flight simulator—a fixed, but visually responsive mock-up of a real plane that provides an early test of proposed modifications. With a new aircraft, says Schneider, "you may fly ten hours in the simulator for every hour in the air." Then, at day's end, he takes a five-mile run through the Mojave Desert. Exercise not only helps Schneider let off steam; it also helps him stay in shape for work that is as demanding physically as it is mentally.

Despite the fact that his predecessor was killed on the job, Schneider views NASA as a place where test pilots can grow old gracefully. Military pilots tend to be rotated out of testing while still young. "At 60, I'll stop," he declares. So far, nothing has happened at NASA to change his mind. In fact, when pressed to recount his most frightening experience, Schneider must go back to

his navy days and an episode in 1982 that he admits was scary.

Schneider and a radio-intercept officer had been assigned to production test an F-4 Phantom fighter that had been extensively modified. Most of the systems were given close preflight tests while the plane was still on the ground, but the airplane's nose radar could not be tested at full power except in flight. As Schneider notes wryly, testing radar on the ground would "essentially involve microwaving your friends." Thus, ground tests had failed to reveal that, months earlier, a technician had unwittingly drilled through the plane's main radar cable, located behind some newly installed avionics gear.

Fifteen minutes into the flight, at an altitude of 35,000 feet, Schneider was bringing the plane up to supersonic speed to test the operation of new wing slats, and the nose radar was at full power for the first time since the repairs. Suddenly, the perforated radar cable ignited, and Schneider had what he calls a "major fire" in the plane's nose. Worse, an electrical domino effect followed: As other wires melted together, multiple short circuits swept through the plane's control and electrical systems. One of the engines stalled, and the cockpit depressurized. "We were 120 miles out to sea and going like a bullet," recalled Schneider, too fast to eject. Schneider and his radio-intercept officer concentrated on the procedures that had been drilled into them for dealing with multiple emergencies. "The bottom line was, we got it all sorted out, slowed down, climbed up, came back, and landed," he says. "But it was pretty interesting while it was going on." □

Gold's Fools

In 1980 what is considered the richest single find of gold in the 20th century was discovered deep in the Amazon rain forest on Brazil's Serra Pelada—"Naked Mountain." The timing could not have been better: Brazil suffered from crippling debt and a poor balance of trade, and gold seemed to offer a heaven-sent cure. By the time the Serra Pelada mine was shut down at the end of the decade, however, the site had lost its lucky connotation, becoming a shocking symbol of desperation and greed. The quest for gold has always driven people to do appalling things, but few gold diggers have ever labored under worse conditions than the *garimpeiros,* or "prospectors," of Serra Pelada.

According to legend, a small, serious prospector named Oscar Soares Silva discovered gold there in February 1980 and announced his find in the nearby town of Marabá with a fist-size nugget. Within 48 hours of Soares's news, a thousand garimpeiros had converged on the site, cutting their way from the nearest highway 50 miles away. Four days after Soares made his claim, another prospector found a 22-pound nugget, and the gold rush was on. Within a month 10,000 men were dividing the earth into claims, or *barrancos,* that measured 7 by 10 feet and hiring others to help carry out the dirt and ore. At the peak of mining, more than 150,000 men, caked in red mud, swarmed over Serra Pelada. While a few were full-time prospectors, most were amateur miners determined to strike it rich—refugees from wretched shantytowns, poor peasants from ⊅

A smiling Ed Schneider *(left)* steps down from NASA's experimental X-29 fighter after completing his first test flight in the novel aircraft, which incorporates new computerized systems and materials as well as an innovative forward-swept wing.

91

the arid northeast, even middle-class professionals, all willing to do the barranco owner's dirty work for a share in the action.

Because the claims were placed right next to one another, there was no way to dig but straight down. Nearly 1,000 feet high in 1980, Serra Pelada had lost some 300 feet by the summer of 1984; soon, what had been a mountain was a wedge-shaped declivity, and, finally, a 200-foot-deep pit, its sides terraced with barrancos. Garimpeiros climbed down into the pit on primitive wooden ladders. At the bottom of the *acava,* or "hole," some clawed out the dirt; others, their waterlogged hands cut by carrying cords, climbed out with 75-pound bags of dirt to be dumped or sluiced or panned. One false step, and they could fall back into the pit and possibly drown in the slurry. In one month in 1986, 12 men suffocated in a mud slide caused by heavy rainfall.

The misery of the pit was not restricted to the mud. In the early days of the rush, almost every man was armed and fired at the slightest provocation—to protect boundary stakes, which tended to slip into the slime, to settle a quarrel over a payout, even to celebrate the unearthing of a nugget. This ceased with the arrival of Major Curio, a renowned guerrilla hunter formerly with the Brazilian security police, charged with bringing law and order to Serra Pelada.

The richest part of the mine, a narrow strip at the bottom, was called the Malvinas, the Argentine name for the Falkland Islands, because it was a site of endless dispute. Mercury used to leach gold from the dirt and mud also menaced the health of the prospectors, exposing them to the risks of kidney failure and cancer. But, for some, the payout was immense. Officially, the 150,000 miners extracted a ton of gold worth about $11 million from Serra Pelada each month; in all likelihood, far more was smuggled out to avoid paying the government its due. There were stories of peasants buying airplanes, soccer teams, and hotels on Rio's Copacabana beach. For others, the fast wealth proved ephemeral. Leaving the mine with their treasure, many garimpeiros were sidetracked—and swiftly impoverished—by bars and brothels on the outskirts of the Serra Pelada camp.

Nor did the gold provide the economic salvation that had been hoped. Although Serra Pelada made Brazil one of the world's top gold producers in the 1980s, it hardly dented the country's raging debt: The total volume of gold pulled out of Serra Pelada even in its best year would service Brazil's total debt for only one month. Like major gold strikes throughout history, Serra Pelada also left in its wake what one reporter described as a "tribe of violent nomads"—hundreds of thousands of impoverished prospectors who continue their destructive foraging at more than 2,000 wildcat sites in the Brazilian rain forest, searching for another Naked Mountain. □

Like a teeming mass of worker ants, impoverished Brazilian gold prospectors swarm across the muddy pit of Serra Pelada *(right)* at the height of the 1980s gold strike there. Above, the white-shirted supervisor of a successful mining plot directs workers hauling sacks of precious gold-bearing earth up the primitive wooden ladders leading out of the 200-foot-deep pit.

Tasting, as always, from the center of a sliced-open carton, ice-cream tester John Harrison *(right)* analyzes a gold-plated spoonful of Chocolate Chip Cookie Dough ice cream.

Frozen Assets

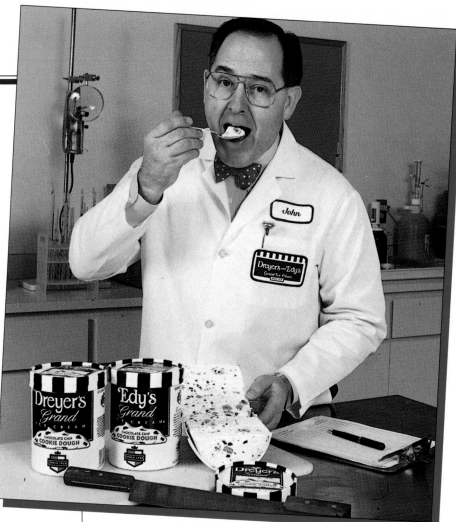

"There's nothing worse than a bad bowl of ice cream," insists John Harrison. That might not be high on most people's list of crimes, but Harrison has an unusual perspective. Since 1982 he has been the official taster and flavor developer for a leading ice-cream manufacturer, Dreyer's Grand Ice Cream of Oakland, California—sold as Edy's ice cream in the American East and Midwest. He cheerfully admits he has a job any child would give his milk teeth for.

Harrison sounds like a winetaster when he describes his work. Starting his day at 7:30 in the morning, when a human's 9,000 or so taste buds are at their most acute, he spends the next few hours visually inspecting and taste testing the beginning, middle, and end of 20 ice-cream production runs. To avoid having the flavor of one sample contaminate another, he works through the flavors in a specific order, beginning, as he puts it, with "the white wines of ice cream, the vanillas," and progressing through the other flavors being produced to "the heavy bordeaux of ice cream, the mochas,

chocolates, and fudge."

Harrison begins each test by cutting the ice cream in half to check for an even distribution of nuts, fruit, and other ingredients. Then he dips his gold-plated spoon—any other material would alter the taste—and deftly flips the resulting sample into his mouth, where he swirls the ice cream, smacks his lips to help "the top note of the bouquet" reach his nose, then spits the stuff into a cup. Like a winetaster, he never swallows what he samples.

In addition to flavor, Harrison checks for texture. "We are looking for two words: smooth and creamy," he explains. "Some of the defects

would be cold, coarse, icy, fluffy, gummy." Each year, he says, some 400,000 gallons of ice cream fail the test and are donated to local food banks; improperly mixed ice cream is almost impossible to correct. "Let's say we put too much fudge in the Marble Fudge," he explains. "If you try to rework it, you're melting it down, and it'll get a light brown color."

Harrison may have inherited some of his expertise. His great-grandfather had a chain of ice-cream parlors in New York City at the turn of the 20th century, his grandfather started the first dairy cooperative in Tennessee, and his father owned an ice-cream ingredients factory in Atlanta. Born in 1942 Harrison has spent his whole career in the ice-cream business, coming to Dreyer's as a taster in 1982. He spends half the year at the company's California headquarters, tasting. The other half, he travels around the country to train his counterparts at Dreyer's other plants and to promote the brand.

In his lifetime, Harrison has passed judgment on more than 100 million gallons of ice cream, from plain vanilla, which remains his favorite, to such seasonal specials as Apple Pie, Egg Nog, and Pumpkin. He has also helped formulate a handful of highly successful flavors, including Cookies 'n' Cream, which mixes Oreo cookies into the ice cream, and Chocolate Chip Cookie Dough ice cream. Those sound like desserts strictly for youngsters, but as Harrison notes, "all of us are kids when it comes to ice cream." To his regret, he has had to veto some flavors, such as cantaloupe and jalapeño; he was proud of an apricot ice cream he formulated, but in that case the public did not agree.

Like the winetasters whose vocabulary he borrows, Harrison has to make certain sacrifices to keep his sense of taste intact. He shuns spicy foods during the work week, does not smoke or drink alcohol, and will not wear cologne because it throws off his sense of smell. He has to be extra careful not to catch a cold. And, for all his precautions, his taste buds are likely to go as he gets into his 60s. Until that happens, however, Harrison has no plans to come in from the cold. "As long as my buds can take it," he vows, he will continue. "I love ice cream." □

The Boys of Summer

As if sun, sand, and surf were not perquisites enough, the lifeguard has long been the bronzed icon of summer pleasures, a teenage sun god fallen to earth. Never was that truer than in 1966. Bikinis were in, the Beach Boys were kings of the airwaves, and brothers Ron and Glenn Hoffman, then 17 and 16 years old, took their thrones—two nearby lifeguard stands on Jones Beach, outside New York City. They loved their work in the sun so much that for more than 25 years they have returned to the East Bathhouse section of Jones Beach each summer weekend. They have become lifeguards for life.

A wooden stand on an urban beach is not where one would expect to find two middle-aged lawyers. For all its glamour, ocean lifeguarding is a job that demands physical strength and occasional acts of derring-do—to the Hoffmans, that is part of the job's appeal. They are dedicated amateur athletes, and being a lifeguard is an extension of that passion. A civil-litigation attorney whose startled clients sometimes recognize him on the beach, Ron calls lifeguarding "forced recreation." Glenn, a bookish legal researcher, speaks of the Atlantic Ocean as a "formidable opponent." That opponent inflicts its share of injuries, however. The physical exertion of rescue can cause back pain, sore shoulders, and what doctors call lifeguard's calf, an inflammation of the foot and calf caused by running hard on bare sand.

Like the other guards, who are less than half the Hoffmans' ages, the brothers survey the ocean from stands 8 to 10 feet tall, built high so the lifeguards can study danger areas where unwary swimmers may be sucked into the undertow. ◊

Near-mirror images in sunglasses and swimming briefs in this photograph from the *National Law Journal*, New York lawyer-lifeguards Ron (*left*) and Glenn Hoffman stand ready to defend the bathers of Jones Beach from undertow, riptides, exposure, and fatigue.

From their vantage point, for example, it is easy to detect the riptide areas—the water is brownish from sand kicked up from the ocean floor. For people in the ocean, however, a riptide is often imperceptible until the swimmer has been trapped in it. "High tide turning to low," says Glenn in lifeguardese, "a rip occurs—it's Air France, baby, and you're gone!"

When they spot a swimmer in trouble, all the guards go into action, with three playing primary roles. One jumps from the stand and swims out to the victim, towing a flotation device on a rope. A second takes a coiled rope out of a bucket, gives one end to a third guard, and holding the other, also swims to the victim. The third guard, holding the swimmer's lifeline, waits on shore to reel him in.

Over the years, the brothers have saved hundreds of weak or panicky swimmers from potential drowning—some more than once. Both participated in three rescues of a hapless but determined New Yorker named Virgil, who got in over his head twice in a single day, then again later that summer. After the third rescue, the Hoffmans decided to give Virgil lessons, and he now swims from beach to beach to visit his lifesavers.

The swimmer they rescued closest to death was a man Glenn spotted going down in a riptide on an unguarded stretch of the beach. Glenn and Ron were exhausted that day, having already rescued several people. Glenn recalls he ran for it, hoping other guards would plunge in, too. By the time he found the victim, the man was unconscious and purple—but Ron was instantly at his side, and Glenn administered mouth-to-mouth resuscita-

tion as they swam to shore. A helicopter flew to the scene to take the victim of the near drowning to a local hospital, where he survived.

Even when lifeguarding is not a matter of life and death, it tends to be lively. Because the work requires intense concentration, the guards spend alternate hours on the sand—jogging up and down the beach, taking out the rowboat, or on "decency patrols," reminding women to wear their bikini bras. As a lawyer, says Ron, he is swayed by the women's arguments that they're asserting their right to express themselves—but as a guard, he insists the tops go on. Then there was the blustery day when Glenn and Ron rowed into 10-foot waves to honor the request of a dead man who wanted his ashes scattered at sea. "It was part of the job," Ron shrugs.

In fact, lifeguarding is more than a job for the Hoffman brothers; it is also a lifestyle. As teenagers, they were members of the all-American swim team and were New York State springboard-diving champions. Ron even went through college on a swimming scholarship, and in 1985 he married Jones Beach's first female surf lifeguard—one who deploys a 12-foot rescue "surfboard." Even today he waxes lyrical about the "lure of the Lorelei," the siren call of the waves—although he concedes he hears it mostly before the beach fills up with screaming children and adults slathered with sunblock. Ron's metaphor may be more apt than he realizes. In German myth, the Lorelei was a Rhine River nymph who lured men to their deaths. Back then, of course, Glenn and Ron were not yet lifeguards. □

Foot Soldier

As a rule, the Chinese set great store in their ancient skilled occupations. Yet foot repair, one of the oldest professions in the country—going back more than 3,000 years to the first recorded patient, King Zhouwen of the Shang dynasty—attracts little respect. "Why are you so stupid as to live with stinking feet?" someone once asked Dr. Du Deshun, the acknowledged master of Beijing's foot repairers. The attitude behind that question, he says, is all too familiar.

Like most of his colleagues in the business, which addresses many of the same problems as the Western discipline of podiatry, Du works in a public bathhouse, hunched for hours over the naked, often malformed feet of strangers. Usually, the foot is soaked in hot water before it is offered up for inspection and diagnosis. Du studies it with silent intensity, then reaches for one of the 20 tools used in the profession. By tradition, there are eight ways to handle the feet and eight ways to handle the knife. He snips away at the damage left by ancient barbarities—the clawed hooves of old women whose feet were bound—and such modern torments as high heels and tight shoes. On an average day, Du sees some 30 pairs of feet, for a total of about 200,000 in his career so far. For this, he receives about $50 a month.

Born shortly after World War II, Du remains passionately loyal to his vocation, which he chose after being assigned to the bathhouse as a teenager. He had to accept a brief hiatus when foot repair was banned as "irrelevant" during the Cultural Revolution; at that time,

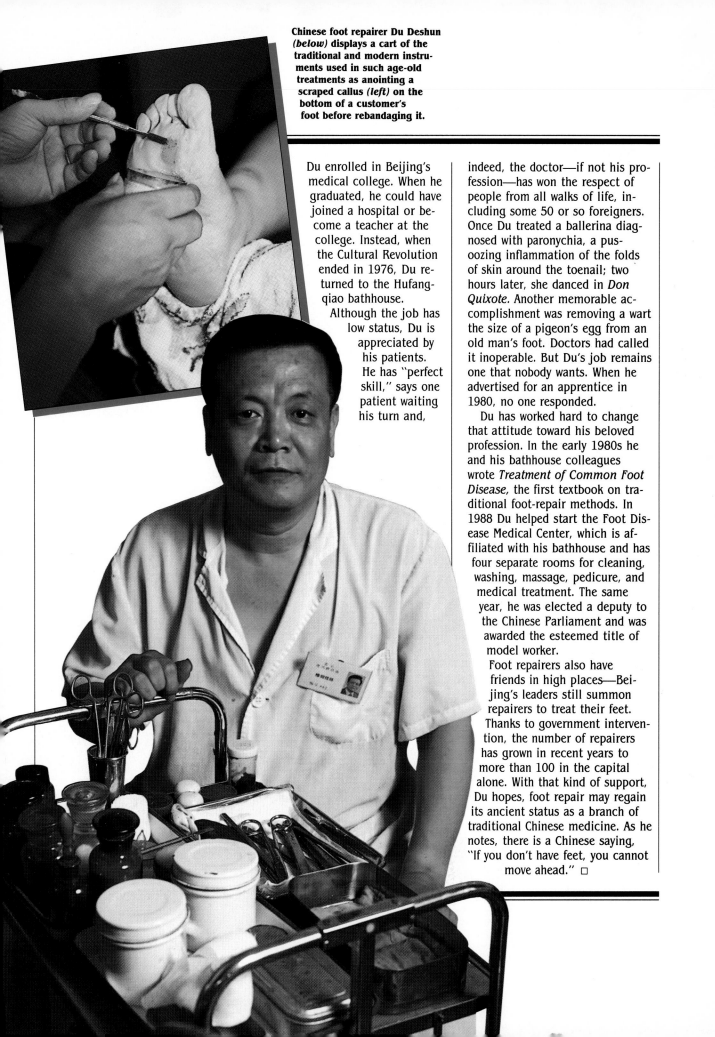

Chinese foot repairer Du Deshun (*below*) displays a cart of the traditional and modern instruments used in such age-old treatments as anointing a scraped callus (*left*) on the bottom of a customer's foot before rebandaging it.

Du enrolled in Beijing's medical college. When he graduated, he could have joined a hospital or become a teacher at the college. Instead, when the Cultural Revolution ended in 1976, Du returned to the Hufangqiao bathhouse.

Although the job has low status, Du is appreciated by his patients. He has "perfect skill," says one patient waiting his turn and, indeed, the doctor—if not his profession—has won the respect of people from all walks of life, including some 50 or so foreigners. Once Du treated a ballerina diagnosed with paronychia, a pus-oozing inflammation of the folds of skin around the toenail; two hours later, she danced in *Don Quixote.* Another memorable accomplishment was removing a wart the size of a pigeon's egg from an old man's foot. Doctors had called it inoperable. But Du's job remains one that nobody wants. When he advertised for an apprentice in 1980, no one responded.

Du has worked hard to change that attitude toward his beloved profession. In the early 1980s he and his bathhouse colleagues wrote *Treatment of Common Foot Disease,* the first textbook on traditional foot-repair methods. In 1988 Du helped start the Foot Disease Medical Center, which is affiliated with his bathhouse and has four separate rooms for cleaning, washing, massage, pedicure, and medical treatment. The same year, he was elected a deputy to the Chinese Parliament and was awarded the esteemed title of model worker.

Foot repairers also have friends in high places—Beijing's leaders still summon repairers to treat their feet. Thanks to government intervention, the number of repairers has grown in recent years to more than 100 in the capital alone. With that kind of support, Du hopes, foot repair may regain its ancient status as a branch of traditional Chinese medicine. As he notes, there is a Chinese saying, "If you don't have feet, you cannot move ahead." □

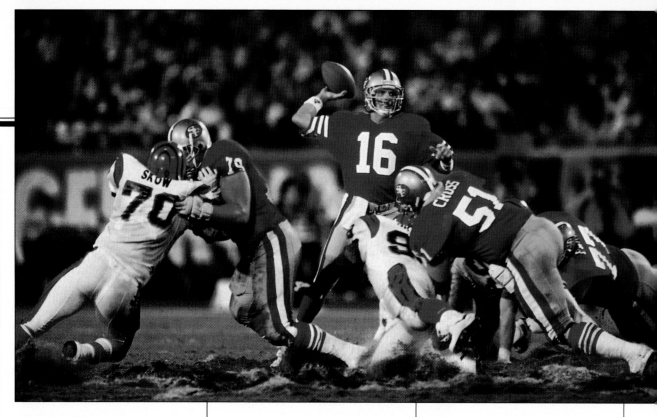

Joe Cool

For everyone who plays or watches American football, there is much power and balletic grace everywhere on the field, and there are many stars—but only one quarterback. On offense he is the general and genius of the game, the athletic intelligence behind a team's wins and losses. To those with the ability, the position is the apex of what is possible in professional sports—and correspondingly difficult to attain. When Joseph Montana, Jr., tried to break into professional football in 1979, he seemed an unlikely candidate. He did not fit the big, strong stereotype who could fling a football a hundred yards or more. Instead, the former Notre Dame quarterback was a short to midrange passer and was on the skinny side.

Yet less than three years after the San Francisco 49ers took a chance on him in the third round of player selection, Montana revealed that inside that slender frame lived a quarterback to be

reckoned with. He led the team to its first Super Bowl victory—and won the game's Most Valuable Player award. In subsequent years, he would lead the 49ers to triumph after triumph, transforming them into the team of the 1980s and becoming in the process what some sportswriters consider the best quarterback of all time.

Great quarterbacks seem to be a specialty of western Pennsylvania, which gave the sport such immortals as Johnny Unitas and Joe Namath. Joe Montana grew up in the town of Monongahela and credits his father with passing on his love of sports—and a grounding in the proper fundamentals of football. But Montana appears to have brought strong inner qualities of his own to the profession. One writer has lauded his "intuitive feel for the role of a passer, for throwing a football at just the right time to just the right place," while another marvels at his "great escape talent," which allows him to dodge opponents and sometimes even throw successfully from within

their grasp. Still another sportswriter has praised his "jazzman's ability to improvise" under pressure. But it is Montana's nearly uncanny ability to remain composed when the odds are long, coupled with his gritty determination to win, that journalists find most remarkable. In the words of the sports pages, he is "Joe Cool" and "the Comeback Kid."

Montana had begun to earn his reputation earlier, playing with the Fighting Irish of Notre Dame from 1975 to 1979. Although he was in the starting lineup during his senior year, for much of his college career Montana served as a second- or third-string quarterback and was called in to play late in the game. On six occasions, the backup player rallied the Irish to spectacular wins in the fourth quarter when a loss seemed certain. Montana pulled off his most extraordinary comeback during a freak ice storm at the 1979 Cotton Bowl in Dallas. As the fourth quarter began, he lay in the locker room suffering from hypothermia, buried under blan-

Surrounded by falling football players, 49ers quarterback Joe Montana coolly prepares a pass during Super Bowl XXIII. With his team trailing in the fourth quarter, Montana led the team to the kind of last-minute victory that has become his trademark.

kets and gulping cups of bullion.

When the quarterback finally returned to the frigid field, seven and a half minutes remained and his team trailed 12 to 34. In a quick succession of plays, the Comeback Kid hacked away at Houston's lead. Still, with only two seconds left in the game, Notre Dame lagged by six points. Running an all or nothing play, Montana threw a final pass—for a touchdown. With the game tied, the Irish kicked the extra point for a 35 to 34 victory in a contest that had seemed a certain defeat.

Montana has gone on to equally dramatic victories in the NFL and has been showered with wealth and fame. But like many celebrities, he has found that being at the pinnacle of his profession has its downside. A dinner out can become a circus of uninvited strangers. Worse, he and his fellow players are the subjects of constant scrutiny. If a player's performance falters, there is talk of drug abuse. After the 1982 Super Bowl win,

Montana says, he stopped using public rest rooms because he was afraid someone might comment, "He's gone to the bathroom twice. He must be doing cocaine."

Rumors circulated hinting that police had found drugs in Montana's car and that he had checked into a drug treatment center, allegations Montana denied. One day, the beleaguered quarterback carried his sick child to the car to take her to the hospital. A bus blocked his drive. "The driver, a woman, was sitting there making faces at me and turning thumbs down," he wrote later, "and all the people on the bus were staring." In his 1986 book, *Audibles,* Montana warns the ambitious: "The next time you think you would like to leave what you're doing and trade it for the life of a high-profile athlete, think twice."

In 1985, following his second Super Bowl win, Montana began suffering from severe back pain, which affected his playing enough to put his future in doubt. It was

hardly his first injury; Montana has suffered innumerable strains and bruises in the NFL. "Anyone who knows anything about the game," he once explained, "knows that a quarterback is putting his body on the line every time he takes the snap from center." But it was not a charging linebacker who was to blame when he threw out his back in 1986—during the season opener, Montana threw a pass, and his ailing spine went with it.

The incident led to an operation to repair a ruptured disk and a congenital spinal defect; many believed he would never play again. Not surprisingly, the Comeback Kid was determined to prove them wrong. Some 55 days after surgery, he was back, inspiring the 49ers to new victories. In 1989 Montana won another Super Bowl, capping his best season ever. The next year, he led the 49ers to a fourth Super Bowl victory. "As long as I love doing the job, feel like I can do the job," said Montana, "I'm going to do the job." □

Paid Vacation

For most vacationers, the brief interludes of rest and play rush past at light speed, restoring one to the real world after little more than a pleasurable instant. During these intervals, however, one often sees another kind of job that seems to possess the soothing texture of a lifelong holiday—the life, perhaps, of a ski instructor, a competitive surfer, or a cruise director on one of the world's great "loveboats." Bruce Chaffkin, a

cruise director for Norwegian Cruise Lines, might happily endorse the fantasy, which has been his reality since 1977. "I get to be a manager," he explains, toting up the benefits. "I get to be a performer. I get to be a director. And I get to travel the world."

A former stage entertainer who began working for the line at 19 and became its youngest cruise director ever at the age of 23, Chaffkin brings seemingly endless energy to his task of organizing shipboard fun. During his career,

he has worked ships visiting ports from St. John, in the U.S. Virgin Islands, to St. Nazaire in France. In 1979 he weathered the rough fringes of hurricane David aboard a cruise ship, organizing commemorative hurricane-cruise T-shirts for the shaken passengers once the worst was over.

Making all go well, as might be expected, consumes an enormous amount of time and effort. On a typical day, Chaffkin works from 7:30 a.m. to 2:00 the following morning. And the pace is always ◊

frantic: On any one day, there are 25 to 45 activities on the agenda, scheduled and overseen by Chaffkin and a staff ranging from 45 to 60, depending on the size of the ship. Intended to suit every possible passenger taste, the events range from classes in ice carving, "swim-nastics," golf, and scarf tying to a chance for couples to renew their wedding vows.

When the sun goes down, Chaff-kin's day swings into high gear, for evening is devoted to parties—parties for singles, honeymooners, grandparents, and others. One night the theme may be country and western, with a hog-calling competition; the next night brings a 1950s-style sock hop, with twist and Hula-Hoop contests.

It is at the nightly cabarets, however, that Chaffkin comes into his own. He rehearses the band, emcees the shows, sings songs, tells jokes, and does skits. When the celebrity talent has stayed ashore, Chaffkin sees that the show goes on, sometimes improvising with takeoffs on TV game shows. Unlike an ordinary entertainer, he has the blessing and the curse of playing to a captive audience.

"They don't just get in their cars and drive home," he says. "I've got these people for a week or two. It's like I'm part of their family."

As for his own family, Chaffkin also met his wife, Annette, at sea—she was traveling with her mother—and courted her every Sunday when the ship docked in Miami. Their wedding was on the ship; so was the luncheon, which featured an ice carving of a bride and groom and another of a ship laden with champagne bottles.

Like other cruise-director spous-es, Annette is allowed to live aboard for as much as two weeks of each three month contract peri-od, although her shore job makes it difficult to take full advantage of it. As in their courting days, the Chaffkins see each other mainly on Sundays in Miami, catching up with family life primarily in the unpaid four-week gap scheduled between each of Bruce's extraordi-narily busy, satisfying, working holidays at sea. □

Bearded cruise director Bruce Chaffkin (left) looks the picture of relaxation as he supervises oddly hatted passengers in 1992. Chaffkin has served as cruise director on many of his line's ships, in-cluding the Norway (below).

Dressed in dashing green and gleaming white, the *agents d'entretien* of the glamorous city of Paris whisk away canine leavings with vacuum-equipped motorbikes called *caninettes*, emblazoned with slogans promoting *les trottoirs nets*—"clean sidewalks."

Dog Stars

According to certain estimates, there is one dog for every 10 residents of Paris, a canine density so unusually high that France's vaunted City of Lights seems at times to lie under a blanket of what the French call *les déjections canines*. Despite the renowned affection of the French for their dogs, canine dejecta ranks third among Parisians' complaints about their city, after traffic tie-ups and car fumes. The slippery litter also reportedly lands 650 people in the hospital each year. In 1983, sensing that something should be done, the city hired a fleet of 100 green-and-white *caninettes—mobylettes*, or "small motorbikes," equipped with special hose attachments to vacuum up the offending piles.

Little is done without style in Paris, and the *agents d'entretien*, or "maintenance agents," who drive the caninettes, cut a dashing figure in their green uniforms and white helmets. But, particularly at first, the workers had a job unfit for a dog. For one thing, until the equipment was modified, their scent was detectable from a distance. For another, early models of the vacuum tended to smear fresh deposits across the pavement.

The main flaw, however, was that the caninette initiative did not solve the problem. Although the fleet harvested five tons of waste a day, six tons remained on Parisian pavement. In 1992 the city's leaders put new teeth in their cleanup: Steep fines were imposed on any owner failing to clean up after his or her dog, with tickets issued by a force of 50 plain-clothes *agents de propreté*. In some ways less glamorous than going undercover to fight dangerous crime, the agents had one consolation: Unlike their mobile colleagues, they never had to touch the *évidence*. □

Shear Misery

With the single exception of the introduction of electric shears in about 1890, the task of separating a sheep from its fleece has remained a task of the preindustrial age. "It's still bloody hard work," says Australian sheepshearer Les Bernie, one of thousands of workers, mostly migrants, who annually fleece the continent's tens of millions of sheep. "It's hard and it's long, but for most of us it's the only skill we have," says Bernie, the son of a sheep drover in the Australian outback.

Bernie left school in 1946, when he was 14, to start a two-year apprenticeship picking up after the shearers, collecting the sheared fleeces, and clearing the cutting floor of debris. "There wasn't much work about in the rural towns," he recalls. "It was a case of taking whatever chance came your way." Now, after a half-century in the sheds, he is one of the continent's most experienced shearers.

On a typical day, the veteran shearer handles 200 frightened, flighty sheep. At a dollar a sheep, that makes for a fairly good living in a year when the wool market is strong and there is plenty of shearing to be done. In a bad year, though, Australian farmers raise fewer sheep, and Bernie may work only six months.

So strenuous is the work, which ranks among the hardest physical labor on the planet, that a sheepshearer expends about as much energy in one day as a marathon runner. For Bernie and other shearers, therefore, the day begins with a hearty breakfast—steak, sausages, bacon, and eggs—and ends with an even more substantial din-

ner, both of which are prepared by a cook supplied by the contractor who links up sheepshearers with prospective employers.

After breakfast, Bernie heads for the sheep sheds, where he and other shearers hunch over excitable 90-pound animals and wield mechanized clipping shears that vibrate at 6,500 oscillations a minute. The veteran shearer guides the vibrating, four-inch wide clipper across the sheep's back in one sweep,

from tail to head, just above skin level, then clips the underbelly, head, and legs separately.

It takes a deft touch not to cut the sheep—bloodstains lower the wool's value—or oneself, and other risks are added if the sheep is a ram with sharp horns. Bernie's arms bear the scars of his work, including one gash on his arm that required 16 stitches. Cuts and injuries are occasions worthy of comment and some excitement,

With a door behind him ajar for ventilation, veteran Australian sheepshearer Les Bernie *(left)* braves noise and odor to fleece a defiant 90-pound sheep, clipping in customary fashion from the back to the front.

but they are not nearly as pervasive as the wool's grease, which inexorably covers every shearer in a slippery layer that irritates the skin. To ease this grueling routine, the day includes an hour break for a sizable lunch, as well as midmorning and midafternoon "smokos."

Had Dante known about sheepshearing, his *Inferno* might have taken inspiration from the working environment where all this takes place, for the sheds are as hellish as the task itself. The noise is utter bedlam: sheep bleat, shears whir, and sheepdogs bark. Because the sheep are generally gathered in from the fields the previous day, the sheds are humid with the moist heat generated by hundreds of animals cooped up overnight.

Along with the hard work, the cuts, and the grease, there is the smell. Daunting to newcomers, it has long since ceased to trouble Bernie. In fact, he feels few regrets about his long, hard years as a shearer. "It's been an interesting life," he says. "Always on the move around the country. It's been good to me and I'd do it again if I had my time over." Indeed, he points out, the noisome sheds are an improvement from his early days as a shearer. Back then, shearing was done outdoors under tarpaulins that the shearers erected to shield themselves from the outback's scorching sun or winter winds. At day's end, they slept on the ground on mattresses filled with straw. Although outdoor sleeping is no longer the norm, some aspects of the job never seem to change. "As soon as he finishes a sheep and stands upright," says Bernie, "every shearer puts his hand to his lower back to massage it and ease the stiffness." □

Repo Man

Although most car buyers may not like to think about it, behind the smiles and handshakes that launch every purchase there lurks an unpleasant legal reality: unless the buyer has paid for the car outright, it is actually owned by the bank, or in some cases the dealership, until the final payment. If too many payments are missed, the lender can seize the car, auction it off to cover most of the outstanding loan—and sue the now carless debtor for the rest of the amount owed.

When a repossession happens, the ticklish assignment of actually getting the car back is farmed out to specialists commonly known as repo men. Despised by the public, abused—or worse—by their prey, and barred in some states from carrying weapons, repo men operate in a gritty no man's land between criminality and the law. Staying alive in that world can require the skills of a car thief and the nerve of a spy.

Perhaps no one does it with more gusto than Jeff Friedman, the self-styled James Bond of Repossessors. A short, husky figure who often wears gold chains, Friedman runs Sherlock Recovery Services in El Monte, California, a suburb of Los Angeles, where he has reclaimed speedboats, tractors, forklifts, lunchwagons, diesel trucks, motorcycles, and even—with a little help from a pilot—airplanes. In one massive raid, he simultaneously retrieved 15 vans from a chain of florists, using a team of employees and friends equipped with synchronized watches. For the most part, however, he repossesses cars; his record for one day is 30 automobiles, and his agency recovers 200 to 300 cars a month. "I don't believe there is a car that can't be repossessed," ◊

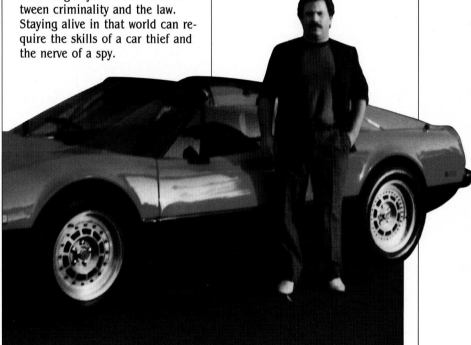

In a photograph from the late 1980s, repo man Jeff Friedman *(above)* stands proudly beside a red Ferrari he retrieved from a delinquent Mafia member, then purchased himself.

Friedman asserts. "It just takes a little imagination."

Even as a youth, Friedman was always scrappy, eager to take on all comers. A childhood bout of polio left him with a mania for fitness, and he acquired a black belt in karate. In 1976, at age 26, he set himself up in business as a private investigator and bodyguard. It was a logical—and lucrative— step to repo work. Friedman averages between $300 and $375 per repo, but the rate can soar to as much as $5,000 when the car is pricey and the risk high.

At the beginning of each repossession, Friedman insists, he does not go looking for trouble. He always tries to recover cars the friendly way, with a phone call to the owner. But when that fails, as it usually does, he faces a considerable challenge. Unlike a car thief, who can select a careless driver from the entire motoring public, Friedman must recover specific vehicles from drivers very much on the alert for signs of repo men. Locating the car at all, and then finding a time when it will be accessible and unattended, can be difficult. One good time, he finds, is when the driver leaves the car momentarily for an errand. Friedman can then slip in, with duplicate keys supplied by the lender, a lock pick, or, in the worst case, a crowbar, start the car, and drive away. When there is enough maneuvering room, an even better solution is to tow the vehicle.

If he takes a car from a home driveway or parking lot, Friedman tries to avoid confrontation by working at about 3:00 a.m.—repo men are the "warriors of the night," he says—and alone. Sometimes his son Robert comes along in the Eagle Claw truck, which can latch onto and tow a car without the operator leaving the safety of the cab; wife Lorraine, who works for Sherlock in the office, waits anxiously by the phone.

Lorraine Friedman has good reason to worry, since even relatively law-abiding car buyers seem to regard the hated repo man as fair game. In the line of duty, her spouse has been shot at—the first time occurred on his second repo job—and has faced down Dobermans, a pit bull, and even a real bull. He has been mistakenly handcuffed by police and once broke his foot in a 30-foot drop into an underground parking lot. He has hunkered down under the dashboard of a BMW as its owner discussed a drug deal a few feet away, and he once had a 400-pound, seven-foot man in the San Bernardino Mountains try to stop him by sprawling across the vehicle's hood and windshield. Unable to talk his way out of that situation, Friedman squirted the man away with windshield-washer fluid. All in all, though, the repo man has been lucky; two former employees who started their own businesses were fatally shot during repossessions.

When the towing gets that tough, however, the tough get going. Friedman says he is more than ready to get out of repo work. Like many other up-and-coming residents of Los Angeles, he wants to get into show business. He hopes to parlay his repo experiences into a TV series—with himself as technical advisor. "I definitely don't want to do this much longer," he says of his current occupation. "The reality is that, if you do this long enough, sooner or later you're going to be killed." □

UNCOMMON PURSUITS

A century or so ago, a gentleman in need of an income had to choose between the military and the clergy—the red and the black—and ladies had few options outside the home. Since then, the entire spectrum of occupational colors has become accessible to everyone, female and male, highborn and humble. And yet, some men and women settle into jobs that, but for their idiosyncratic incumbents, might not even exist.

Not surprisingly, many of them labor in the arts, distinguished mainly by their medium—art that results in a castle of sand or three-dimensional images that seem to float. In these narrowest niches of employment, even the vast jetsam of humanity becomes both the stuff of art and a unique workplace; there are celebrators, curators, and explorers of waste.

Some of these highly individualized professions are reached now, as always, by way of birth and station. To others, workers merely follow their unique abilities and their wit, which may take them where few can, or wish to, go. The fact is that those who pursue such unusual fields of endeavor are often peculiarly acute and fascinating in their own right, living proof, perhaps, that one-of-a-kind jobs are best filled by one-of-a-kind people.

4

Catnip king Leon Seidman *(below)*
holds back his eager pet, Tiger, from
an array of toys packed with the high-
grade Maryland catnip *(inset)* that is
Seidman's specialty.

The Cat's Meow

When Leon Seidman drove to a friend's house one day to help him move, six or seven cats from the neighborhood gathered around Seidman's van, irresistibly attracted by its smell. It was a sight Seidman has become accustomed to. Although the van was empty at the time, Seidman uses the vehicle to transport his crop of intoxicating weed: high-grade catnip, the aromatic delicacy that acts as a stimulant and a delight to cats who smell or eat it.

Seidman's entry into the exotic world of catnip farming began while he was still a graduate student at the University of Maryland in the early 1970s. When he offered one of his three cats an assortment of store-bought catnip, he received a firm feline rejection. At a friend's suggestion, he tried growing the oily plant, a member of the mint family, in his yard. His cats loved the result, in part because it was so fresh, nibbling at it and rolling around in the full feline ecstasy catnip is supposed to induce.

The budding grower gradually began sharing his crop with friends, then selling it to pet stores. Eventually, he says, "I had people knocking at my door saying, 'Are you the guy with all this great catnip?'" At that point, Seidman recalls facing an unusual life choice: Should he stay at the university to finish his thesis on the history of the American nude, or should he devote himself to growing the world's most exquisite catnip? He chose the second course and has never looked back.

Today, as president and owner of Cosmic Pet Products, based in Hagerstown, Maryland, Seidman boasts that he is the "largest supplier of catnip in the world." The firm dominates the market in Canada and the United States and has made inroads in Britain. Its Hagerstown headquarters is part of the secret, since that area offers the highly alkaline soils in which the best catnip is grown, and the summer's hot days and cool nights provide an optimal climate.

Catnip is planted in the fall and harvested the following year. Afterwards, the leaves must be kept indoors in a cool, dark space as they dry; sunlight can leach out the oils that give catnip its punch. The dried plant should then be stored in airtight containers to keep it fresh and attractive to cats.

Seidman uses an ordinary tractor to plant the catnip and keep down weeds, but at one time he experimented with an alternative approach to weeding. Having read that Chinese geese are sometimes used to weed mint fields because they prefer any plant to mint, he bought a gaggle and turned them loose in a test catnip field. The geese duly ate the weeds but had to be removed just before they began eating the main crop. "It was cute, but not efficient," Seidman says. "Once I got beyond 10 acres I would have needed over a thousand geese."

Cosmic Pet Products got its name in part as an outgrowth of the 1960s, Seidman admits, but he also defends the corporate title on strictly factual grounds. The catnip is "cosmic," says the avid farmer, "because the aroma is heavenly; it truly is." □

Waste Not, Want Not

Like most archaeologists, Andrew Jones makes a living finding out about the people of long ago from the fossils and artifacts they left behind. But the ancient remains he turns to for information are not sherds of pottery or old thigh bones: Instead, Jones looks for the secrets of the past in specimens of ancient excrement.

A world leader in the obscure specialty of paleo-scatology, the study of fossilized dung, Jones studies fecal remains for clues about diet, sanitation, and health among humans and beasts that lived centuries ago. Fascinated by a line of research that others consider odd at best and disgusting at worst, he contends "there are few things that make my

heart beat so vigorously" as a new-found fossil.

Like many scientists, Jones came to his particular field of study by way of a logical progression of interests. Born in Malta and brought up on a farm, he majored in zoology at England's Portsmouth Polytechnic, specializing in parasitology. Jones returned to the study of things intestinal when writing his doctoral thesis in biology. For that project, he tested his theory that fish-bone fragments found in a Viking-era archaeological dig in York proved that the former inhabitants had eaten fish without first removing the bones.

To explore his hypothesis, Jones decided to find out what would happen to fish bones during the rigors of digestion. For about a week, he fed herring—bones and all—to a trio of subjects: a pig named Marilyn, a dog named Sally, and himself. Jones then sifted bone frag- ◊

Among files and specimens stored at York University's Archaeological Resource Centre, paleo-scatologist Andrew Jones contemplates a 1,000-year-old coprolite, or fossilized stool, a rare clue to the diet of Britain's Viking invaders.

ments out of the resulting wastes and found a close resemblance to similar fragments from the Viking site, suggesting that today's preference for deboned fish is a relatively modern affectation.

Jones went on to author such scholarly paleo-scatological papers as "The Worms of Roman Horses" and "Intestinal Parasite Ova from Archaeological Deposits." He also continued to use his unusual type of archaeological research to investigate the diet of the ancient Yorkshire Vikings. By studying fossilized wastes at old Norse sites, he found that the Vikings lived on a surprisingly healthy diet of fish, grains, seeds, and berries. "Hippies, really," he quips. Jones also

found that the Vikings played host to all manner of intestinal worms, which they combated, he has determined, by eating noxious plants.

In 1990 Jones left pure academic research to become director of a new museum in York, the award-winning Archaeological Resource Centre, where visitors explore exhibits intended to show the techniques of working archaeologists. Although his work there is broad ranging, paleo-scatology remains an important focus. On display at the museum, for instance, is a fossilized segment of 1,000-year-old human feces *(page 107)* that Jones considers "the most exciting piece of excrement I've ever seen."

He makes this extravagant claim

because the eight-inch-long fossil is a rare coprolite, a complete, mineralized stool. Usually, paleo-scatologists must study fragments since bacteria quickly reduce the samples to soil. This unusual specimen managed to escape decomposition, Jones speculates, because of a rare combination of climatic and geologic factors that limited bacterial growth.

The find is also popular with young visitors and the local press, whose interest may be less scholarly than Jones's. Still, the researcher believes his brand of archaeology is more accessible than most. "Looking down microscopes is dull," he says, "but this is something everybody can relate to." □

Puzzling Behavior

In 1924, 11 years after newspaper editor Arthur Wynne invented the crossword puzzle, the *New York Times* sneered that the game was at best a "primitive form of mental exercise." Since then, the *Times* and the crossword puzzle have evolved; today the most important crossword in the United States is the one in the *Times*'s Sunday magazine. That puzzle, as well as its smaller daily counterparts, is the creation of Eugene T. Maleska, one of the few "cruciverbalists" to make a living at the trade.

A Latin major, Maleska began dabbling in the puzzles in college and even used them to court his future wife. Reportedly, he gave her a puzzle in which the answer to

"the best-looking girl on campus" was Jean Merletto, her name. Friends urged him to create puzzles for money, and in 1934 he sold his first to the New York *Herald Tribune*, which had rejected 40 previous attempts. Later, a *Tribune* editor told Maleska the first 40 had been so good that the newspaper assumed he had plagiarized.

From that first sale, Maleska led a double life professionally, working as a prize-winning educator in the tough reaches of Manhattan's East Bronx District while he continued a flood of freelance contributions to the crossword-puzzle *oeuvre*. A crossword trendsetter as early as the 1940s, he became the first at that time to use a phrase as an answer, rather than a single word. His stylistic flair and erudition made him a favorite of the first editor of the Sunday *Times*

puzzle, Margaret Farrar, for whom he invented the step-quote—an utterance that wends its way from the upper left to the lower right of the puzzle and is only deciphered by solving other clues.

By the time Maleska became the third *Times* crossword-puzzle editor in 1977, following Will Weng, he had retired from the school system. Among his honors was being Harlem's Man of the Year in 1971 for his work as a Bronx superintendent of schools. Not surprisingly, fanciers of the Sunday puzzle were quick to note a slightly more informative tone. The first goal of the puzzle is to entertain, Maleska told one interviewer, "but there is a role to enlighten."

Toward that end, Maleska puts in 12-hour days editing puzzles and puzzle clues contributed by some 500 freelancers, rewriting about

45 Module
46 Memorable silver-smith
48 Ignoble
50 Rearrange Governor W. Daly to make a very long word
56 Kismet
58 Actor Billy —— Williams
59 His motto is "Can Do"
60 Hibernia
61 Rousseau classic
63 Chanteuse Horne
64 Scourge of serge
65 Descartes and Coty
66 Verve
67 Doesn't keep up
68 High-hat someone
69 Geometric line

DOWN

1 Silent ones in an Oscar film
2 Juliet's emotion
3 Most brilliant planet
4 They're old and often sold
5 What chairpersons do
6 Conducted
7 Quarter figure
8 ". . . —— of dread-
ful note": Macbeth
9 Maid, e.g.
10 Resinous tree
11 Atonement
12 Astronaut Bean
13 Something to pitch
21 Type of buoy
25 Hustlers after rustlers
26 Traveller's rider
29 "The King ——"
30 Caesura
31 Polo team
32 Uprear
33 Like good literature
35 Bar bill
36 Crockett's last stand
40 Where topsides and decks meet
42 Three, in Torino
43 Cattlemen
44 Most obtuse
47 Parts of meets
49 Vital statistic
51 Arabian land
52 Finnish literary giant: 1878-1926
53 Printers' daggers
54 French historian: 1832-92
55 He recruited Lafayette
56 Hew yews
57 Sortita, e.g.
62 Summer sign

ACROSS

1 Etna's output
5 Appeals
10 Headcheese, e.g.
14 Preacher's sign-off
15 Aptly named author
16 Car part
17 —— Blanc, Alpine
peak
18 Lawn tool
19 Bridge
20 Boston's NHL team
22 Bulgarian's coin
23 Shading
24 Very long words
27 Ruin
28 Any delicious drink
31 Manumit
34 Patrimony
37 Suffix with hero
38 Wyeth's medium
39 Songdom "gal"
40 Olympians
41 Manipulate
42 "—— Seed," M. Anderson play

one-third of those he accepts. The resulting puzzles, created by laying down the longer words, then filling in shorter answers around them, follow a unique aesthetic. Black spaces, for example, make up no more than one-sixth of the total. The puzzle is also designed symmetrically, with long words on one side matched by long words on the other. Then there is a *Times* quirk: Puzzles never include diseases.

Puzzles still play their part in Maleska's personal life. A few years after his first wife, Jean, died in 1983, Maleska wooed another woman, a family friend. This time, he says, his secret weapon was an amorous cryptogram. □

Surrounded by well-thumbed tomes, *New York Times* crossword editor Eugene T. Maleska *(right)* ponders a puzzle in his Massachusetts home. He devised the crossword above especially for *Odd Jobs;* answers appear on page 133.

Sandman

Like many people who choose unusual professions, Gerry Kirk believes that "if you don't do what you want to do, you're not happy." To him, being happy means playing in the sand.

A Californian, Kirk is one of the world's few full-time sand sculptors, a work-for-hire artist who creates dreamlike castles, fantastic scenes, and all manner of other gritty marvels for conventions, festivals, and other customers. In the course of business, he and his staff have built a huge Christmas tableau out of sand for the Seaport Village District of San Diego, a 330-ton sand version of the United States Capitol for a Fort Lauderdale Independence Day celebration, and still other sand sculptures that have appeared in television commercials for Nissan cars and McDonald's restaurants.

The busy sand shaper has also secured two places in the *Guinness Book of World Records.* Kirk's 48,000-ton artist's conception of a fabled lost city on Atlantis is considered the largest sand sculpture ever created, while a fantasy castle he constructed in Kaseda, Japan, is the tallest—56 feet 2 inches high. Kirk currently plans to top himself with a 60-foot sculpture.

Creating such enormous custom sculptures out of sand is not the child's play it may seem. A trained artist who worked in aerospace design and homebuilding before turning to professional sand sculpting in his early 40s, Kirk employs one or more paid helpers, often aided by eager volunteers, to produce his gritty constructions. He and his crew use bulldozers and cranes to mass tons of sand on the statue's planned site, which may be a beach, a park, or a floor indoors. Depending on the location, the sand may be trucked in or taken directly from the beach. Before work begins, the material is wetted thoroughly, often with seawater, to avert crumbling.

The bulldozers are also used to push wooden blocks against the great mound of wet sand to pack it together. The blocks then serve as a scaffolding that provides the sculptors with a place to stand. The team works from top to bottom; once a level is completed, there is no going back. Unlike children at the beach, who make ◊

Leafy plants fashioned from dampened sand encircle two battling dinosaurs *(above)* in a scene crafted for the San Diego Wild Animal Park in 1992 by sand sculptor Gerry Kirk, seen touching up a giant triceratops at right.

their castles by building up bucketfuls of sand, Kirk and his assistants create by taking sand away—like stone sculptors, they use their tools to discover the figure in a block of sand.

Trowels and palette knives come in handy for carving, and the sculptors blow excess sand from hollows with drinking straws. A large sculpture may take several days to complete, but for Kirk that period of construction is also part of the show; he encourages people to watch the creative process and, under supervision, to participate.

One of the more intriguing organizations attracted to Kirk's blend of art and entertainment is the American Psychiatric Association, which hired Kirk and his associates to create 60-ton sand busts of psychoanalytic patriarchs Sigmund Freud and Carl Jung for a 1987 convention in Chicago. The next year they called Kirk back to their convention in Montreal to sculpt a 28-ton model of the left lobe of the human brain. The lobe stood for five days indoors and was taken down after the convention.

Like the lobe, most indoor sand sculptures are temporary, although they can be put in protective glass if desired, allowing the work to last for years. Outdoors, Kirk and his crew often spray glue solutions on finished works to guard them against wind and rain, but the protection is only temporary: An outdoor sculpture will not survive much past a week before succumbing to the elements. For his part, Kirk keeps his fleeting masterpieces from being as ephemeral as castles in the air by photographing each one. "This way," he says, "I can carry a 180-ton sand castle in my back pocket." □

Refusenik

Trash and those who collect it are for many people a phenomenon to be kept out of sight and mind. In the works of professional artist Mierle Laderman Ukeles, just the opposite is true. As the New York City Sanitation Department's artist in residence, an unpaid position she lobbied to create, Ukeles celebrates the city's often-overlooked sanitation workers with elaborate events, known as performance art, that are paid for by corporate and government grants. "I want to show how we all have a place in sanitation," she says. "After all, the public makes the garbage."

A 1961 Barnard College graduate with a masters in art, Ukeles believes much of the hard work that bonds society goes unrecognized, an insight that first struck her as a new mother in 1969. To offer sanitation workers some belated recognition, she set out on her first major trash-art project in 1979, shaking the hand of every one of the 8,500 "sanworkers" in New York's 59 sanitation districts.

The piece, *Touch Sanitation Performance*, required more than 11 months to complete, from July

1979 to June 1980. Ukeles followed it in November 1980 with a 22-hour performance involving roughly 100 London dustmen, as that city's trash collectors are called. Entitled *After the Revolution, Who's Going to Pick Up the Garbage on Monday Morning?*, the piece focused again on the hands of sanitation workers. This time, Ukeles walked trash routes with the dustmen, then exchanged brand-new American trash-collecting

In New York performance artist Mierle Ukeles's *Maintenance City (inset)* sanitation is symbolized by a ceiling city map and walls covered with work-shift forms and clocks. Below, Ukeles wields the sixth broom from the left in "Ceremonial Sweep."

gloves for the dustmen's own. At the event's finale at a Marine Transfer Station, she presented a pair of New York City sanworker gloves to the head of the London City Council, who was dressed in a formal morning suit. "It was great!" she says of the ceremony.

For the next few years, Ukeles worked largely behind the scenes, raising funds and presenting proposals for a series of major projects. Then, in 1983, she staged *Sanitation Celebrations,* a show in which waste-handling equipment rolled down 32 blocks of Manhattan like a Sanitation Department version of a military parade. The event featured a "mobile sanitation sculpture" Ukeles constructed from a garbage truck, as well as a "Ballet Mechanique" of six sweeper vehicles that whooshed about the street in choreographed movements. In a typical Ukeles touch that she calls "reversing the hier-

archy," Sanitation Department officials, union leaders, and members of her family were among those who cleaned the streets after the main performance *(below).*

Since then, Ukeles has continued to support herself with refuse-related performance art, launching a major project every year or so, usually in coordination with the New York Sanitation Department. In 1992 she prepared to unveil her biggest project of all. Entitled *Flow City,* the display focuses on the Marine Transfer Station at 59th Street and the Hudson River, where 3,000 tons of New York's garbage are loaded each day onto barges for shipment to a dump on Staten Island. With funds from the National Endowment for the Arts, the New York Art Council, and the Department of Sanitation, Ukeles designed a public walkway through the entire length of the Marine Transfer operation, allowing visi-

tors to see trash up close. Along the way, they encounter what Ukeles has called the "Violent Theater of Dumping," where trucks unload their hauls, and an innovative "Media Flow Wall" where audio-visual monitors display scenes from the plant, the river bottom, and the Staten Island dumpsite, planned as one of the world's largest.

"There's so much for people to see and learn," Ukeles told *Waste Age,* the journal of the trash industry. People should see how sanitation workers "make 400 million objects seem to disappear," she explained. "They make magic with this stuff every day." The trash does not actually disappear, of course, a fact that is also a concern in Ukeles's work. In the future, says Ukeles, trash collection will figure ever larger in the public mind; given the increased need for recycling, she says, "we're all going to become sanworkers." □

Hotdoggin'

Each spring, the Oscar Mayer Foods Corporation selects 12 recently graduated college seniors from an applicant pool of about 500. Like many companies, Oscar Mayer is looking for bright, outgoing young people, but the firm also requires applicants to have good driving records. Driving is an essential part of the highly visible—and highly unusual—position of hotdogger.

Those who pass the selection process to become hotdoggers are in due course entrusted with the Oscar Mayer Wienermobiles, the company's hot-dog-shaped promotional vehicles. Before the Wienermobilers set out, they train for a week at Oscar Mayer headquarters in Madison, Wisconsin. There, teachers familiarize the drivers with the Oscar Mayer family of products and lead them in motivational cheers.

They also encourage the young people to form a habit of spouting wiener-related puns—"relishing" the opportunity to drive the vehicle, for instance, or "cutting the mustard" as a hotdogger. Other instructors help the trainees learn to maneuver the massive 8-foot-wide Wienermobiles, which measure 23 feet in length and weigh some 5,800 pounds.

At the end of the session, the hotdoggers are assigned in pairs to the six stateside Wienermobiles. Four additional Wienermobiles are operated intermittently by affiliates in Japan and Spain. During the drivers' year-long tour of duty, Oscar Mayer provides them with a decent salary and a daily allowance to put toward food and lodging. The vehicles themselves, each of which is built on the chassis of a Chevrolet van, are decked out with such creature comforts as a microwave oven, a refrigerator, a cellular phone, a sunroof, and seating for six people.

The unabashed purpose of the Wienermobiles—which Oscar Mayer has deployed in various forms on and off since 1936—is to generate excitement about the company's meat products. From a vent in the side of each Wienermobile, for instance, wafts the tantalizing scent of freshly grilled hot dogs. Hotdoggers can entertain passersby by playing tapes of the Oscar Mayer wiener jingle in 21 musical styles, including bossa nova, rap, and Cajun. They also pass out wiener whistles and extol the virtues of Oscar Mayer products to anyone who lends an ear.

As part of the never-ending quest to promote the name of Oscar Mayer, each Wienermobile covers a particular region of the 48 contiguous states and ticks up about 50,000 miles over the year. Hotdoggers take the vehicles to such events as Mardi Gras in New Orleans, the Boston Marathon, and the Indianapolis 500 auto

Hotdogger Royce Mitchell *(below)*
strikes a comfortable pose atop a
Wienermobile shortly after his grad-
uation from Oscar Mayer's Hot Dog
High in June of 1992.

race. They also frequent communities, taking part in parades, appearing at festivals, and visiting
schools. Sometimes they even escort newlywed couples, festooning
the Wienermobile with pun-filled
signs reading ''Just Linked'' and
''For Better or Wurst.''

The public response to the
Wienermobile is usually enthusias-
tic. In one instance, however, a few
seventh-graders found the vehicle
more embarrassing than entertain-
ing. Hotdogger Cathleen Dum-
baugh had agreed to drive a group
of the youngsters to school. She
found that the children were so
mortified when they saw the
Wienermobile, though, that ''they
begged us to drop them off

behind the school'' so as not to be
seen emerging from it. On a more
auspicious occasion, a member
of the rock band ZZ Top flagged
down one of the Wienermobiles
and treated the drivers to dinner—
at a sushi bar.

While some of the hotdoggers
grow weary of talking about hot
dogs every day, and some wish
they could drive an ordinary car for
a change, most look back on their
year aboard with nostalgia. After
all, when no longer linked to the
Wienermobile, says one former
hotdogger, ''you aren't famous any
more. You go to the mall and no
one cares.'' □

Name That Tune

Twenty-four hours a day, seven
days a week, the answering machine of England's Birmingham
Library Services Humline stands
ready to receive melodic inquiries
from around the world. Inaugurat-
ed in 1992, Birmingham's special
year of music, and intended to
promote the city library's extensive
music holdings, the phone-in service offers to identify any tune or
melody specified by the caller.

Although answering humline
inquiries requires a daily invest-
ment of time and thought, the
service is not the primary job of
any one librarian. Instead, it has
become something of a group effort and a fairly jolly one at that.
Each day, a group of four or five
humline answerers on the library
staff, all said to be ''mad about
music,'' come together to listen to
the latest recorded calls. Often one
or more of those present knows
the answer right away, and a return
telephone call with the correct
identification is duly made.

Sometimes, several callers request the same tune, usually because it has been played, but not
identified, in a film or commercial. When Ernest Bucalossi's
''Grasshopper's Dance,'' a 1905
military tune, served as background music to a dancing milk
bottle in several British commercials, the obscure melody
produced a number of humline
inquiries, as did ''Good Night,
Sweetheart,'' by The Spaniels,
which got a double boost when it
was featured in cough-mixture
commercials and in the 1988 film
Three Men and a Baby. ◊

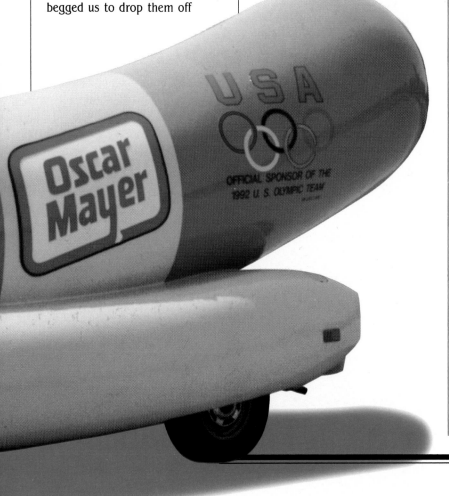

In a cheerful 1992 group portrait of the Birmingham Library Services Humline team *(below),* Christina Rickard checks recorded phone queries, backed up by *(from left)* Isobel Mills, Mohammed Sultan, Garry Pye, and John Gough.

When a tune is more difficult to identify, the staff has a chance to flex its research muscles, turning to the extensive resources of the Birmingham library's music department, which holds the largest single British collection of musical scores, recordings, and music books. They may also consult nearby music schools as well as music libraries throughout Britain—or turn to one of the many volunteer friends of the humline. Humliners say a retired gentleman who frequently visits the library has proven adept at identifying problem tunes, for example, and at least one local record-shop owner is always eager to participate as well.

The humline answers about 80 percent of all calls within a few days; more obscure tunes may take months, if they can be identified at all. Some inquiries are also hard to answer for other reasons. Embarrassed callers are sometimes too self-conscious to hum, sing, or whistle the tunes they want to identify. Instead, they may recite something like DEE DAH DEE DAH DEE DAH in hopes of conveying the tune or offer verbal descriptions that require still further research: "It was in a television program about hospitals in June or July," a caller might say. "I'm not sure whether it was BBC or ITV, and it was played during a particularly delicate operation."

From time to time, the emotions associated with remembered music also claim a victim. One call came from an anonymous German who yodeled the desired melody, then began to shriek. Ever helpful, the humline staff consulted a German employee at the library. She said she almost—but not quite—recognized the tune. Perhaps more disconcerting was a call from a man who wanted to know the name of a tune used in a commercial—which he hummed while banging himself on the head with a pan. That sound eventually did the trick; the tune, the humline realized, must be "Mule Train." □

Dressed in blue working coveralls, Nedis Tramontin (*left*) and son Roberto pause beside one of the two or three gondolas they produce every year, its distinctive prow already crafted and set in place.

Rare Craft

Five hundred years ago in Venice, the job of gondola maker was hardly an unusual one. The shiny black wooden boats, each about 36 feet long, routinely ferried Venetians from house to market and from market to work. On any given day the canals that serve as Venice's streets were jammed with an estimated 10,000 to 15,000 gondolas. Today, only a few hundred gondolas remain, the unique craft displaced by motor launches. As if to add insult to injury, rough waves raised by the motorboats batter the small surviving fleet, causing the gondolas to wear out more rapidly than in their heyday.

Despite this diminution, gondolas are still being fabricated, primarily for the tourist trade, by a handful of gondola makers employed by one of two old-style shops. The most distinguished of these is operated by Nedis Tramontin and his son Roberto, whose family has been in the business for more than 100 years. The Tramontins' fame goes back to 1884, when Roberto's great-grandfather Domenico designed the first modern gondola, a craft somewhat more maneuverable than its predecessors. Domenico built his craft with the left side 9½ inches wider than the right, an asymmetry that made the gondolier's single oar less likely to spin the boat.

Domenico trained his four sons in gondola building, and his ◊

descendants Nedis and Roberto have been trained as well. They use no prefabricated parts and no designs or workbooks—the technology of making gondolas is kept in their heads and passed on in long, careful apprenticeships. After 22 years working in his father's shop, Roberto told one visitor that he had "started to understand the work" only in the last five years.

Indeed, a young gondola maker has much to learn. To begin with, every gondola includes 280 parts, all handmade. The Tramontins use cherry, walnut, fir, lime, and four other kinds of well-seasoned wood to fashion the parts for a single boat, adapting the design to the specific properties of each piece of wood because, as Roberto says, "each tree is different."

Every gondola they make is different, too. "It's made like a balance, to fit the gondolier," Roberto says. A heavy gondolier would need a gondola built high at the stern, for instance, while makers compensate for a lightweight gondolier at the bow. It takes the Tramontins about 500 hours to build one boat. Only part of that time is assembly; once it is put together, a craft is sandpapered to a smooth finish and coated with at least six layers of glossy black paint.

Producing only two or three boats a year, the Tramontins cannot keep up with demand—or with the rate at which existing gondolas are vanishing. The craft now disappear from the canals of Venice about twice as fast as they can be replaced, a situation that seems unlikely to improve. Still, the gondola refuses to go away. The Tramontins' backlog of orders for new boats will take them well into the 21st century. □

Fine Line

It is one of the West's last bastions of hereditary pomp and privilege, seemingly the most British of institutions. Yet for more than two decades the aristocratic servitors that make up the queen's personal household have included a former American heiress. A blithe spirit once described by the *Times* as "witty and unconventional," she sometimes avoids London traffic by riding her old "bone-shaker" bicycle to Buckingham Palace, where she is a lady-in-waiting.

Virginia, countess of Airlie, known to friends as Ginnie, was born Virginia Fortune Ryan of Newport, Rhode Island, granddaughter of German-American financier and philanthropist Otto Kahn, one of the founders and first directors of New York's Metropolitan Opera Company. She was just 19 in 1952 when she married David Ogilvy, son of the 12th earl of Airlie, still one of the landowning British titles. Guests at their wedding in Westminster included five members of the royal family, reflecting the Ogilvy tradition of close ties to the Crown. David's grandmother Mabell, the 11th countess, spent more than 50 years as lady-in-waiting to Queen Mary; his younger brother Angus would later marry Princess Alexandra, a cousin to Queen Elizabeth II.

Upon his father's death in 1968, David became the 13th earl of Airlie, making Ginnie a countess. In 1973 came the next step; the queen appointed the countess, who had two years earlier given birth to her sixth and last child, as a lady-in-waiting, one of the discreet aristocratic handmaidens who accompany and serve the queen at home

and on her travels. That appointment made the American-born noblewoman part of a tiny yet obscure elite. Elizabeth II has seven regular ladies-in-waiting, as well as four others who fill in as standbys and part-time help. These women are most often seen hovering behind the queen at public affairs, ready to take flowers and gifts handed to the monarch, hold her coat, or help out with conversation. They travel abroad with the queen, serve as constantly available advisers, and handle a variety of personal chores, including the queen's shopping.

For all this they receive no wages, only traveling expenses and a small clothing allowance. "Those who have the privilege of being appointed lady-in-waiting serve Her Majesty out of love and loyalty," the countess of Airlie said in a rare public comment in 1985. "The badge of office," literally, a tiny diamond brooch in the shape of an *E*, "is its own reward."

Like the countess, all the ladies-in-waiting are members of the British aristocracy, but on the job they are not all equal. The top-ranking lady is the mistress of the robes, a position occupied since 1967 by the duchess of Grafton, considered one of the queen's closest confidantes. Privileged to wait upon the queen at the State Opening of Parliament and accompany her to the House of Lords, the duchess also assists Elizabeth at Buckingham Palace garden parties and on royal tours, acting as a kind of extension of the royal personality. Her title stems from another, rarely called-upon function of the office. Should another female monarch one day assume the throne, the mistress of the robes designated by the new queen would, at the appropriate moment, remove the crimson robe of the monarch-to-be and replace it with the royal Pall of the Cloth of Gold.

The countess of Airlie and her colleague Lady Farnham are the queen's two ladies of the bedchamber, a rank just below mistress of the robes. The mistress "may do the grandest things," an anonymous lady of the bedchamber once explained, "but we do the next grandest." They too wait upon the queen at the opening of Parliament and on other ceremonial occasions, but they travel overnight with the queen only when her consort, the duke of Edinburgh, is a member of the party.

When the queen travels alone, the duty of accompanying her falls to the third and final rank of aristocratic helpmate, the women of the bedchamber—there are currently four. The women of the bedchamber also attend the queen at home, each serving two-week shifts on a rotating schedule. In years past, the women were required to remain in London even when off-duty, on the chance their monarch might unexpectedly need them. That custom changed decades ago, during the World War II bombing of London.

Despite their plenitude of duties, which require them to do "anything but wait," in the words of one, the workload of ladies-in-waiting is lighter than it once was. Ladies no longer serve meals on bended knee, as in an earlier age, and the queen's private secretary handles most of the correspondence that was once their lot.

As for their remaining tasks of fetching, carrying, and running errands—one of Queen Victoria's attendants said that the dullness of her occupation was "impossible to describe"—the current waiting ladies, even the one known for "her lively American ways," evidently have no complaints. □

The countess of Airlie *(above, right)* takes a bundle of flowers in stride during a 1992 walkabout by her royal mistress outside Guildford Cathedral in Surrey. Members of the royal protection and diplomatic squad accompany the pair.

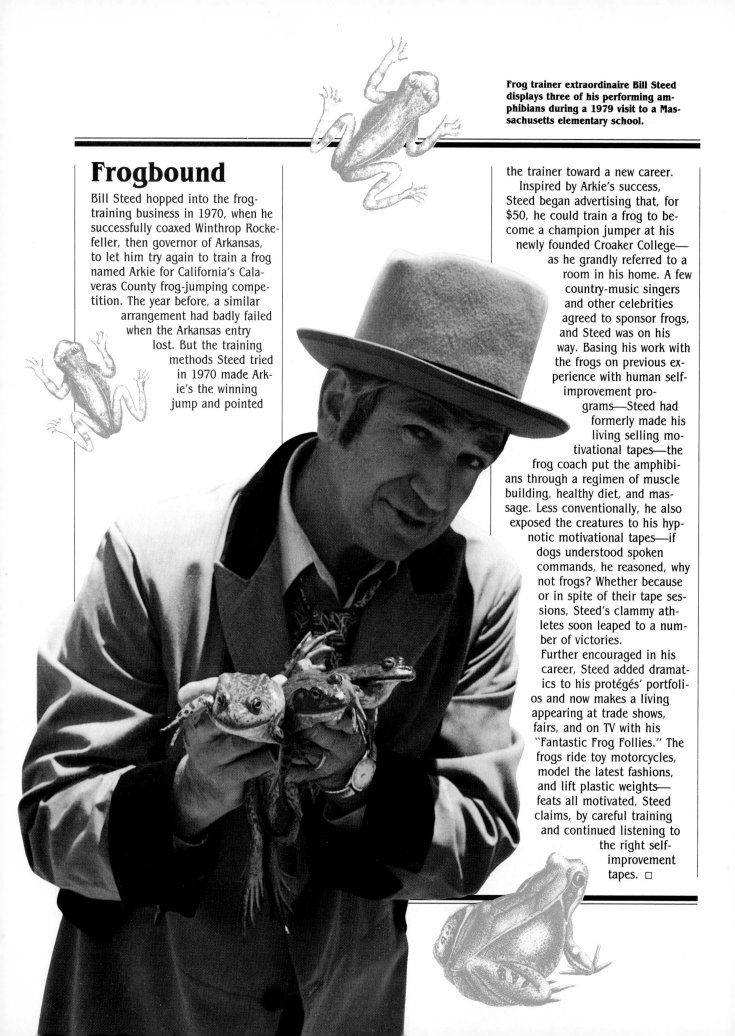

Frog trainer extraordinaire Bill Steed displays three of his performing amphibians during a 1979 visit to a Massachusetts elementary school.

Frogbound

Bill Steed hopped into the frog-training business in 1970, when he successfully coaxed Winthrop Rockefeller, then governor of Arkansas, to let him try again to train a frog named Arkie for California's Calaveras County frog-jumping competition. The year before, a similar arrangement had badly failed when the Arkansas entry lost. But the training methods Steed tried in 1970 made Arkie's the winning jump and pointed the trainer toward a new career.

Inspired by Arkie's success, Steed began advertising that, for $50, he could train a frog to become a champion jumper at his newly founded Croaker College—as he grandly referred to a room in his home. A few country-music singers and other celebrities agreed to sponsor frogs, and Steed was on his way. Basing his work with the frogs on previous experience with human self-improvement programs—Steed had formerly made his living selling motivational tapes—the frog coach put the amphibians through a regimen of muscle building, healthy diet, and massage. Less conventionally, he also exposed the creatures to his hypnotic motivational tapes—if dogs understood spoken commands, he reasoned, why not frogs? Whether because or in spite of their tape sessions, Steed's clammy athletes soon leaped to a number of victories.

Further encouraged in his career, Steed added dramatics to his protégés' portfolios and now makes a living appearing at trade shows, fairs, and on TV with his "Fantastic Frog Follies." The frogs ride toy motorcycles, model the latest fashions, and lift plastic weights—feats all motivated, Steed claims, by careful training and continued listening to the right self-improvement tapes. □

In a cozy workplace nearly as old-fashioned as the pens he repairs, Phillip Dunn *(below)* examines a worn instrument, working over blotting paper to absorb any ink. The racks in front of him hold 20 sizes of plastic and rubber ink sacs.

Penmanship

In 1985, 17-year-old Phillip Dunn answered a want ad for a pen repairperson. He got the job and ever since has made his way by fixing and restoring pens for a small London company called Penfriend, one of the world's mere handful of pen-repair firms. Wearing the official title of writing-instrument technician, Dunn repairs both old and new fountain pens—nearly 80 a week. With brand names such as Swan, Conway Stewart, and Mentmore, some of the vintage pens date back to the turn of the 20th century and would be irreplaceable if they could not be repaired. Many hold great sentimental value for their owners, Dunn explains, because they are "old pens they may have used to take exams with or been given by a special relative."

Working with elderly pens is a delicate business, since many parts have become brittle. Often, the rubber ink sac must be replaced—not always an easy task since spare parts for some older, more obscure pens are almost impossible to find. In most cases, however, the technicians are able to substitute a similar piece from a newer model. Penfriend's success rate with repairs is about 98 percent.

With modern brands, Dunn is more likely to face such wear-and-tear problems as leakage. He is also learning one of Penfriend's specialty services: grinding custom-tailored nibs. Left-handers, for instance, sometimes have trouble making a consistent line with standard penpoints. Under the supervision of veteran penman Roy Zeff, Dunn is learning how to analyze a client's way of writing and alter the nib accordingly—a skill that takes years to master.

In addition to its repair workshop, Penfriend owns a pen retail showroom that includes a collection of older writing instruments. Dunn's favorite there is the so-called Prohibition pen. Originally designed for court stenographers, who needed to write for long periods without stopping to refill their pens, this 1920s Waterman had a barrel that held six times the ink of a standard pen. But the design was not only a favorite of court reporters. Others, wanting an unobtrusive drink during America's Prohibition period, are said to have drained the oversize ink barrel—and loaded it with liquor. □

Skeeter Breeder

At any given moment, there are about 100 trillion live mosquitoes in the world. Few people would argue that the planet needs any more. Nonetheless, Douglas C. Seeley, supervisor of mosquito husbandry at the National Institutes of Health, spends his days breeding the stinging pests.

Since 1965 Doug Seeley has been one of a handful of mosquito breeders working in medical research. He and a small staff at the organization's Maryland headquarters currently breed six species of mosquitoes used by researchers seeking a cure for malaria, a mosquito-borne parasitic disease that kills about a million people each year. At any given time, the NIH mosquito-husbandry group has about 30,000 insects, and breeding is continuous, for even the healthiest mosquito succumbs to old age after four to six weeks.

Each day, feeding is the first order of business for the breeders, who give the mosquito larvae a meal of bacteria and the adults a dilution of corn syrup on sugar pads placed in their cages. Seeley also feeds what are known as blood meals to the adult female mosquitoes. Although male mosquitoes and nonlaying females do not need animal blood, females require blood proteins in order to lay their eggs. Most of them happily imbibe the blood of laboratory animals reared for the purpose, but certain species prefer human blood and will produce fewer eggs if offered anything else. Seeley allows these finicky malaria-free mosquitoes to dine upon his arms —not because it is part of his job description, he says, but because he does not mind. He has become so habituated to the stinging, he claims, that his arms return to normal within a few hours if he resists scratching.

With the blood meals completed, Seeley next collects any recently laid mosquito eggs and places them in rearing pans filled with water. The larvae swim around in the rearing pans for 7 to 12 days before passing into the pupal phase, an intermediate stage that lasts only 2 days.

To prevent mosquitoes from swarming the laboratory after they hatch, Seeley makes sure to transfer the pupae into smaller pans in the cages that will house them as adults. The laboratory has tried cages made out of many different materials, but the mosquitoes seem most relaxed, Seeley says, in enclosures fashioned from one-gallon ice-cream containers. "The mosquitoes like

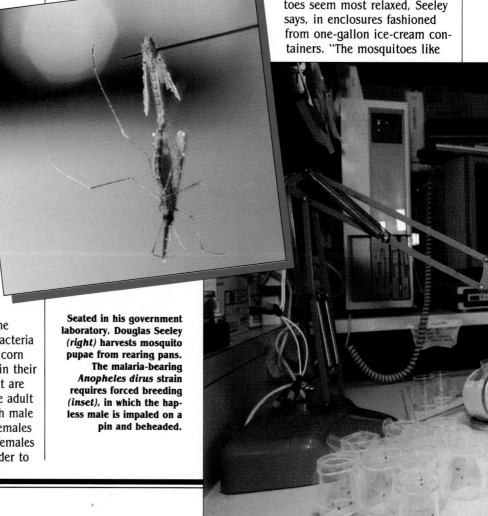

Seated in his government laboratory, Douglas Seeley *(right)* harvests mosquito pupae from rearing pans. The malaria-bearing *Anopheles dirus* strain requires forced breeding *(inset),* in which the hapless male is impaled on a pin and beheaded.

the paper walls for grasping," he explains. "They are very comfortable, at rest, on the paper sides."

Just 24 hours after hatching into maturity, the mosquitoes are ready to mate. Some species reproduce successfully in the laboratory, but others do not. In such cases, Seeley and his assistants must turn to "force-mating," a delicate but grisly business performed on a very small scale.

People are fascinated by this procedure, which Seeley calls "one of our dog and pony shows." To begin, he anesthetizes a female mosquito with ether and lays her on her back on a piece of filter paper. Then, he sticks a pin through a male mosquito's thorax in order to manipulate the insect

more easily. Seeley insists that this piercing "bothers the mosquito practically not at all." Next, he takes an even more violent step: He removes the male's head. Instead of killing the insect immediately, the decapitation stimulates the male sexually, because the ganglia that inhibit mating are no longer connected to the body. Seeley then rubs the genitalia of the male mosquito against those of the female, and the two clasp in a procreative embrace. After that, the male dies and the female is pampered with blood meals while she prepares to lay her eggs.

One purpose of such breeding is to try to use genetic selection to develop mosquitoes unable to transmit malaria. In the wild, mosquitoes ingest the malaria parasite when they sting an infected human or animal. Normally, the organism undergoes sexual reproduction in the mosquito's gut, then moves into the salivary glands, from which it may be transferred to another human or animal when the mosquito next feeds on blood. Seeley and his colleagues have bred a mosquito strain with a genetic trait that arrests the development of the parasite in the stomach, so the malaria never becomes infective— one breakthrough of many needed to stem the spread of this disease. □

Inclined to Fall

Five years after its construction began in 1173, the partially completed Tower of Pisa began to tilt gently toward the south, a subsidence that was the inevitable effect of soft soil and a too-narrow base. The project was halted until 1275; the masons of that day cut their blocks to accommodate the tower's lean but were unable to correct it. By the time the structure was completed in 1350, its unplanned inclination had become an accepted fact—even an unexpected blessing, as the novelty attracted visitors. Still, the slowly increasing list to southward has caused centuries of anxiety among Pisa's citizens.

By official count, at least 17 commissions have studied the matter of rescuing Pisa's leaning tower, 14 in the 20th century. Yet to date not one has slowed or halted the tower in its gradual surrender to gravity. Indeed, a 1934 attempt to brace it up by pouring concrete into the ground only worsened matters and led to a long interval of acceptance. Then came the alarming collapse of a medieval bell tower in nearby Pavia in 1990, followed by a new study that found the Pisa tower was tipping over faster than expected. Desperate to save its famous landmark and biggest tourist attraction, the city hired a rare kind of engineer—a tower straightener.

Their choice was Michele Jamiolkowski, a distinguished Polish-Italian professor who has his own international engineering firm in Milan. During his decades-long career, he has built Egyptian dams, Norwegian refineries, and Argen- ◊

His leaning nemesis listing in the background, tower straightener Michele Jamiolkowski pauses for a snapshot portrait after a 1992 meeting in Pisa.

tinian nuclear reactors. He also served as a consultant to the 1966 Pisa tower commission and worked in Venice on a group trying to preserve St. Mark's Square. Moreover, his academic pursuits reflect the Pisa problem: soil mechanics and dynamics, soil-structure interaction, soft-ground construction, and soil improvement.

A deep-voiced engineer who sometimes comes to work in fresh-pressed blue jeans and a sports jacket, the new president of the Committee for the Conservation of the Tower of Pisa brought what one tower worker called "a special charisma" to the Pisa assignment. "Apart from its astonishing beauty, the leaning tower of Pisa arouses an intriguing curiosity and a special interest," Jamiolkowski said of

his new task in a 1991 speech. "The international geotechnical community has chosen it as a sort of symbol of Soil Mechanics."

As they ponder the long-term stability of this symbol, Jamiolkowski and his committee have moved to relieve the worst of the immediate stresses, wrapping the tower's lowest stone tier in steel bands that could be tightened or loosened by a series of cables anchored deep underground. Jamiolkowski has since reported that monitors show the stress in the most dangerous sections of masonry has been reduced, "improving the situation a little."

A more permanent solution must somehow correct for the tower's inadequate foundation, stabilize the structural problems that

have already arisen, and pull the tower back toward the vertical by about half a degree—all without "endangering the tower's historical character" or even visibly affecting its appearance, according to Jamiolkowski. One possibility: Adding a series of massive lead counterweights under the ground on the tower's north side. Whatever the solution, it needs to come soon. "Otherwise the tower will be lost for sure in the next 30 to 40 years," Jamiolkowski says. "If the lean goes on increasing there will be a structural collapse before a foundation failure and this could occur absolutely without warning."

Before he can act, however, the tower straightener must continue to study the problem and conduct trial approaches on soil nearby. In the meantime, the residents of Pisa—and perhaps Jamiolkowski too—may find comfort in the fact that the green area encompassing the cathedral, the baptistry, and the tower is known as *la piazza dei miracoli*—"the plaza of miracles," which may be all that can save Pisa's tilting tower. □

Ears pricked forward attentively, a race-horse *(below)* submits to a lip-tattoo examination by Illinois horse identifier Mary Erickson just before a 1991 race.

Lip Reader

When Mary Erickson came to work at Illinois's Arlington International Racecourse on June 15, 1979, she found there had been a serious accident. Her boss, who was responsible for identifying each racehorse by the number tattooed inside its lip, had been rushed to the hospital for an emergency leg amputation. A diabetic with poor circulation, he had suffered a crushed foot from a horse early that morning. Under Illinois law, horses must be identified before each race, so the track needed a horse identifier in a hurry. Although the profession had been exclusively male, "I was the only race board employee with the necessary experience to do the job," Erickson later explained, "so I did."

A self-described "middle-aged lady who keeps six cats and a retired race horse," Erickson has remained a member of the tiny community of Illinois horse identifiers ever since, a group that now includes other women. She brings a lifelong love of horses to her position, having worked as a groom for several years before taking up the clerical racetrack duties that eventually led her to the present job.

Horse identifiers, who work directly for the state of Illinois and are used everywhere in the United States where there is horse racing, are one of the sport's main lines of defense against fraud involving the substitution of one horse for another. A variation on that trick occurred in the Sherlock Holmes story "Silver Blaze," upon which Erickson, a Holmes enthusiast, has written a small monograph. Although Erickson says she has yet to uncover a deliberate fraud, she has found some accidental mix-ups, including one she spotted in her second week on the job. An investigation found that two mares, "one cheap and one *very* expensive," had been inadvertently exchanged during a long trip in the same van. By the time Erickson spotted the switch, one mare, intended for racing, had been bred twice; the other, intended for breeding, had won a few races.

Unquestioned integrity and good eyesight are key job requirements, Erickson says, but a horse identifier must also be strong nerved and agile. Because she checks the horses moments before they are saddled up for the race, her job can be difficult and dangerous; excited horses do not always cooperate with the lip-checking routine. "I like to compare it," she says, "to a reporter trying to interview the Chicago Bears in the locker room five minutes before they go out to play the Super Bowl. It can be done, but it requires a certain degree of finesse."

Although a horse identifier has to be ready at any moment to dodge half a ton of frantic horse, it is also important to stay as calm as possible. "I take pride in the fact that I can usually accomplish my purpose without upsetting the horse very much," says Erickson. The alternative is a battle of wills between lip reader and mount that could cause the horse to "leave his race in the paddock." Indeed, the Illinois horse identifier's approach to her subjects seems far more friendly than confrontational. "What I like about this job," she says, "is that I get to pet everybody's horse, but I don't have to clean anybody's stables." □

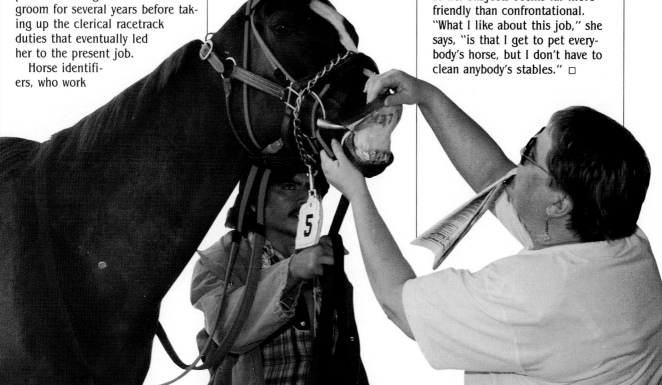

Like luminous visitors from another world, elements in an untitled holographic work in progress seem to hover beside holographer Dan Schweitzer *(below)* in his New York studio in 1992.

Alternate Reality

"As a student," Dan Schweitzer recalls, "I summarily rejected all of science for lack of patience." But in the past 20 years, his distaste for physics and mathematics has vanished. As an artist in the relatively new field of holography, he has acquired a deep knowledge of laser physics and even relies on mathematical equations to create his palette of colors.

Schweitzer, who is the codirector of the New York Holographic Laboratories in Manhattan, was drawn to the almost magical quality of this modern art form. De-scribed simply, a finished hologram assembles every visual detail of a three-dimensional scene onto a flat two-dimensional surface. The result is a type of photograph with remarkable depth and dimension that allows an observer to look around objects in the foreground by changing the viewing angle.

To make a hologram of a single object, Schweitzer illuminates his subject with light from a laser, an energy source that produces a tuned, highly coherent beam of light in which all the waves have the same frequency and oscillate precisely in phase with one another. In a typical session, he splits this orderly beam of light in two, directing some of the beam onto a glass photographic plate while reflecting the other part of the original beam off the object to be photographed, then onto the plate.

Since the second beam takes a less direct path to the plate, it arrives imperceptibly later, throwing the two beams out of phase. As they interfere with one another, they create microscopic light and dark lines—"fringes"—on the photographic plate. An image of the original three-dimensional subject can then be created by shining ordinary light on the seemingly meaningless fringes. The holographic image often appears to jump out of the plate, hovering somewhere between the viewer and the illuminated object.

An art major who worked in the theater during the 1960s, Schweitzer started to experiment with video art in New York in the early 1970s. There he saw his first holograms. He was so haunted by the images' three-dimensional quality that he left the theater for holography, opening his first show in 1975. Two years later, he cofounded the laboratory where he works.

Typical of Schweitzer's work is *The Movie Theater,* which he first exhibited in 1978. The piece shows an audience in a darkened theater; on the screen in front of them is an image of the artist with his hand reaching out toward the people in the foreground. The special qualities of the hologram make it appear as though the hand is emerging from the screen.

Another work from the same period, entitled *Thendara,* depicts a man deep in thought gazing out the window; the scene is viewed simultaneously from the spectator's point of view and from the subject's. Schweitzer says *Thendara* represents "a turning point for me, marking the end of the theater and the beginning of a commitment to the visual arts."

In the 1980s and early 1990s Schweitzer's holographic works of art have continued in much the same style, which he describes as sculptural in approach. For the former technophobe, who teaches holography, sells holographic works, and runs his holographic center, holography has become another window on reality. His current project: To create a hologram in which the viewer seems to view the image from within, what Schweitzer calls "a different way of looking at virtual reality, a new way of 'seeing' seeing." □

Anything, Anywhere

Behind their manicured lawns and dark-glass modernity, big pharmaceutical research firms often find themselves dealing with decidedly low-tech materials, fragments of animal and vegetable matter that may hold the secret to new cures and treatments. In 1987, for example, researchers at Dow Chemical, Genentech, and Merck & Company decided that the clot-dissolving properties of the saliva of certain leeches and bats might help in learning how to avert excessive blood clotting in heart disease and stroke patients. The firms duly placed an order for leech and bat spit with Terry Fredeking, one of the world's few collectors of pharmaceutical research specimens.

To tackle that particular assignment, Fredeking turned to the Amazonian rain forest of French Guiana, where his crew eventually secured a number of giant leeches. The 18-inch-long bloodsuckers were at first "almost impossible" to locate, he admits, since his team inadvertently arrived during the animals' six-month hibernation, which is spent deep underground. Fredeking then made three expeditions to the mountainous jungle outside Cuernavaca, Mexico, in search of the saliva of a thumb-size vampire bat, which lives on the blood of other mammals.

To reach the bats, Fredeking and his assistants explored several Mexican caverns, some of which had been filled with poison gas by government workers to kill the vampires. Fredeking's group wore gas masks against the vapor and also to avoid breathing the dangerous

spores of a rare cave fungus. On the first and second trips to the caverns, the team extracted samples of bat saliva, capturing and holding the animals with thickly padded gloves, then releasing them unharmed. On the third trip, the collectors captured live bats and took them to the United States. Since bats often carry rabies, it was tricky getting them through customs, Fredeking says.

On another occasion, Merck asked Fredeking to get some 10,000 black widow spiders to help the company's researchers develop an antidote to the spiders' venom. In the event, the resulting expedition did not take him very far from home. Using tweezers, he and his colleagues collected the requested number of black widows from a West Texas culvert.

An air-force veteran who worked as a General Dynamics factory hand before turning to his own peculiar line of work, Fredeking describes himself as a combined "soldier of fortune and humanitarian." He first became interested in the specimen-collecting business in the early 1970s, influenced by his father, an obstetrician with an interest in blood disorders. As the younger Fredeking picked up assignments from pharmaceutical makers, he began to hire assistants. After working together for years, the group was finally incorporated as Antibody Systems in 1991, with Fredeking as president.

Fredeking now has six full-time employees. He also gets regular assistance from a former United States ambassador, who helps negotiate permits and visas with foreign governments. Antibody Systems undertakes no more than five projects a year—"three is com- ◊

fortable," says Fredeking—because months are needed to plan each expedition. Between assignments, Fredeking looks for another kind of trophy—as a bowhunter of wild boar and other game.

The firm's philosophy is simple, Fredeking says: "If you can afford it, we will get it for you." One request he did turn down, however, was an order for human brain tissue for use in hormone research. Fredeking, who gets many of his specimens from relatively unsettled areas where there is little or no law, was worried that any brain he was offered by the locals "might be a little too fresh." □

Invitation Only

Since childhood, Marc Friedland has enjoyed communicating with his friends on unusual, homemade greeting cards and stationery. As a boy, he wrote letters on airsick bags acquired on frequent flights to visit relatives. The bags are ideal, he says, "they fold real nicely." And they were distinctively his. As an adult, Friedland's view of correspondence as uniquely personal has earned him a handsome living as one of the few—if not the only—custom designers of jet-set party invitations.

Certainly, the invitations and stationery Friedland develops at his Creative Intelligence firm in Los Angeles eclipse anything a regular card store might sell. He and his assistants make each invitation individually, often from an unexpected material—copper or vinyl, bamboo or bark. Invitations commissioned for one 1987 garden party, for instance, arrived upon a backing of a synthetic grass called Astroturf. Summons to an event to celebrate the film industry's Academy Awards came in film canisters stuffed with popcorn and tiny Coca Cola bottles.

For the stationery itself, Friedland uses cotton, handmade, marbleized, and other types of special

Specimen hunter Terry Fredeking (*above*) uses a pistol to scare away an aggressive rattlesnake he encountered while seeking poisonous black scorpions in Texas for a pharmaceutical firm.

paper, often incorporating pressed wildflowers. The invitation itself is individually inked in a distinctive calligraphy. And always, he tries to reflect the personality of the event's host. A set of dinner-party invitations for actor Alec Baldwin were "rustic and earthy, very masculine," according to Friedland, who had them printed on a bark-like paper embellished by a bold tribal pattern. "I ask the person if they like black and white," Friedland says, "are they conservative, offbeat, do they like concrete or organic things, glitzy things. It's almost like working with them as a therapist."

Like psychotherapy, Friedland's products are not cheap. But in the elite social and corporate circles Creative Intelligence often serves, where invitations are as common as junk mail, Friedland's invitations stand out. One corporate client reports that "when I do an invitation with Marc, we get an 80 percent 'yes' response." With a standard engraved card, only half the invitees come to the party. □

Wedding invitations with painted borders and wax seals (above, left) and romantically ribboned Valentine's Day dinner invitations (above, right) are among the creations of Marc Friedland, shown at right in an exuberant mood.

Using a cardboard illustration, Tokyo storyteller Tameharu Nagata *(below, far left)* relates the story of Jado Maru, the great boy samurai, to an enthralled band of children—many sucking on Nagata's homemade sweets *(opposite)*.

The Last Storyteller

A little before 3:00 each afternoon, Tameharu Nagata prepares to leave his home to go to work. First, he loads a big wooden box on the back of his bicycle, putting in about 35 illustrated placards made from large pieces of heavy cardboard. Then he stows a selection of sweet-

meats into a milk crate strapped to the front of the bike. As a final touch, he dons a light blue apron printed with playing cards—the distinctive uniform of the profession he has followed for 40 years. The 64-year-old performer is Tokyo's only full-time *kami shibai,* or professional children's storyteller.

Each day Nagata rides his heavily laden bicycle to a park not far from his home, where between 10 and 60 children await his arrival. Before beginning his work, he beats together two wooden clackers to summon still more. The children line up to buy treats: sugar candies on a stick and sweet-and-sour pickled radishes he and his wife have made, as well as store-bought wafers topped with jam. Then the young ones, sweets in hand and mouth, gather around the storyteller, ready for a traditional Japanese tale.

Nagata selects an illustration from his big box and, displaying it in a frame attached to the bicycle, begins to tell a story. It might be "Goku the Monkey," in which an evil ghost transforms herself into a spider and captures the good Goku and his friends in her web. Or it could be "The Jungle Boy"—the exploits of a boy hero and his comrade Golden Bat—or any other of the 70-some tales in Nagata's repertoire. With octave-spanning vocal chords that have earned him the nickname The Seven-Colored Voice, Nagata impersonates each character. Rather than simply reading the stories off the back of the illustrations, Nagata tells them from the heart, with passion, occasionally varying the tale in small particulars for a given audience.

Well aware of children's limited

attention span, Nagata usually tells just three stories, each one lasting four or five minutes and involving about 10 illustrations. Then he gives a quiz by displaying one of the pictures and asking the children to explain what it depicts. Those who give correct answers win points good toward more candies. After the quiz, many of the children come through the sweets line again, and then Nagata pedals off to his next stop, where another group of children is eagerly waiting.

Candy sales from his three performances a day bring in about $75, and Nagata augments this modest income by appearing for a fee at parties and schools. His wife also works, and they are able to live comfortably. Still, it is hard nowadays for an urban storyteller to make a living.

Indeed, thanks largely to electronic diversions, the storytelling profession has all but died out in Japan's cities, although some 20,000 of the storytellers still work in the provinces. All of them are members of a well-respected pro-

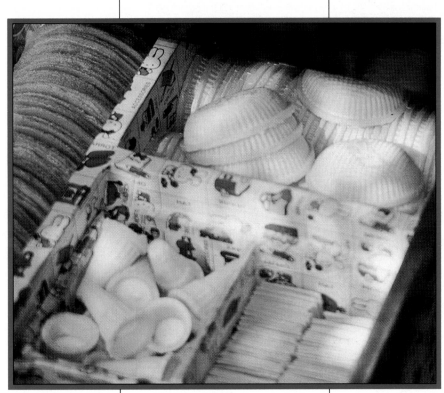

fession. Accredited by a national association, they are considered educators—a position of considerable status in Japan.

In the past, this meant they were often called upon to serve as mouthpieces for the state. Before and during World War II, the government encouraged storytellers to tell allegories of Japanese supremacy. After the war, the education ministry mandated stories of peace. Now that the government no longer regulates their stories, Nagata and others in his profession have reverted to the well-loved tales of old.

Storytellers find that many parents deeply appreciate the time the tale spinners spend with the children. One very poor mother, for instance, had no money to send with her child to buy candies from Nagata. Instead, she prepared a simple dish of vegetables and soy sauce for the storyteller as a way of signifying her respect.

Poverty is no stranger to Nagata, whose own impoverished parents gave him up in childhood to a more prosperous couple. He says he left school at the age of 10 and tried various apprenticeships over the next dozen years, finally finding satisfaction in acting.

From there, he drifted into a troupe of storytellers, and although he gave up the profession once, he was happy nowhere else and soon returned to it. Nagata is proud to serve the children he entertains. As in other countries, parents in modern Japan seem to have too little time to spend with their children, and he hopes his presence helps fill the void. Nagata plans to continue telling stories as long as he can, he says, for he worries that when he is finally silent, no one will take his place. □

Lower Depths

Sewage plants are at least as necessary as power, police, and adequate transportation, but they rarely attract much public attention except when something goes wrong. Then, in some towns, area residents must turn off their taps and toilets for days while the municipality stops processing at the plant, drains out the sewage, and fixes the problem. Frequently, however, someone must go down into this underworld of waste, find the failure, and repair it on the spot. Willing divers are, understandably, difficult to find; one of the very few to specialize in such work is the imperturbable John Stapp of Austin, Texas.

A former welder with a lifelong fondness for diving, Stapp works submerged in sewage for four hours or more on a typical job. One assignment lasted 12 hours, he says. During a dive, he replaces pipes, remedies various mechanical problems, and does underwater welding in total darkness; even underwater flashlights cannot dent the opaque sludge. For the squeamish, the work would be nightmarish; but to Stapp, who named his company simply Weld/Dive International, it is "just a job"—one that requires "a lot of skill that not everybody has."

Stapp prepares carefully for each sewage dive. He builds full-scale mockups of some of his jobs and, to simulate sludge-blindness, puts duct tape over his faceplate to make himself work entirely by feel. Because he built water and wastewater treatment plants before setting out on his own, Stapp knows the nuts and bolts that lurk in the turbid darkness. Often, with his eyes closed, he sits on the white silk sofa in his off-white carpeted living room, rehearsing a task he may need to perform blind the next day. Stapp has become so

Not quite fully submerged, diver John Stapp *(left)* waits to be handed a set of tools before plunging into the depths of the Southwest Travis County Municipal Utility District No. 1 sewage treatment plant near Austin, Texas.

adept that he can identify different materials and machinery through his rubber gloves.

The meticulous preparations continue on location. Stapp often spends several hours setting up his radio-communications system, pneumatic tools, and surface-based breathing apparatus—he uses an "umbilical" hose that houses both a radio cable and an airline connected to a compressor. Finally, he strips off his jeans, puts on several layers of insulated underclothes, boots, a sealed rubber suit adapted from a diving "dry suit," and a 27-pound helmet. After Stapp lowers himself into the murky depths, the only way for surface observers to follow his movements is by watching his exhaled air bubbles and the eddies he stirs up while tromping through the sludge down below, where, he says, it is "really very quiet and peaceful."

It can also be intensely dangerous. Stapp often has to work in a plant's lift station, where the first onslaught of raw sewage is received. To minimize the risk of having his suit cut open by glass shards, razors, needles, or the sheer force of the incoming flow, Stapp prefers to work at 2:00 or 3:00 a.m., when the community's outlets are relatively quiet.

But there is always the unexpected. In July 1992, for example, Stapp was repairing a water-intake system in Austin's Lake Travis when he encountered a pump with a broken seal—and a hot wire. Zapped with 480 volts, the unconscious Stapp sank in 60 feet of water, inaccessible to rescuers because of the powerful electrical field around him. Finally, with the current switched off, Stapp revived and groggily returned to the surface,

equipped, he said later, with a new outlook on life and a new appreciation for electricity.

Stapp also dives with a backup team that is very trustworthy, for Weld/Dive is in essence a mom-and-pop business. During each dive Stapp's wife, Cleta, perches atop the tank, directing topside operations, monitoring Stapp's air supply, and chatting with him via radio. The crew she supervises can number as many as 15, usually including Stapp's stepson. Among other duties, they keep Stapp sup-

plied with buckets of tools—he cannot take everything with him on a single dive—and haul the air and power tool hoses in and out of the sludge. When Stapp surfaces, crew members wash him down repeatedly with disinfectants and soap before he takes off his rubber suit. During this process, his helpers need to hold their noses, but Stapp smells only rubber and oxygen inside his protective cocoon. In fact, at the end of a long dive, he says, the first thing on his mind is food. □

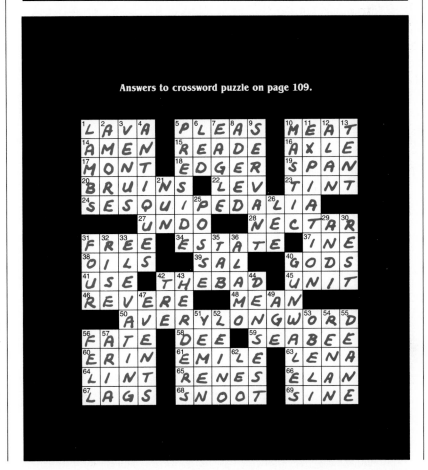

Answers to crossword puzzle on page 109.

ACKNOWLEDGMENTS

The editors wish to thank these individuals and institutions for their valuable assistance in the preparation of this volume:

Jolynn Attoe, Oscar Mayer Foods Corporation, Madison, Wisconsin; Elizabeth Bain, Fairfax, Virginia; Kathleen Bain, Fairfax, Virginia; Robert Bain, Fairfax, Virginia; James Barnett, Bothell, Washington; Dan Berger, Santa Rosa, California; Daniele Billitteri, Palermo, Sicily; Kathy Black, Louis M. Martini Winery, St. Helena, California; John D. Bruen, Springfield, Virginia; Bruce Chaffkin, Norwegian Cruise Lines, Coral Gables, Florida; Kenneth X. Charbonneau, Benjamin Moore & Company, Montvale, New Jersey; Jean-Louis Cheminé, Paris; Bruce A. Colvin, Bechtel/Parsons Brinckerhoff, Massachusetts Highway Department, Boston; Ann Cooper, Berkeley Heights, New Jersey; Robert H. Dick, Tea Room, FDA, Brooklyn, New York; Paul Dunn, Fairfax, Virginia; Phillip Dunn, Penfriend, London; Mary Erickson, Arlington International Race Course, Arlington Heights, Illinois; Dixie Evans, Exotic World, Helendale, California; Amanda Fish, Fairfax, Virginia; Richard S. Fiske, Department of Mineral Sciences, Smithsonian Institution, Washington, D.C.; Terry Fredeking, Antibody Systems, Inc., Bedford, Texas; Marc P. Friedland, Creative Intelligence, Los Angeles; Jeff Friedman, Sherlock Recovery, El Monte, California; Don Gatlin, NASA Ames-Dreyden Flight Research Facility, Edwards, California; Robert Gheyssens, Paris; R. A. Gilbert, Bristol, England; John Gough, Birmingham Library Services, Birmingham, England; Howard Green, Walt Disney Company, Burbank, California; Judith Harris, Rome; John Harrison, Dreyer's and Edy's Grand Ice Cream, Oakland, California; Richard Hill, Museum of the American Indian, Sanborn, New York; Glenn Hoffman, Melville, New York; G. Ronald Hoffman, Melville, New York; Ollie Johnston, Flintridge, California; Andrew Jones, Archaeological Resource Centre, York, England; Gerry Kirk, Sand Sculptors International, Solana Beach, California; Charles Kuster, Pioneer Hybrid Seed Company, Johnston, Iowa; David Lees, Florence; Mario Lugari, Rome; Diane McIntyre, Dreyer's and Edy's Grand Ice Cream, Oakland, California; Eugene T. Maleska, Wareham, Massachusetts; William R. Maples, C. A. Pound Human Identification Laboratory, Florida Museum of Natural History, University of Florida, Gainesville; Michael Martini, Louis M. Martini Winery, St. Helena, California; Roderick Conway Morris, Venice; Michele Moses, Burlington, Vermont; Stacy Moyer, Kloster Cruise Limited, Coral Gables, Florida; Ray Nalpant, Merrick, Long Island, New York; David Nitta, Amchick, Lansdale, Pennsylvania; Fonda Ryan, Sea World of Florida, Orlando; Judith Ryan, Halifax, Nova Scotia; Edward T. Schneider, NASA Ames-Dreyden Flight Research Facility, Edwards, California; Dan Schweitzer, New York Holographic Laboratories, New York; Douglas Seeley, National Institute of Health, Bethesda, Maryland; Leon Seidman, Cosmic Pet Products, Hagerstown, Maryland; Don Sewald, Lasalle, Colorado; Luiz Simas, Rio de Janeiro; Cleta Stapp, Pro-Weld Company, Austin, Texas; John Stapp, Pro-Weld Company, Austin, Texas; Bill Steed, Croaker College, Emeryville, California; Paula Sturdivin, St. Joseph, Illinois; Jim Thornton, Miss America Pageant, Atlantic City; Chuck Tompkins, Sea World of Florida, Orlando; Joan Torino, Jersey City, New Jersey; George Turoff, Arlington, Virginia; Mierle Laderman Ukeles, New York; Charles Vickiels, Greely, Colorado; Philippe Virat, Paris.

PICTURE CREDITS

The sources for the illustrations that appear in this book are listed below. Credits from left to right are separated by semicolons; from top to bottom by dashes.

Cover: C. Leroy/Sipa Press, New York, background, Benn Mitchell/The Image Bank, New York. **3:** C. Leroy/Sipa Press, New York. **7:** University of Florida, photo by Walter Coker, Gainesville, background, W. Cody/West Light, Los Angeles. **8:** Marine Art Center, Tokyo. **9:** *Amherst Daily News* Photo, from the Collection of the Springhill Miner's Museum, Springhill, Nova Scotia. **11:** Skyline Engineers Inc., Fitchburg, Massachusetts. **12, 13:** QA Photos Ltd., Hythe, Kent, England/© The Channel Tunnel Group Ltd., England. **14, 15:** C. Leroy/Sipa Press, New York. **16, 17:** Zambelli Internationale Fireworks, New Castle, Pennsylvania. **18:** Courtesy Johnny Kazian—courtesy Jessie Woods and Ann Cooper. **19:** Ron Taylor Film Productions, Sydney, Australia. **21:** Larry Burrows for *LIFE*—Mark Godfrey for *LIFE*. **22, 23:** Katia Krafft, Explorer, Paris. **24:** © Mike Holist/*Daily Mail*, London—David Rolfe/Howletts & Port Lympne Zoo Parks, Bekesbourne, Nr. Canterbury, Kent, England. **25:** University of Florida, photo by Walter Coker, Gainesville. **26, 27:** © Victoria Ivleva/Magnum, New York. **29:** © 1991 Chris Noble. **30:** Keith E. Goggin. **32:** © Russell Munson 1989—courtesy Jim Newman. **34:** Courtesy Joseph McCormick. **35:** Eric Valli. **36:** George Kramer. **37:** Courtesy B. J. Lowe. **39:** Tom Radcliff, Point of View Studio, Takoma Park, Maryland. **40, 41:** Publifoto, Palermo, Sicily; © Poani-Baldelli/Contrasto/SABA, New York. **42:** © Poani-Baldelli/Contrasto/SABA, New York. **43:** Debby Burley, background,

Skycraft/West Light, Los Angeles. **44:** Courtesy Robert H. Dick, FDA, Brooklyn, New York—Suzanne Opton. **45:** © Ben Swedowsky for Avon Products Inc. **46, 47:** © Ben Swedowsky for Avon Products Inc.; Renée Comet, courtesy Benjamin Moore & Company, Montvale, New Jersey; courtesy Benjamin Moore & Company, Montvale, New Jersey. **48:** © The Walt Disney Company; courtesy Ollie Johnston. **50:** Team, Rome. **51:** UPI/Bettmann, New York. **52, 53:** Courtesy Nintendo of America, Inc., Redmond, Washington (2)—Renée Comet (4). **54, 55:** Renée Comet; used with permission, Mattel Toys, El Segundo, California; Dick Berry (2)—Renée Comet (5). **56:** Ice Carving Kubodera, Tokyo. **57:** South West News Service, Bristol, England—Clifton Suspension Bridge Trust, Bristol, England. **58:** Randy Olson. **60:** Oscar Cabral/Abril Imagens, Rio de Janeiro. **61:** Calus C. Meyer/Agencia Tyba, Rio de Janeiro. **62:** Photo provided by and reproduced with permission of Binney & Smith Inc., Easton, Pennsylvania—Hamidullah Nuriddin. **63:** Photo Original, Tokyo—Noritoshi Iwanaga from Jiji Gaho, Tokyo. **64, 65:** Lee Boltin. **66, 67:** Debby Burley. **68:** Sygma, New York. **69:** Deborah Gichan/*The Hudson Reporter,* Hoboken, New Jersey. **70:** Renée Comet, courtesy Joan Torino. **71:** Brian Hamill/Photoreporters, New York. **73:** © Stephane Compoint/Sygma, New York, background, M. Angelo/West Light, Los Angeles. **75:** Courtesy of The Trustees of The Victoria and Albert Museum, London. **76:** Courtesy Dr. Sylvia Earle. **78:** Renée Comet—courtesy Dwight D. Eisenhower Library, Abilene, Kansas. **79:** From *Animals: 1419 Copyright-Free Illustrations of Mammals, Birds, Fish, Insects, etc.,* selected by Jim Harter, Dover Publications, New York, 1979. **80:** From *Animals: 1419 Copyright-Free Illustrations of Mammals, Birds, Fish, Insects, etc.,* selected by Jim Harter, Dover Publications, New York, 1979 (3)—bottom left, © Andy Ryan. **81:** Frank Clarkson. **82:** Bruce Cotler/*New York Post,* New York—courtesy Ray Nalpant. **83, 84:** Courtesy William R. Maples, Ph.D. **85:** Courtesy Sea World of Florida, Orlando. **87:** Courtesy Jim Barnett. **89:** © Stephane Compoint/Sygma, New York. **90:** Courtesy Ed Schneider. **92, 93:** © Sebastiao Salgado/Magnum, New York. **94:** Courtesy Dreyer's and Edy's Grand Ice Cream, Oakland, California. **95:** Courtesy Ron and Glenn Hoffman. **97:** Forrest Anderson. **98:** Richard Mackson/*Sports Illustrated.* **100:** Courtesy Norwegian Cruise Line, Coral Gables, Florida. **101:** Vioujard/Gamma, Paris. **102:** Helen Blunt, Longreach, Australia. **103:** Courtesy Jeff Friedman. **105:** Courtesy Larry Kolvoord, background, M. Angelo/West Light, Los Angeles. **106:** © 1985 Dennis F. Paxenos, Baltimore—Evan Sheppard. **107:** Pete Addis ©, Twickenham, England. **109:** Courtesy Eugene T. Maleska/art by Time-Life Books—Bert Lane. **110, 111:** Foto Fantasy/© Robert E. Jensen, Canoga Park, California. **112, 113:** D. James Dee, courtesy Ronald Feldman Fine Arts, New York; courtesy Ronald Feldman Fine Arts, New York. **114, 115:** Oscar Mayer Foods Corporation, Madison, Wisconsin. **116:** Birmingham Library Services, Birmingham, England. **117:** © Mark Smith. **119:** © Photographers International Ltd., Guildford, Surrey, England. **120:** From *Treasury of Animal Illustrations from Eighteenth-Century Sources,* edited by Carol Belanger Grafton, Dover Publications Inc., New York, 1988 (3)—bottom left, courtesy Bill Stead/Croaker College, Emeryville, California. **121:** John David Begg, London. **122, 123:** Douglas C. Seeley. **124:** © Massimo Sestini/Farabola Foto, Milan. **125:** Mary Erikson and Four Footed Fotos, Inc., Arlington Heights, Illinois. **126:** Photo by J. Barnes, New York Holographic Laboratories, New York. **128:** Antibody Systems, Inc., Bedford, Texas. **129:** Creative Intelligence/Sidney Cooper, Los Angeles—Creative Intelligence/Jeffrey Meyer, Los Angeles. **130, 131:** Dick Berry. **132:** Courtesy Larry Kolvoord. **133:** Courtesy Eugene T. Maleska/art by Time-Life Books.

BIBLIOGRAPHY

Books

Ambrose, Stephen E. *Eisenhower: Soldier, General of the Army, President-Elect, 1890-1952* (Vol. 1). New York: Simon & Schuster, 1983.

Arnot, Michelle. *What's GNU?* New York: Vintage, Random House, 1981.

Barnes, G. W., and Thomas Stevens. *The History of the Clifton Suspension Bridge* (19th ed.). Bristol: W. B. Harris, 1977.

Bearden, H. Joe, and John W. Fuquay. *Applied Animal Reproduction.* Reston, Va.: Reston Publishing, 1980.

Benson, Ragnar. *Action Careers.* Boulder, Colo.: Paladin Press, 1978.

Brendon, Piers. *Ike: His Life and Times.* New York: Harper & Row, 1986.

Brouwer, Alexandra, and Thomas Lee Wright. *Working in Hollywood.* New York: Crown, 1990.

Conley, Andrea. *Window on the Deep: The Adventures of Underwater Explorer Sylvia Earle.* New York: Franklin Watts, 1991.

Evers, Dora R., and S. Norman Feingold. *Your Future in Exotic Occupations.* New York: Richards Rosen Press, 1972.

Friedman, Jeff. *License to Steal.* Hacienda Heights, Calif.: Gumshoe, 1991.

Givens, Bill. *Son of Film Flubs: More Memorable Movie Mistakes.* New York: Citadel Press, 1991.

The Great Themes (Life Library of Photography series, rev. ed.). Alexandria, Va.: Time-Life Books, 1982.

Hankinson, Alan. *Man of Wars: William Howard Russell of the Times.* London: Heinemann Education Books, 1982.

Hill, Richard. *Skywalkers.* Brantford, Ontario: Woodland Indian Cultural Educational Centre, 1987.

Koskoff, David E. *The Diamond World.* New York: Harper & Row, 1981.

Larry Burrows: Compassionate Photographer. New York: Time-Life Books, 1972.

Longford, Elizabeth (Ed.). *Louisa, Lady in Waiting.* New York: Mayflower Books, 1979.

Masters, Brian. *The Passion of John Aspinall.* Great Britain: Coronet Books, 1989.

Moeller, Susan D. *Shooting War.* New York: Basic Books, 1989.

Montana, Joe, and Bob Raissman. *Audibles: My Life in Football.* New York: William Morrow, 1986.

O'Neil, Paul, and the Editors of Time-Life Books. *Barnstormers and Speed Kings* (Epic of Flight series). Alexandria, Va.: Time-Life Books, 1981.

Ryan, Judith Hoegg. *The Mine* (Growth of a Nation series). Canada: Fitzhenry & Whiteside, 1984.

Sacharov, Al. *Offbeat Careers.* Berkeley, Calif.: Ten Speed Press, 1988.

Scotti, Paul C. *Police Divers.* New York: Julian Messner, 1982.

Somerset, Anne. *Ladies in Waiting.* New York: Alfred A. Knopf, 1984.

Taylor, Valerie, and Ron Taylor (Eds.). *Great Shark Stories.* New York: Harper & Row, 1978.

Thomas, Frank, and Ollie Johnston. *Disney Animation: The Illusion of Life.* New York: Abbeville Press, 1981.

Periodicals

Abramson, Elinor W. "You're a What? Purser and Cruise Director." *Occupational Outlook Quarterly,* Winter 1989.

Acton, Doug. "Scot Schmidt." *California Boardsailor,* Fall II, 1987.

Arcidi, Philip. "Projects: Nine Proposals on Behalf of the Environment." *Progressive Architecture,* March 1991.

Aspinall, John. "Opinions That Are Designed to Shock, Alarm and Appal." *Independent,* February 11, 1990.

Bache, Ellyn. "Leon Seidman, Catnip Magnate." *Maryland Magazine,* Spring 1986.

Bailey, David. "Pizarro's Bones." *Today,* Fall 1984.

Baker, David M. "Revolution in Diamond Cutting: Laser Sawing of Diamond Crystals." *Gems & Gemology,* Fall 1981.

Barron, James. "Which White Is the Right White?" *New York Times,* August 10, 1989.

Beam, Alex. "On the Ready for the Rat War." *Boston Sunday Globe,* June 14, 1992.

Belisle, Richard F. "Closer to God." *Morning Herald,* May 29, 1980.

Blume, Mary. "To the Barricades! But Please Curb the Dog." *International Herald Tribune,* November 18, 1991.

"Bone Jones' Amazing Passions!" *Lifestyle Magazine,* July 16, 1991.

Bove, Alfred A. "Diving Medicine." *Skin Diver,* July 1986.

Breen, Bill. "The Greatest Flow on Earth." *Garbage,* January-February 1992.

Bush, E. A. "A Conversation with Dan Schweitzer." *Holosphere,* January 1981.

"Cabeças Cortadas na Avenida." *Veja,* February 13, 1991.

Carey, Patricia M. "The Great Taste Test." *North American International Business,* March 1991.

Carter, Graydon. "The Joker." *Rolling Stone,* November 2, 1989.

Casimiro, Steve. "Getting Big Air with Scot Schmidt." *Powder: The Skier's Magazine,* November 1986.

"A Chronology: Westray Mine Disaster." *Chronicle-Herald/Mail-Star,* May 15, 1992.

"Clifton Bridge Ready for 21st Century Traffic." *Surveyor,* April 25, 1985.

Cohen, Marcia. "I Wanted to Take On the World." *Parade,* November 24, 1991.

Cohn, Lowell. "At Croaker College, Good Students Reach the Top by Leaps and Bounds." *Sports Illustrated,* April 9, 1979.

Colacello, Bob. "Who's That Girl?" *Vanity Fair,* December 1990.

Cook, William J. "Battle under the Sand." *U.S. News & World Report,* March 11, 1991.

Cowell, Alan. "Bomb Kills Anti-Mafia Official and 5 Others in Sicily." *New York Times* (International), July 20, 1992.

Craven, Scott. "Here's the Scoop." *Phoenix Gazette,* May 17, 1991.

Cube, Bob. "Puzzles, Poetry and Pedagogy." *Sunday Enterprise,* no date.

Daut, Virginia. "President Bush Should Be Pleased the Green Wasn't Called Broccoli." *Wall Street Journal,* March 11, 1991.

DeYoung, Bill. "Kent Vliet, a True Gator Fan." *Gainesville Sun,* November 21, 1988.

Dillon, Cathy. "Walk on the Wild Side." *Today,* June 1989.

Dolan, Carrie. "If You Really Cut the Mustard, You Will Relish This Job." *Wall Street Journal,* July 7, 1992.

Erickson, Mary. "Of Horse Identification." *Varieties of Ash,* January 1992.

"Federal Tea Examiners Help Consumer to Get a Quality Cup." *Specialty Food Merchandising,* March 1986.

Federman, David. "The Hidden World of America's Diamond Cutters." *Jeweler's Circular-Keystone,* April 1977.

Ferrell, David. "Hard Road to Tow for Repo Men." *Los Angeles Times,* December 27, 1991.

Field, Eunice. "Script Supervisors Annoyed at Being Blamed for 'Bloopers.'" *Hollywood Reporter,* December 21, 1979.

Fox, Catherine. "Public Art's New Wave." *Atlanta Journal,* August 4, 1991.

Franzheim, Roberta. "Going against the Grain." *Art Cellar Exchange,* May 1990.

Freeman, Alan. "The Fourth of July Is Boom or Bust Day for George Zambelli." *Wall Street Journal,* July 3, 1985.

Gardner, Joseph L. "'Bull Run' Russell." *American Heritage,* June 1962.

Gargan, Edward A. "Field Is Lush, and Yanks Are Undefeated at Home." *New York Times* (Metropolitan), April 15, 1991.

Gildea, William. "Ever So Simply, Montana." *Washington Post,* August 28, 1990.

Gourse, Leslie. "A Deadly Delicacy." *Science,* May 1982.

"The Greatest Show on Earth." *RioLife,* January 16-31, 1988.

"The Greatest Show on Earth—II." *RioLife,* February 1-15, 1988.

Greene, Mary. "Falling between Two Stools." *Observer* (London), February 16, 1992.

Hall, Howard. "Anatomy of a Shark Bite." *Skin Diver,* April 1981.

Hamblin, Dora Jane. " 'Delicious! Ah! What Else Is Like the Gondola?' " *Smithsonian,* July 1987.

Harris, Judith. "Death of a Drug Warrior." *Wall Street Journal,* May 27, 1992.

Hauser, Hillary. "Ron and Valerie Taylor." *Skin Diver,* April 1982.

Hertzberg, Hendrik. "Summer's Blood." *Time,* August 10, 1992.

"The High Cost of Golden Dream." *World Press Review,* May 1992.

Hinckle, Pia. "The Grip of the Octopus." *Newsweek,* June 8, 1992.

Hirshberg, Charles. "Hell on Earth." *Life,* July 1991.

Hogan, Mary Ann. "His Students Croak, but Don't Die." *Oakland Tribune,* August 21, 1978.

Hollander, Neil, and Robert MacLean. "Mud-Caked Amazon Miners Wallow in Newfound Wealth and Power." *Smithsonian,* April 1984.

Holloway, Marguerite. "Fire in Water." *Scientific American,* April 1992.

Hopkins, Harold. "The Smell That Tells." *FDA Consumer,* December 1974-January 1975.

Horngren, Barbara. "Never an Adult Moment." *Westways,* July 1992.

Horswell, Michael. "Third Keeper Killed in an Aspinall Zoo." *Times,* April 9, 1984.

Horwitz, Tony. "Endangered Feces: Paleo-Scatologist Plumbs Old Privies." *Wall Street Journal,* September 9, 1991.

Jackson, Donald Dale. "The Ins and Outs of a Dangerous and Boring Subject." *Smithsonian,* May 1986.

"Japan's Fugu Is a Delicacy—but Is It *Poisson* or Poison?" *People,* January 22, 1990.

Jaworski, Margaret. "Miss America's Shadow." *Family Circle,* September 3, 1991.

Jefferson, David J. "Creativity Isn't All That's Needed by a Creative Business." *Wall Street Journal,* March 19, 1990.

Jenish, D'arcy. "A Desert Inferno." *Maclean's,* July 8, 1991.

Johnston, Bruce. "Mafia Mole Sought as Italy Mourns." *Daily Telegraph,* May 26, 1992.

Johnston, Bruce, and Robert Fox. "Mafia Blamed as Top Judge and Wife Die in Explosion." *Daily Telegraph,* May 25, 1992.

Karp, Jonathan. "At Ballparks, a Question of What to Play." *Washington Post,* August 31, 1986.

Kaufman, Joanne:
"He Makes the Frocks They're Paid to Shed." *Wall Street Journal,* September 5, 1991.
"Miss America's Shadow." *Wall Street Journal,* September 13, 1991.

Keen, Cathy. "UF Scientist Researches Gator 'Language of Love.' " *Gainesville Sun,* May 11, 1992.

Keen, Larry. "Those Courting Alligators." *Gainesville Sun,* June 26, 1983.

"Keeper Killed by 'Aroused' Elephant." *Times,* May 25, 1984.

Keer, Richard A. "Dancing with Death at Unzen." *Science,* July 19, 1991.

Keith, Fred. "An Interview with Scot Schmidt." *Steep Technician,* no date.

Kleiman, Dena. "Food Styling: The Art of Making the Basil Blush." *New York Times,* November 7, 1990.

Kluge, P. F. "The Man Who Is a Diamond's Best Friend." *Smithsonian,* May 1988.

Koncius, Jura. "Where Did They Find That Paint?" *Washington Home,* September 27, 1990.

"Ladies in the Shadows." *Sunday Telegraph Magazine* (London), August 4, 1985.

"Lawyers Always in the Swim of Things." *National Law Journal,* August 18, 1986.

Leerhsen, Charles, Pamela Abramson, and Frank Washington. "Montana's Passing Fancy." *Newsweek,* January 23, 1989.

Logan, Michael. "Repo to the Stars." *Los Angeles Magazine,* November 1991.

Lyons, Richard D. "A Good Nose for Coffee Is a Job Requirement." *New York Times,* March 1, 1992.

McCoy, Bob. "Froggy Fame." *Sporting News,* June 6, 1983.

MacFie, Rebecca. "Women Take Up the Shears." *World Press Review,* June 1988.

MacNeil, Paul, and Pam Sword. "Rescuers Delayed in Search for Miners." *Mail-Star,* May 12, 1992.

Maier, Anne. "Two Houston Psychologists Are Proving the Best Defense Is Picking a Good Jury." *People,* February 21, 1983.

Maples, William R., et al. "The Death and Mortal Remains of Francisco Pizarro." *Journal of Forensic Sciences,* July 1989.

Mathews, Jay. "DeLorean Jury Selected with Expert Help." *Washington Post,* August 18, 1984.

Miller, Cheryl. "Out of the Trashcan." *Public Art Review,* Spring-Summer 1990.

Miller, Marjorie. "Evangelists in an Old Plaza Sell Hope Found in Literacy." *Los Angeles Times,* September 4, 1990.

Mitchell, Joseph. "The Mohawks in High Steel." *New Yorker,* September 17, 1949.

Mulvagh, Jane. "Beastly Table Manners." *You Magazine,* November 19, 1989.

Munson, Russell. "Crop Dusters." *Flying,* December 1989.

Murray, Iain. "Digging Dirt on the Facts of Life." *Marketing Week,* September 22, 1989.

Needham, Edgar H. "Larry Burrows: A Photographer's Own Story." *Popular Photography,* July 1971.

Nestlebaum, Karen Berman. "Great Cutters: The Men Who Cut New York's Legendary Stones." *New York Diamonds,* Winter 1990.

Newman, Andy. "Dressing the Well-Dressed Stripper." *Hudson Current,* October 17-23,

1991.

Oates, Bob. "He Passes NFL Test of Time." *Los Angeles Times,* February 22, 1989.

Okie, Susan. "Federal Tea-Tasting Rite Is Steeped in Tradition." *Washington Post,* March 22, 1989.

O'Neill, Sean, and Martin Whitfield. "Workers 'Being Put at Risk in Rush to Meet Deadlines.' " *Independent,* May 9, 1990.

Oppel, Richard A., Jr. "Short on Bat Saliva? Bedford Collector Will Fetch You Some." *Fort Worth Star-Telegram,* January 18, 1992.

Orenstein, Peggy. "Oceanographer Sylvia Earle." *New York Times Magazine,* June 23, 1991.

Parmelee, Jennifer. "Imagine—Venice without Gondolas?" *International Herald Tribune,* January 3, 1989.

Perkins, Carol. "Women in Horse Racing: The Myth and the Reality." *Sentinel,* October-November 1989.

Perlman, Eric S. "Scott Schmidt's Kind of Freedom." *Ski West,* Winter 1987-1988.

Petche, Nicholas. "St. Valentine Love Keeps Scribes Busy." *News* (Mexico City), February 14, 1992.

Peters, Nizam. "Diamond Cutting Is Still a Viable Profession." *Lapidary Journal,* June 1981.

Philips, John. "Anti-Mafia Powers Free Italian Police to Pounce on 700 Suspects." *Times,* June 10, 1992.

Pierson, John. "Dead-Animal Trade Is Still the Lifeblood of One Hardy Soul." *Wall Street Journal,* March 12, 1991.

Ranier, Desmond M. "How the Cutter Unleashes Diamond's Fire." *Jeweler's Circular-Keystone,* April 1971.

"RCMP Say 24 Remaining in Pit." *New Glasgow Evening News,* November 1956.

Rebeyrol, Yvonne. "Maurice et Katia Krafft, Deux 'Fous' des Cratères." *Le Monde,* June 7, 1991.

Richards, Charles. "Palermo Mourns as Mafia Kills Its Bravest Son." *Independent,* May 25, 1992.

Riechman, Deb. "Cosmic Catnip's Blend Has the Smell of Success." *Washington Post,* March 9, 1992.

Rose, Matthew. "Dead Men Don't Float." *Interview,* September 1990.

Rosen, Marjorie, and Tom Cunneff. "As His Fantasia Creatures Charm Moviegoers Again, Ollie Johnston Draws on His Memories of Disney." *People,* October 29, 1990.

Rudolph, Barbara. "Supermodels, Beauty and Bucks." *Time,* September 16, 1991.

Saar, John. "A Frantic Night on the Edge of Laos." *Life,* February 19, 1971.

Sautter, Bill. "Fire Power." *Washington Post Magazine,* April 5, 1992.

Shepard, Richard F. "Bambi Is a Stag and Tubas Don't Go 'Pah-Pah.' " *New York Times Magazine,* February 16, 1992.

Shields, Jan. "Classy Croakers." *Sunday Record,* January 11, 1987.

Simons, Marlise. "Gondola Makers, an Endangered Species." *International Herald Tribune,* July 17, 1991.

Simons, Mary, and Daniele Billitteri. "A Wounded Mafia." *Life,* March 1985.

Smith, David Hugh, and Glynis Gordon. "Castles Built to Order, to Crumble." *Christian Science Monitor,* August 25, 1989.

Smith, Gary, and Alan Maki. "World's Most Dangerous Shell Game." *Soldier of Fortune,* July 1992.

Solnit, Rebecca. "Trash, Talk and Politics." *Sierra,* July-August 1990.

Stone, Judith. "The Rat Stuff." *Discover,* July 1991.

Stuckey, Scott. "The Dizzy World of Wing Walking." *Boys Life,* May 1989.

Summers, Diane. "Facing the Bees." *International Wildlife,* May-June 1990.

Swift, Harriet. "Fanfare for the Common Trash." *Tribune* (Oakland), May 8, 1989.

Taylor, Valerie. "All Knights of Mettle True." *Oceans,* March 1982.

Taylor, Wilkie. "The '56 Explosion and '58 Bump: A Veteran Newsman Looks Back." *Chronicle-Herald,* May 12, 1992.

Thorne, Stephen:

"Draegermen Clear Rock by Hand, Squeeze through Tiny Gaps." *Chronicle-Herald/Mail-Star,* May 13, 1992.

"Tearful Draegermen Describe Their Ordeal." *Chronicle-Herald/Mail-Star,* May 15, 1992.

Tianen, Dave. "Ribit(ing) Show." *Milwaukee Sentinel,* January 3, 1991.

Tillander, H. "Six Centuries of Diamond Design." *Journal of Gemology,* July 1965.

Tobin, Richard. "Our View." *A. I. Breeding News,* April 1992.

Tomsho, Robert. "When You Need Vampire-Bat Saliva, He's the Man to Call." *Wall Street Journal,* January 16, 1992.

Touby, Frank. "The End of a Firestorm." *Maclean's,* December 30, 1991.

"Track People." *Chicago Reader,* August 8, 1986.

Tyrer, Robert. "The Hellhole." *Times Magazine* (London), May 24, 1987.

Valli, Eric, and Diane Summers. "Honey Hunters of Nepal." *National Geographic,* November 1988.

Van Housen, Caty. "Success in the Sand." *Business Action,* December 1990.

Vietmeyer, Noel D. "The Preposterous Puffer." *National Geographic,* August 1984.

"A Vintage in Hand." *Times* (London), November 25, 1988.

Walker, Christopher. "Gulf War Weapons Keep on Killing." *Times* (London), February 22, 1992.

Wayne, George. "Naomi: The Hard Facts." *Interview,* May 1990.

Werne, Jo. "Paint Power." *Miami Herald,* January 3, 1992.

Wernicki, Peter G., and John Glorioso. "Lifeguarding: The Sport, the Profession, the Hazards." *Physician and Sportsmedicine,* April 1991.

White, Wallace. "Her Deepness." *New Yorker,* July 3, 1989.

"Who Put the Poo in Poodle?" *Economist,* October 26, 1991.

Wiersema, Brian. "Castles of Sand Make Hard Cash." *San Diego Union,* December 14, 1989.

Wilson, Janet. "It's a Dirty Job and John Stapp Does It." *Austin American-Statesman,* February 8, 1992.

Winter, Christine. "Identifier Takes Lip from Horses." *Chicago Tribune,* July 1, 1991.

Woo, Elaine. "Novel Detective." *Los Angeles Times,* July 29, 1991.

Woods, Randy. "The Art of Waste Transfer." *Waste Age,* August 1991.

"Write in Style." *Lady,* July 31, 1986.

Zimmerman, Paul:

"Born to Be a Quarterback." *Sports Illustrated,* August 6, 1990.

"The Ultimate Winner." *Sports Illustrated,* August 13, 1990.

Other

"The Birmingham Humline." *News from Birmingham Library Services.* Birmingham, England: Birmingham City Council Library Services, 1992.

"Calaveras County Fair & Jumping Frog Jubilee." Press Packet. San Andreas, Calif.: Calaveras County Chamber of Commerce, June 18, 1992.

"Celebrate!" Press release. Madison, Wis.: Oscar Mayer Foods Corp.

Colvin, Bruce, et al. "Planning Rodent Control for Boston's Central Artery/Tunnel Project." Davis: University of California Davis, 1990.

Creative Intelligence. Press clippings. Los Angeles: Paul Burditch & Associates and Creative Intelligence, 1986-1992.

"Croaker College Resume." Pamphlet. Emeryville, Calif.: Bill Steed.

"Dovea, A.I. Sires 1992." Brochure. Dovea, Ireland: South Eastern Cattle Breeding Society, 1992.

"Holography: Notes on the Technique." New York: New York Holographic Laboratories.

"Hotdoggin'—Hilarious Highway to Humor." Press release. Madison, Wis.: Oscar Mayer Foods Corp.

Jamiolkowski, M. "The Leaning Tower of Pisa—Present Situation." Paper presented at the Nikken Nakase Geotechnical Institute. Tokyo,

September 1991.

"Judging the Jurors!" *20/20* transcript, program 1217. New York: ABC News, April 24, 1992.

"Penfriend (London) Limited." Press release. London: Penfriend (London) Ltd.

"Picking the William Kennedy Smith Rape Trial Jury." *Nightline* transcript, program 2725. New York: ABC News, November 1, 1991.

"Sand Sculptors International." Brochure. Solana Beach, Calif.: Sand Sculptors International, 1989.

Schweitzer, Dan. Unpublished abstract. New York: December 26, 1990.

"Suicide Mission to Chernobyl." *Nova* transcript, program 1815. Boston: WGBH-TV, October 22, 1991.

"What Is a Wienermobile?" Press release. Madison, Wis.: Oscar Mayer Foods Corp.

"Wienermobiles Hotdoggin' through History." Press release. Madison, Wis.: Oscar Mayer Foods Corp.

INDEX

Time-Life Books is a division of Time Life Inc.,
a wholly owned subsidiary of
THE TIME INC. BOOK COMPANY

TIME-LIFE BOOKS

PRESIDENT: Mary N. Davis

MANAGING EDITOR: Thomas H. Flaherty
Director of Editorial Resources:
Elise D. Ritter-Clough
Executive Art Director: Ellen Robling
Director of Photography and Research:
John Conrad Weiser
Editorial Board: Dale M. Brown, Janet Cave,
Roberta Conlan, Laura Foreman, Jim Hicks, Blaine
Marshall, Rita Thievon Mullin, Henry Woodhead
*Assistant Director of Editorial Resources/Training
Manager:* Norma E. Shaw

PUBLISHER: Robert H. Smith

Associate Publisher: Sandra Lafe Smith
Editorial Director: Russell B. Adams, Jr.
Marketing Director: Anne C. Everhart
Director of Production Services: Robert N. Carr
Production Manager: Prudence G. Harris
Supervisor of Quality Control: James King

Editorial Operations
Production: Celia Beattie
Library: Louise D. Forstall
Computer Composition: Deborah G. Tait (Manager),
Monika D. Thayer, Janet Barnes Syring, Lillian
Daniels
Interactive Media Specialist: Patti H. Cass

© 1993 Time-Life Books. All rights reserved.
No part of this book may be reproduced in any form
or by any electronic or mechanical means, including
information storage and retrieval devices or systems, without prior written permission from the
publisher, except that brief passages may be quoted
for reviews.
First printing. Printed in U.S.A.
Published simultaneously in Canada.
School and library distribution by Silver Burdett
Company, Morristown, New Jersey 07960.

TIME-LIFE is a trademark of Time Warner Inc. U.S.A.

**Library of Congress
Cataloging-in-Publication Data**
Odd jobs / by the editors of Time-Life Books.
p.   cm.   (Library of curious and unusual facts).
Includes bibliographical references and index.
ISBN 0-8094-7767-X (trade)
ISBN 0-8094-7768-9 (lib. bdg.)
1. Occupations. 2. Professions.
I. Time-Life Books. II. Series.
HB2581.O33 1993
331.7—dc20   92-30493 CIP

LIBRARY OF CURIOUS AND UNUSUAL FACTS

SERIES EDITOR: Carl A. Posey
Series Administrator: Roxie France-Nuriddin
Art Director: Alan Pitts
Picture Editor: Sally Collins

Editorial Staff for *Odd Jobs*
Text Editors: Esther Ferington (principal),
John R. Sullivan
Associate Editor/Research: Katya Sharpe
Assistant Editors/Research: Michael E. Howard,
Ruth Moss
Writer: Sarah Ince
Assistant Art Director: Sue Pratt
Senior Copy Coordinators: Jarelle S. Stein
(principal), Colette Stockum
Picture Coordinator: Jennifer Iker
Editorial Assistant: Terry Ann Medlin

Special Contributors: Eliot Marshall, Peter Pocock,
George Russell, Sandra Salmans (text); Ellen C.
Gross, Catherine B. Hackett, Kathryn B. Pfeifer (re-
search); Louise Wile Hedberg (index)

Correspondents: Elisabeth Kraemer-Singh (Bonn),
Christine Hinze (London), Christina Lieberman (New
York), Maria Vincenza Aloisi (Paris), Ann Natanson
(Rome). Valuable assistance was also provided by
Forrest Anderson, Mia Turner (Beijing); Peter Haw-
thorne (Johannesburg); Caroline Alcock, Caroline
Wood (London); John Dunn (Melbourne); Andrea
Dabrowski, Libby Williams (Mexico City); Juan Sosa
(Moscow); Elizabeth Brown, Katheryn White (New
York); John Maier (Rio de Janeiro); Leonora Dods-
worth, Miriam Murphy, Ann Wise (Rome); Dick Berry,
Mieko Ikeda (Tokyo).

Other Publications:

THE AMERICAN INDIANS
THE ART OF WOODWORKING
LOST CIVILIZATIONS
ECHOES OF GLORY
THE NEW FACE OF WAR
HOW THINGS WORK
WINGS OF WAR
CREATIVE EVERYDAY COOKING
COLLECTOR'S LIBRARY OF THE UNKNOWN
CLASSICS OF WORLD WAR II
AMERICAN COUNTRY
VOYAGE THROUGH THE UNIVERSE
THE THIRD REICH
THE TIME-LIFE GARDENER'S GUIDE
MYSTERIES OF THE UNKNOWN
TIME FRAME
FIX IT YOURSELF
FITNESS, HEALTH & NUTRITION
SUCCESSFUL PARENTING
HEALTHY HOME COOKING
UNDERSTANDING COMPUTERS
LIBRARY OF NATIONS
THE ENCHANTED WORLD
THE KODAK LIBRARY OF CREATIVE PHOTOGRAPHY
GREAT MEALS IN MINUTES
THE CIVIL WAR
PLANET EARTH
COLLECTOR'S LIBRARY OF THE CIVIL WAR
THE EPIC OF FLIGHT
THE GOOD COOK
WORLD WAR II
HOME REPAIR AND IMPROVEMENT
THE OLD WEST

*For information on and a full description of any of
the Time-Life Books series listed above, please call
1-800-621-7026 or write:*
Reader Information
Time-Life Customer Service
P.O. Box C-32068
Richmond, Virginia 23261-2068

This volume is one in a series that explores
astounding but surprisingly true events in history,
science, nature, and human conduct. Other books in
the series include:

*Feats and Wisdom of the Ancients
Mysteries of the Human Body
Forces of Nature
Vanishings
Amazing Animals
Inventive Genius
Lost Treasure
The Mystifying Mind
A World of Luck
Hoaxes and Deceptions
Crimes and Punishments
Odd and Eccentric People
Shadows of Death
Manias and Delusions
Above and Beyond
Science Astray
All the Rage*